C000234734

# *The History* *of* **S***t. Francis Xavier's College* *1842 - 2001*

## Pat Heery

The History of St. Francis Xavier's College, Liverpool, 1842-2001

Designed and typeset by Stephen J. Baker, Dolphin Design
Printed and bound by K. & N. Press
Published by Pat Heery

The History of St. Francis Xavier's College, Liverpool, 1842-2001

# To Fred Devereux

not only for the the assistance he has given me throughout,
but also as the representative of all those who have served the College and its pupils so well
for so many generations

*The main entrance to the College, Salisbury Street, 1842 - 1961*

*Front entrance: St. Francis Xavier's College, Salisbury Street, 1842 - 1961*

# The History of St. Francis Xavier's College
## Liverpool
## 1842 - 2001

## Contents

| | | page |
|---|---|---|
| Preface | | vii |
| Acknowledgements | | viii |
| List of Illustrations | | x |
| Introduction | | xiii |
| Glossary of Terms | | xiv |
| Chapter 1 | England's First Catholic Day Secondary School | 17 |
| Chapter 2 | College Premises | 29 |
| Chapter 3 | The College, The Government and The Law 1842-1918 | 53 |
| Chapter 4 | The College, The Government and The Law 1919-2001 | 67 |
| Chapter 5 | Curriculum : Drama | 85 |
| Chapter 6 | Curriculum : Other Areas | 111 |
| Chapter 7 | Scouse | 133 |
| | a.    The Ferula | 135 |
| | b.    Prefects of Studies 1842 - 1918 | 138 |
| | c.    The Woodlock Years 1919 - 1937 | 143 |
| | d.    The Neylan Years 1939 - 1953 | 151 |
| | e.    The Warner Years 1953 - 1961 | 158 |
| | f.    The Doyle Years 1962 - 1974 | 162 |
| | g.    The Brother Francis Years 1979 - 2001 | 165 |
| Epilogue | SFX in 2042 by Jonathan Murphy | 171 |
| Annex 1 | Cardinal Acton and his Report to Propaganda | 175 |
| Annex 2 | Three Letters of Bishop Brown Conceding | 177 |
| Annex 3 | Catholic Liverpool 1800 - 1860 | 179 |
| Annex 4 | Letter sent by Fr. Wilcock to St Anthony's Parishioners | 182 |
| References | | 191 |
| Bibliography | | 193 |
| Index | | 194 |

# Preface

**M**ost school histories adopt a strictly chronological approach - with the result that they often read like a list of people, places and events. Consequently ex-pupils find themselves mainly interested in the sections that deal with the years they attended.

To widen the interest I have taken a thematic line, where selected topics in the life of the College are dealt with at some length. Such choices may be personal, but they are not necessarily arbitrary. The items on Sadler's Report in Chapter 3 and on Jesuit Drama in Chapter 5 show the virtues of concentrating on topics where there is information available, but not readily accessible. Chapter 7 resorts to chronological listing, since there has to be a place in an account such as this for readers to locate themselves and switch into 'reminiscence' mode. In spite of an initial determination to give equal prominence to both the Everton and the Woolton sites, the proportions have ended up skewed in the direction of Salisbury Street. Given my stance perhaps this was in the end inevitable and I can only apologize for this lack of balance.

A word about style: the book does not aim to be academic, and it is not meant simply as a popular chronicle, although in places it leans very definitely in both these directions. The writing is at times deliberately journalistic, and it is hoped that this adds to, rather than detracts from, its enjoyment.

Finally, it hardly needs pointing out that the honours of the College are not primarily in Oxbridge scholarships awarded or in football Shields won, but in the unrecognized achievements - great and small - of the thousands of pupils and staff who have passed through the doors of St Francis Xavier's since 1842. I hope that the contents of this book can be seen to recognize in some way the contributions they have all made to Salisbury Street and Woolton.

## 1842 -1942
## PORTRAIT OF A COMMUNITY

"Ere the parting hour go by,
Quick, thy tablets, Memory!"

A hundred years hence (long after the writer
and his readers have gone to their reward)
someone perhaps will sit down to write the
history of the College during the second
century of its existence, or even to rewrite
the whole anew. We can but hope that he will
be able to record that in the present emergency (World War 2) we rose to the height of
our opportunities, and that, in the truly
Ignatian spirit of Fr. Randal Lythgoe, whilst
praying as if everything depended upon God,
we worked as if everything depended upon ourselves.

W.F.F.G.

(The last paragraph of the article 'Portrait of a Community"
written for the College Magazine in 1942 by Dr. Grace to
celebrate the Centenary)

# Acknowledgements

There are three people whose help has been vital in the preparation of this book.

Professor Maurice Whitehead, of The University of Wales, Swansea, has provided me with direction and advice throughout. There can be no one with a greater knowledge of Jesuit education and he has made this knowledge available to me at every turn. I am particularly grateful, since I was calling upon him as he changed appointments and had more than enough to do in his new post at Swansea. His Ph.D. thesis on the history of SFX 1842-1902 was a valuable reference point for me throughout, being a model of its kind. He has generously allowed me to quote extensively from it as well as from articles he has written on the College. In places, what I have passed off as my own should more rightly appear under his name. I cannot thank him too much for his help.

Fred Devereux likewise has been a mine of information about the College, speaking authoritatively from his unique position as Pupil, Teacher, Head of Department, Deputy Head, Acting Head and Governor. Fred has searched out references for me; provided me with photographs; answered a never-ending stream of questions and sent me details about the College, which could have come from no other source. He has read and corrected chapters, saving me in some cases from serious errors: not only errors of fact, but also errors of style and approach. I had the good sense to realize early on that some sections were much better written by Fred than by me, since he had been an important participant in some of the most vital events in the history of the College. I am grateful for those passages, which are included under his name.

The College has a list of long-serving teachers from Fr. Vaughan and Fr. Woodlock to Putty Grace and Les Bailey. Fred stands in this tradition. But there is a difference. His contributions have been made on a wider front, as the status of the College changed from Direct Grant to Comprehensive to Grant-Maintained to Foundation. The book would be much the poorer without his assistance.

My brother Jack is the third important support I have had. He has been my Liverpool Legs - a vital service, since I was trying to write the book from my home in London. He has interviewed people for me, made innumerable trips to the Liverpool Central Library to find or check on an item, and has been an invaluable sounding board, as I sometimes groped my way uncertainly. But undoubtedly his most significant contribution came from his research in the Liverpool Archdiocesan Archive Offices. Careful reading of uncatalogued papers turned up a number of interesting letters, but none as important as the letter he found from Bishop Brown in Rome to Fr Wilcock, announcing the Pope's verdict on the dispute described in Chapter 1. This letter, possibly not read by anyone since 1842, has been described by Professor Whitehead as an 'important and significant find'. I am especially grateful to Jack for this discovery.

The Headmaster, Brother Francis, has been more than helpful, putting at my disposal files and papers, which have filled out the narrative and put some flesh on what otherwise would have been some rather bare bones. In spite of his busy schedule he has always been ready to answer my questions, provide me with photographs and suggest helpful contacts, for all of which I am in his debt.

I also owe a debt to the staff at a number of institutions. The Public Record Office in Kew, The British Library, The London Library, the Newspaper Archive in Colindale and the Liverpool Central Library. In these instances my Putney address sometimes worked to my advantage. Fr. McCoog and Brother Hodkinson in the Jesuit Archive in Farm Street have been a constant help, without which there would be significant gaps in some of the chapters. I must also express my gratitude to Fr. Provincial, for agreeing to make the resources of the Farm Street Archive available to me.

The quality of the sketches of both college buildings drawn for me by Sun Hai Li add considerably to the text and I am particularly grateful to him. Mick O'Neill, aided by Ted Walsh, drew the remarkably detailed plans of the old College. Brother Vance helped me with some valuable contacts. George Ridge talked at length on several occasions of the affairs of the College over some 50 years; no one else has such detailed knowledge over such a long period.

downs and variava(sic), is the architectural firm responsible for the current Salisbury Street renovations; the generosity of W. Hodge, one of the partners, with both his time and his records has been much appreciated. I am grateful to Dave Monaghan for the use of the photographs of the Everton teams at Melwood in the Twenties and to Jack McCarran for the photographs of Our Lady of Compassion in Formby.

Special thanks must be paid to John Waldron and Steve Baker. To John for the photographs of both college buildings; his images considerably enhance Chapter 2 in particular and I am grateful to him for his patience, his photographic expertise and his willingness to assist. To Steve not only for the skill with which he designed and set the text and illustrations, but also for the tolerance he showed in the face of my frequent changes of direction.

The image of the College on the cover is reproduced by permission of the artist, Frank Green. Prints of this and other views of Liverpool are available from Frank's Gallery at 97 Oakfield, Liverpool L4 0UE or at www.frankgreen.co.uk

Others have helped me in various ways: Tommy Hall, Frank Gibbon, Ray O'Connor, Ted Whitehead, Hugh Kearney, Frank Hart, Kathleen Heery and Hannah Heery. Others agreed to put their recollections on tape or at interview: Larry Pickett, Peter Beardwood, John Reid, Tony Glynn, George Glynn, Sir Peter Baxendell, Graham Ireland, and John Osborne.

I am grateful too to all those who took the trouble to write to me and to those who sent me photographs, College magazines or memorabilia. This is a long list of people who will perhaps forgive me if I do not name them individually.

Bill Bewley has a phenomenal memory for the details of the College in the early fifties and I have profited enormously from talking to him. He also agreed to take on the role of editor, assisted by his wife Jean. I must record that the incisiveness, accuracy and general editing skills they brought to bear have eradicated faults of style and content and in consequence have made the text considerably more understandable and more readable.

Lastly, I wish to thank Margaret, my wife, for bearing her share of the brunt of the disruption that a work like this brings in its train; also for the help she has given in reading the text and making suggestions that have contributed to making the book better than it otherwise would have been.

Her help also enables me to print the example of the perfect dactylic hexameter, which Leo Bond, our Latin Master in 1948, was fond of quoting :-

'Last but not / least to my / wife for her / help in com / piling the / index'.

- with thanks to Ted Walton for making sure I got the scansion right.

# List of Illustrations

The maps, illustrations and photographs listed appear with the kind permission of those credited below.

Front Cover        College at Salisbury Street : Frank Green
Dedication         The Main Entrance to the College, Salisbury Street : Sun Hai Li
Frontispiece       Front Entrance : St. Francis Xavier's College, Salisbury Street : Sun Hai Li
Back Cover         Sketch of Woolton site : Sun Hai-Li

Page        xv     South end of College, Salisbury Street : Sun Hai Li
            17     Advertisement in the Liverpool Mercury : British Library
            18     Map showing Salisbury Street area around 1840 :  L'pool Central Library
            19     Fr. Randal Lythgoe :  M. Whitehead
            19     Bishop George Brown : Liverpool Archdiocesan Archive
            23     Map showing Catholic churches in 1840s
            25     1 mile survey map - St. Francis Xavier's to St. Anthony's  : M. Whitehead
            26     St Anthony's Church Scotland Road : M. O'Neill
            28     Architect's original drawing for SFX : Farm Street Archive
            29     Salisbury Street, 1873 : Sun Hai Li
            30     Soho Street : Sun Hai Li
            30     St. Anne  Street : Sun Hai Li
            31     Map of Rural Everton - Swire 1824: Lancashire Record Office & P. Aughton
            32     Site of SFX 1849 : Farm Street Archive
            33     Ground Plan, SFX College, Salisbury Street, 1860 : Farm Street Archive
            33     Lay-out  of 1856 SFX College : Farm Street Archive
            34     Fr. Vaughan's Rejected Plan : Sun Hai Li
            35     Henry Clutton, Architect :  M. Whitehead
            35     Clutton's French Sketches : H. Clutton, Domestic Architecture of France
            36     Our Lady of Compassion (2), Formby :   Jack Mc Carran
            36     SFX College, Salisbury Street : Building and Engineering News, May 1876
            37     The Original College Hall, SFX College, Salisbury Street : Farm St. Archive
            37     The Hall in 1961 : Farm St. Archive
            38     Church, Presbytery and College 1907 : M. Whitehead
            38     Singing Gallery, School Hall, SFX College, Salisbury Street : Mrs T. Flynn
            39     1908 Extension (2), SFX College, Salisbury Street : J. Waldron
            39     Crucifix and Shrine, SFX College, Salisbury Street : Mrs T. Flynn
            40     St. Francis Xavier's College, Salisbury Street : Mrs T. Flynn
            40     Chemistry Laboratory, SFX College, Salisbury Street : Mrs T. Flynn
            40     Interior, St. Francis Xavier's Church : Mrs T. Flynn
            41     Ground Floor and First Floor Lay-out, SFX, Salisbury Street : M. O'Neill
            42     The Campion, Magazine of SFX Bilateral School : SFX Woolton  Archive
            42     SFX Bi-lateral : Assembly, New Hall 1971 : SFX College Woolton Archive
            42     Hope University at Everton : J. Waldron
            43     Aerial Views (2), Woolton : SFX College Woolton Archive
            43     Ground View of High Lee : J. Waldron
            44     Chapel and Classrooms, Woolton : SFX College Woolton Archive
            44     Foundation Stone laid in 1961 : SFX College Woolton Archive
            45     Beaconsfield Road, Entrance and Gatehouse : SFX College Woolton Archive
            45     The Coach House : SFX College Woolton Archive
            46     The Gables : SFX College Woolton Archive
            47     Entrance Hall, SFX College Woolton : SFX College Woolton Archive

47    College Chapel, SFX College Woolton : SFX College Woolton Archive
47    Assembly Hall, SFX College Woolton : SFX College Woolton Archive
48    Swimming Pool, SFX College Woolton : SFX College Woolton Archive
48    Sixth Form Library, SFX College Woolton : SFX  College Woolton Archive
48    Community House, SFX College Woolton : SFX College Woolton Archive
49    Lower School (Cardinal Newman) : Jonathan Murphy
49    Views of Old Xaverian Club (2) : J. Waldron
50    The Warner Building, SFX College Woolton : J. Waldron
51    The De La Mennais Centre, SFX College Woolton : J. Waldron
51    Old Xaverian Mass 2001, SFX College Woolton : J. Waldron
54    Liverpool Institute for Boys : J. Waldron
54    Liverpool Institute for Girls : J. Waldron
54    The Liverpool Collegiate : J. Waldron
55    St. Domingo House, Everton 1843: Sun Hai Li
65    College Memorial : SFX College Woolton Archive
66    Roll of Honour : Jonathan Murphy
70    Two Views of SFX, Salisbury Street : J. Waldron
70    Miss Edna Lewis : College Magazine : 1971
73    The New College at Woolton 2001 : SFX College Woolton Archive
85    The School Hall, SFX College, Salisbury Street : Mrs. T. Flynn
88    The College Stage, SFX College, Salisbury Street : Mrs. T. Flynn
89    The Baby Elephant : College Magazine, 1932
89    The Ten Minute Alibi : College Magazine, 1936
90    The Safety Match, 1929 : Kevin Reade
90    MacBeth : The Three Witches : College Magazine, 1923
92    Ratio atque Institutio Studiorum : Farm St. Archive
103   Henry IV. Part I, Act II, Scene 2 and 4, 1947 : P. Heery
104   The Mikado : College Magazine, 1968
106   The College Choir 1934 : Farm Street Archive
108   Ted Whitehead : E. A. Whitehead
109   Fr. Gerard Manley Hopkins, SJ : Farm St. Archive
112   Frs. Gerard, Vaughan, Tarleton, Donnelly : M. Whitehead
114   Intercollegiate Prize-winners : College Magazine 1949
120   College Shrine to Our Lady of Lourdes, SFX, Salisbury St.: College Archive
120   The Shrine of Our Lady at Woolton :  SFX College Woolton Archive
121   SFX Pilgrimage Group, Lourdes, 1957 : SFX College Woolton Archive
122   Original Pavilion, Melwood, 1921 : College Magazine, 1922
122   Pavilion Extended, 1932 : College Magazine, 1932
123   The Father Parry Shield : College Magazine, 1922
124   Challenge Cups 1931 : College Magazine, 1931
124   Athletic Sports, 1931. First Prize Winners : College Magazine, 1931
125   Senior Shield Winners, 1947 : College Magazine, 1947
125   Junior Shield Winners, 1959 : College Magazine, 1959
126   Senior Shield Winners, 1942 : College Magazine, 1942
126   Senior Shield Winners, 1920s : D. Hardman
126   Senior Shield Winners, 1950 : College Magazine, 1950
127   Senior Shield Winners, 1971 : College Magazine, 1971
127   Senior Shield Winners, 1976 : College Magazine, 1976
127   Senior Shield Winners, 1987:  College Magazine, 1987
128   Second Eleven, 1947-48 : G. Ridge
128   Junior Shield Winners, 1951 : College Magazine, 1951
129   First Eleven Cricket, 1962 : College Magazine, 1962

129 The Tennis Team, 1962 : College Magazine, 1962

129 First Eleven Cricket, 1960 : College Magazine, 1960

131 Trophies won by College Teams, 2000-2001 : SFX College Woolton Archive

131 Football Representative Honours, 1994-95 : College Magazine, 1995

135 The Ferula - two views : Stonyhurst Archive and G. Ridge

136 A Ferula Bill and a Red Bill : J. Douglas and P.P. Mc Carthy

138 Fr. Harris : M. Whitehead

140 SFX Boys, 1887 : P.P. McCarthy

140 SFX Class, 1883-84 : P.P. McCarthy

141 Masters at SFX, 1896 : P.P. McCarthy

141 V Classical, 1910-11 Football Team : F. Devereux

143 Form 1B, 1918 : Mrs T. Flynn

143 Fr. Woodlock and Fr. McCann (2) : R. W. Parkes

144 Frank Hart : Frank Hart

146 Fr. Woodlock : College Magazine, 1943

147 Junior B, Miss Carroll's Class, 1922 : Mrs T. Flynn

147 Two boys in caps : J. Heery

148 Mr. Checkland with Class 1935 : B. Duffy

149 Mr. Jones with IVB, 1937 : B. Duffy

149 Dr. Grace with Sixth Form, 1937 : F. Hart

150 Annual fixture with Everton F.C.. : D. Monaghan

151 Rev. W. J. Neylan : College Magazine. 1954

152 Boys and Staff at Mia Hall, Dyserth, 1940 : SFX College Woolton Archive

153 Mr. Britt-Compton with 3B, 1949 : J. Walsh

153 Mr. Hornby with 4S, 1948 : J. Walsh

154 The Chicks, 1946-47 : J. Heery

154 First Eleven Football, 1955-56 : G. Ridge

154 Colts Eleven Cricket, 1950 : G. Ridge

154 First Eleven Cricket, 1957 : G. Ridge

154 Senior Shield Winners at Goodison Park : M. O'Neill

154 First XI, 1952-53 : College Magazine, 1953

155 College Lay Staff, 1954 c. : SFX College Woolton Archive

155 Natty Lucas with class, 1950 c. : G. Glynn

156 Fr. Callaghan with class, 1950 c. : G. Glynn

156 Staff Dinner, 1953 : J. Heery

157 Fr. Neylan as seen by Mr. Van de Put : Simon Vandeput

158 Fr. Warner and Fr. Taunton at High Lee : F. Devereux

159 Cutting the First Sod : F. Devereux

161 First Eleven Football, 1961 : College Magazine, 1961

161 First Eleven Cricket, 1961 : College Magazine, 19611

162 Tennis Team, 1969 : College Magazine, 1969

163 Classical Odyssey, 1969 : SFX College Woolton Archive

165 Brother Francis, O.B.E. : Brother Francis

166 Oxford Awards, 1987 : College Magazine, 1987

168 Old Xaverian Cricketers, 1950s and 1960s : E. Frane

168 Basil d'Oliveira and Friends, 1984 : E. Frane

169 Friends and Servants of the College :  F. Devereux

171 Jonathan Murphy : J. Murphy

180 Fr. Price's chapel at corner of Dale St. and Sir Thomas St : H. J. Tiffen

185 Conjectural Map of Liverpool XIV Century : Liverpool Central Library

186 Drawing of Liverpool Mid XVII Century : Liverpool Central Library

187 River Mersey at High Water 1650 : Liverpool Central Library

188 Chadwick's Map Of Liverpool, 1725 : Liverpool Central Library

189 Sketch Map of Old Liverpool, St. Mary's ; R. J. Stonor

# Introduction

The foundation of St Francis Xavier's College in Liverpool in 1842 was an event intimately bound up with the struggle of the Jesuits to secure permission to build a church in Everton.

Between 1840 and 1842 a bitter dispute took place between the Vicar Apostolic (Glossary) and the Jesuits over whether or not permission should be given for the building of a Jesuit church in Salisbury Street, Liverpool. After two years of rancorous argument the matter had to be settled by Rome with the final decision taken by Pope Gregory XVI.

In some quarters this was seen as a struggle between those who were zealously in favour of absolute submission to papal authority, known as the ultramontanes, and those who argued for a degree of local independence, the cismontanes. The Jesuits were thought to imperil this local independence, as well as being accounted a hindrance to the development of Catholic emancipation in England. Others gave the dispute no such significance, seeing it only as a struggle for local control.

This sort of reference to Rome over a local dispute was not unusual at the time. England and Wales were still 'mission territories' and as such were under the direction of the Sacred Congregation de Propaganda Fide. The English and Welsh hierarchy of diocesan bishops was instituted in 1850 partly in order that the rule of law should obtain as against rule by episcopal intuition, which had led to a steady stream of appeals to the Vatican. At a meeting of a Parliamentary Select Committee in 1851 T. C. Anstey, a prominent Catholic MP, quoted Pope Gregory as declaring that he had more trouble in the administration of church officers in his province called England than he had with the church affairs of the Universal Church.

In the final decree, permission was given for the building of a church without any mention being made of the College. But there is sufficient internal evidence in the correspondence to maintain that the Pope was certainly aware of proposals for a school.

Cardinal Acton, an Anglo-Italian Vatican diplomat, was the first to suggest a college in Salisbury Street in a report he prepared for the Sacred Congregation de Propaganda Fide in 1841. Acton was not only the Pope's confidant, but also his close personal friend and it is inconceivable that Gregory would not have read Acton's Report with its proposals for Jesuit schools in England. This decision about the church would therefore probably have been influenced to some extent by the idea that one of the consequences would be the provision of education for the sons of the Liverpool middle classes.

Conflict marked the establishment of the College and it is an ever-recurring theme in the next 159 years. It started off as a struggle between the secular priests and the religious. It continued as a fight against the apathy of Liverpool businessmen and of parents, who readily withdrew boys after only a couple of years schooling for employment in the city. This threatened the survival of the College in its early days. The sectarian nature of local politics towards the end of the nineteenth century and the unwillingness of Government to give proper funding to schools like SFX were the next obstacles the College faced. Then, as the Government took steps to develop a national system of education in 1902, the College joined in the campaign of schools to run their own affairs - not least in deciding on their own religious curriculum. Between 1918 and 1945 there was comparative calm. But from 1945 to 2000 the College once more found itself embroiled in a series of exchanges - intra-Catholic as well as extra-Catholic - which it has successfully survived. It now provides to a high standard an education both secular and religious for the Catholic community of Liverpool.

# A Glossary of Terms

A number of terms used in Chapter 1 may need some explanation.

## Vicar Apostolic

Vicar Apostolic was the official administrative and pastoral title used till 1850 for the Bishop of an English or Welsh District, which was the forerunner of the modern diocese. The title Bishop was only rightfully used in England after Pope Pius IX formally reinstated the English and Welsh hierarchies in 1850. The term "Bishop" nonetheless was commonly used by clergy and laity alike before 1850. The vicars apostolic were consecrated as bishops - albeit of defunct early Christian dioceses often in Moslem countries. Protestant sensitivities had persuaded the Vatican in previous years not to give bishops names of English counties and towns.

## Sacred Congregation for the Propagation of the Faith

Usually referred to in the correspondence as 'Propaganda'. This Congregation, founded in 1622, is one of several powerful Vatican Committees. In the early nineteenth century its director - usually a cardinal - had great power and influence in settling differences amongst the English clergy, such as we are dealing with here in Chapter 1. England and Wales at this time were still formally counted as mission territories and this status meant that their affairs were directly the responsibility of Propaganda.

## The Society of Jesus

The Jesuit Order, founded by St Ignatius Loyola, received papal sanction in 1540. Known as the Soldiers of Christ, they came to exercise great political power in the sixteenth and seventeenth century throughout Europe. Their Superior General was sometimes referred to as the Black Pope, a reference to the black gown all Jesuits wear. For reasons more political than religious the Order was suppressed in 1773 by Pope Clement XIV and was not reinstated till 1814 by Pope Pius VII. It might be noticed in passing that antipathy towards the Jesuits has existed amongst both priests and laity down through the centuries. Bishops in particular resented the claims of religious orders to be exempt from their jurisdiction.

For two hundred years after the Reformation it became extremely dangerous for Catholic priests to operate in England, and numbers of Jesuits risked their lives to minister to the 25,000 Catholics who survived in south-west Lancashire. Their loyal presence in Lancashire during the dark days of the persecution was evinced as an argument in their favour at several points in the dispute of 1840.

## Secular and Regular Priests

The dispute in Liverpool was a struggle for control between the secular clergy and the Jesuit Order, who were regulars. The secular priests, then as now, owed their allegiance to the bishop and served in his parish churches. The regulars were monks, priests and religious who belonged to a religious order (like the Benedictines, the Dominicans, and the Jesuits) who obeyed a rule and owed their obedience to an abbot or a superior general. Such hostility between the two sides in 1840 was not an unusual feature in clerical relations.

## Canonical Distance

Canon Law, which regulates the administration of church affairs, laid down that a new church could not be built within a certain distance of an already existing church. In Liverpool in 1840 this was one mile. Part of the controversy was that the Jesuits, it was claimed, were proposing to build inside this limit.

## Stonyhurst College

This school in Lancashire was run by the Jesuits as a boarding school for the sons of the upper classes. The College was originally founded in France at St Omer in 1593. It moved to Bruges in 1762 and then to

Liege in 1773. When the Jesuits were forced out of the independent principality of Liege at the time of the French Revolution, the College transferred to Stonyhurst in 1794. At the time of the dispute the Provincial, the title of the superior of the Order in England, had his headquarters at Stonyhurst. The misconception that SFX was intended as a prep. school for Stonyhurst was not unusual even in the twentieth century. This was never the case, even though pupils did transfer regularly to Stonyhurst at the age of thirteen.

## Ratio Studiorum or Plan of Studies

The character and objects of the Society of Jesus, its method and its system of administration are laid down in the Constitutions of the Society which were drawn up by St Ignatius. The Ratio, which was first published in 1599, is devoted to the system of studies to be followed in the Order's schools and colleges. Called the *Ratio Studiorum,* or Plan of Studies, it is more method than principle and is essentially a system of school organization, a curriculum and a practical method of teaching and was never meant to be followed to the letter.

## Prefect of Studies

The Ratio gave the title of Prefect of Studies to the office of Headmaster, who was responsible for all academic matters. There was a second senior official known as the Prefect General or the Prefect of Discipline, whose duties covered the general discipline of the college and the management of staff and pupils. Both were answerable to the Rector, the head of the local Jesuit community.

In a small college these two offices were often combined in the  one person, as was the case at SFX from 1842 - 1874. But in 1874 a Prefect of Studies and a Prefect General were appointed separately, although for local reasons the title Prefect General was not used. Instead at SFX - and in no other college - the Prefect General was known as 'Vice-President of the College'. These titles continued to be used at SFX College till 1938, when the roles of Prefect of Studies and Vice-President were combined and the single title 'Headmaster' replaced them.

## The Xaverian

In 1884 the Jesuits who ran St Francis Xavier's Church began to publish a monthly parish magazine which from the beginning was a publication of some substance. It detailed all the activities of the parish  - including those of the College - and printed articles of both a religious and social nature. The sections devoted to life at the College have proved an invaluable source of material. The College entry continued till the *College Magazine* was started in 1920.

*South end of the College, Salisbury Street*

The editor of The Xaverian for 1892 decided to  'rummage amongst the records'. Using contemporary records from 1845-1863 he devoted several issues to a description of the affairs of the College from 1845. These entries were based on ledgers, diaries and record books that the editor had discovered amongst the College papers. It is unfortunate that these primary sources have since disappeared.

## St Francis Xavier's College

The College went under different names in its early years. In the  programmes which date from 1851 it is called St Francis Xavier's Schools or St Francis Xavier's Catholic School. From 1856 it is referred to as St Francis Xavier's Collegiate Schools. In 1857 we have SFX Collegiate Schools and SFX College. Thereafter it is always SFX College. It was officially designated a College by the Provincial in 1857, when it ceased to be a collegium inchoatum or an embryonic college. In these pages it is referred to throughout as 'College".

xvi

The History of St. Francis Xavier's College, Liverpool, 1842-2001

*Chapter 1*

# England's First Catholic Day Secondary School

Even before it had opened, the new school was involved in a rancorous dispute over the building of the new church of St. Francis Xavier. A remarkable feature of this dispute was the unusual, if not unique, way in which the Sacred Congregation de Propaganda Fide in Rome became involved. It seems strange to us today that the Congregation should have had laid before it the case for the opening of a new school some thirteen hundred miles away in Liverpool. Yet the proposal to open a Jesuit secondary school there first saw the light of day in a report which Monsignor Acton, a highly-placed Vatican Secretary and an English aristocrat, was asked to prepare for *Propaganda*. It is perhaps significant that, by the time Propaganda came to consider the Report in 1842, Acton had been made a Cardinal.

St. Francis Xavier's Preparatory, Classical and Commercial Day School welcomed its first pupils at Number 36 Soho Street on 27 October 1842. 'Preparatory' was used in the sense of 'preparing for a career'. Two pupils turned up on the first day in answer to the advertisement placed in The Liverpool Mercury by Father Randal Lythgoe, SJ. Two months later the new school could still only muster three pupils. By March 1843 there were eleven pupils on the register and there must have been real fears for the future of the School. In November of the following year the School moved to 43 St. Anne Street. Then in 1846 it transferred to Number 6 Salisbury Street, using rooms in the newly-built Presbytery for the twenty-four boys now on roll. There it stayed for the next 135 years.

THE

## Liverpool Mercury,

### AND LANCASHIRE GENERAL ADVERTISER.

| No. 1641—Vol. XXXII. | FRIDAY, OCTOBER 21, 1842. | PRICE FIVEPENCE. |

CATHOLIC PREPARATORY DAY SCHOOL

No. 36 Soho Street

THE Rev. R. LYTHGOE begs to announce to the Catholics of Liverpool that he has taken measures for OPENING A PREPARATORY CLASSICAL AND COMMERCIAL DAY SCHOOL, at No. 36 Soho Street, to be conducted by Masters from, and in connection with Stonyhurst. The Religious and Moral Instruction of the pupils will form the first care of the teachers. The Pupils will also be taught different branches of education usually taught in such schools, and when Parents wish it, French, Latin, and Greek also, *without any extra charge.*
The Terms will be Two Pounds Ten Shilling per Quarter; payment to be made in advance. Pens, Ink and Paper will be provided. School Books will be the only extra charge. Application for Admission must be made to the Rev. FRANCIS LYTHGOE. (late of Holywell) No. 36 Soho St. The school will be Opened on Thursday next, the 27th instant

*Liverpool Mercury 21 October 1842*

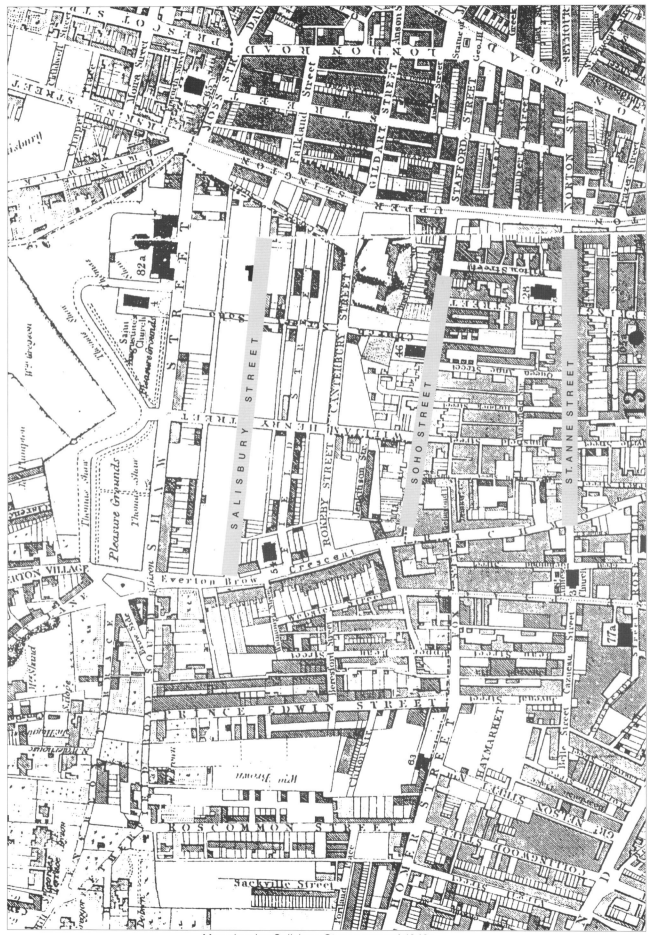

*Map showing Salisbury St area around 1840c.*

# St Francis Xavier's Church : The Dispute

The disagreement between supporters and opponents of the opening of a new Jesuit church and school in Liverpool in the 1840s was seen to have national and canonical importance. It was all to do with the powers of the Vicars Apostolic (Bishops) vis-a-vis the rights of religious orders - particularly with respect to the building of churches in post-Emancipation England and Wales. As such it was recognized as an important test case by both sides. Fr. Bird, the Jesuit Provincial of the day, had perhaps overstated the case when he said in a letter to another Jesuit, Fr. Clarke of Gillmoss, in October 1840 that *'if we are defeated, we must give up London and every other place'.* But such feelings indicate the seriousness of the emerging confrontation.

The main Jesuit protagonist in the dispute was Fr. Randal Lythgoe SJ, who succeeded Fr. Bird as Provincial of the Jesuit Order in 1841. His main opponent was Bishop George Brown, the Vicar-Apostolic of Lancashire. Bishop Brown was a reluctant bishop and no friend of Liverpool or the Jesuits. His predecessor as Vicar Apostolic, Bishop George Briggs, had also opposed the building of the church.

*Fr. Randal Lythgoe SJ.*
*English Provincial 1841-1851*

*Bishop George Brown*
*Vicar Apostolic of Lancashire 1840-56*

Fr. Lythgoe was ably supported in the dispute by Fr. Bird; and Bishop Brown was constantly encouraged by Fr. M. Wilcock, Parish Priest of St. Anthony's, the church that would be most affected by the new building.

# The Preliminaries  January 1840

In January 1840 nine Catholic laymen met at the Rose and Crown Tavern in Cheapside, and the Society of St. Francis Xavier, which was formed there, met regularly for two years. Most of these men had some connection with the Jesuits. Some had relatives in the Order. Some recognized the debt owed to the Jesuits by their families in the dark years when Catholicism was forbidden. Some had been pupils at Stonyhurst, the Jesuits' boarding school for sons of the upper classes in Lancashire.

At their first meeting they signed an agreement.

> 'We, the undersigned, form ourselves into a provisional committee for the formation of a society with the view to erect a Catholic Church in Liverpool to be presented to the President of Stonyhurst College.'

This was signed by a list of prominent Catholic laymen - Polding, Lightbound, Jenkins, Callen, Lennon, Madden, Langsdale, Holme and Moreton.

This was followed later that month with a prospectus.

> 'Such has been the increase of Catholicity in Liverpool during the last few years that it has become absolutely necessary to add to the present number of our places of worship. To assist so desirable an object, we, the undersigned, have resolved with the help of God to endeavour to erect another edifice for the propagation of the Catholic faith. We know that it will be a task requiring energy and industry, but, labouring in a holy cause, we have every confidence that it will ultimately succeed. We propose that the projected church should be served by clergymen connected with Stonyhurst whose predecessors were once the only Catholic Missionaries in Liverpool and to them, under God, we may esteem ourselves indebted for the preservation of our faith at that period.'

It should be noted that at this stage no mention was made of a college. Nor was there for the next two years, as the debate raged over the rights of the Jesuits to build St. Francis Xavier's Church. Only in the last stages was the idea of a college raised on the back of the debate with the result that the school started in 1842. The church did not open its doors till 1848.

**Round One   February - May 1840**

# The Seeds of Disagreement

So far so good. That the signatories were in earnest was left in no doubt when in February 1840 they arranged the purchase of the land on which the church was finally built.

It is an indication of the blurred boundaries between priest and people in relation to power and authority at the time that the Committee had acted without consulting the Vicar Apostolic (Bishop) or the Society of Jesus itself. Fr. Lythgoe SJ met the Committee in January, drew their attention to this lapse and wrote to his Provincial, Fr. Bird, at Stonyhurst, reporting his meeting.

The Committee hastened to correct its mistakes with two letters.

The first letter was sent to Fr. Bird in February.

> "We have secured a plot of land in Salisbury Street, Upper Islington, (extent 3000 square yards) eligibly situated (about midway between the Chapels of St. Anthony and St. Nicholas) in a respectable part of the town  and where a church would be desirable. It is our intention to make over the land and church entirely to the disposal of your Society, as you may direct. We are at present engaged in procuring additional signatures to be presented to our Bishop, which we intend to forward on Thursday 13th inst., craving his blessing on our undertaking."

That blessing was not forthcoming,

By the middle of February a second letter had gone to Dr. Briggs, the Vicar Apostolic of the Northern Vicariate, in which the members of the Committee made plain their intentions, informed him of the purchase of the land and 'solicited any pecuniary assistance' the Bishop might be able to give. Dr. Briggs' reply was curt and unhelpful. He replied in a letter dated 19 February 1840 that he would give their request 'his early and best consideration'.

The Committee responded in somewhat contrite fashion, defending their motives in terms that foreshadowed the disagreements to come.

> 'It has been more than insinuated that our motives are not pure, and that disingenuous means have been employed by us in obtaining signatories to the address we presented 24 February 1840.'

But on 23 March Dr. Briggs wrote back to Mr. Polding 'refusing consent and asking the Society of St. Francis Xavier to cease from making any further public collections.'

# Confrontation

In May 1840 the secular clergy, feeling threatened by what they saw as expansionist plans by the Jesuits, sent a letter to Dr. Briggs, seeking 'to avoid unseemly and discreditable warfare'. In the light of subsequent events the word 'warfare' was appropriate. The letter goes on to object to the proposed new church and to the development of the work of the Jesuits and Benedictines in the city. The Benedictines were already operating at St. Mary's, St. Peter's and St. Austin's. St Anne's in Edge Hill had been sanctioned. Dr. Briggs was asked to pass the letter on to the Sacred Congregation de Propaganda Fide, which he did.

Whether in response to this letter of the seculars or not, later that month the Committee of The Society of St. Francis Xavier took the unusual, yet canonically correct, step of appealing to Rome also. On 3 May the Committee resolved that

> ' A memorial be framed praying for instructions regarding the future proceedings of the Society of St. Francis Xavier in its undertakings, embodying the Address of the Society to Dr. Briggs and his Lordship's definite reply; that the memorial be signed by each member of the committee and that this memorial be addressed to Cardinal Fransoni at Rome, the Director of Propaganda.'

If this was the end of Round One, then the points were shared.

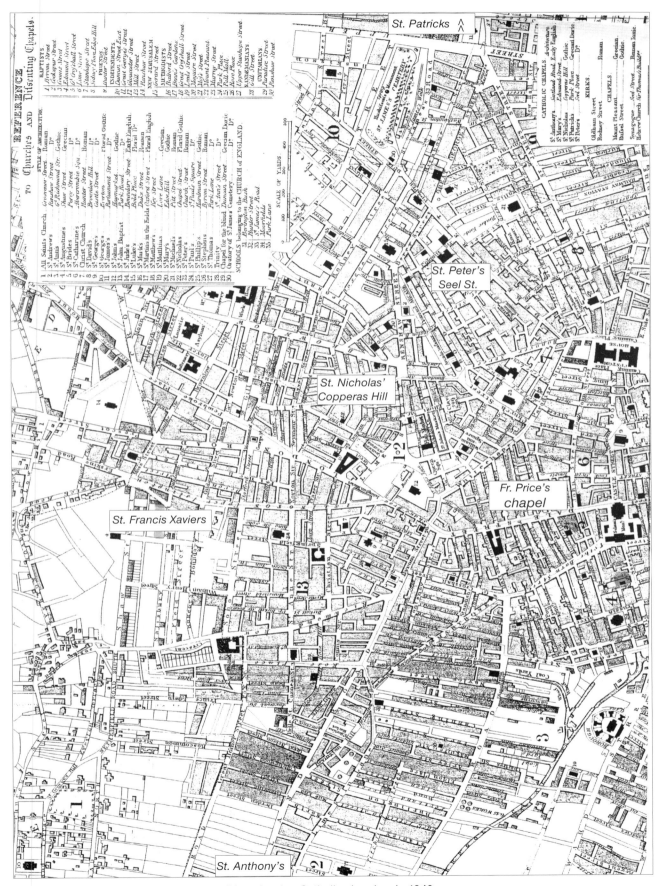

*Map showing Catholic churches in 1840s.*

**Round Two   July - November 1840**

## Settlement - Aborted

Before the Committee's Memorial to Rome could be considered, in July 1840 Pope Gregory XVI redrew the ecclesiastical regions in England and Wales. Four vicariates became eight, and Lancashire, which had been part of the Northern Vicariate, was now a separate administrative unit. Dr. Brown, the new Vicar in Lancashire, met Fr. Bird, the Jesuit Provincial, at Stonyhurst College shortly after and agreement was reached between them for the erection of the church in Salisbury Street.

There were protests from three different quarters against the decision of Dr. Brown to agree to the new church. One group consisted of those Catholics who were simply anti-Jesuit, accusing the Order of snobbery, of being too academic, and of being interested in rich parishes only. The second group, led by St. Anthony's and its outspoken priest, Fr. Wilcock, saw their financial interests threatened by the new-comer. The third and least biased group simply saw no need for another church in that area, which, in truth, at that time embraced a very small Catholic population.

The Committee's case in answer was that the church was not intended as a parish church and therefore presented no threat to revenues. The Members of the Committee claimed that St. Nicholas' and St. Anthony's were in fact incapable of accommodating all the Catholics in their own areas, as things stood, and that the district of Everton was being opened up as a residential area with churches already being built there by other denominations.

A series of letters on the topic reflect the mounting disagreement. From 1 October to 3 November 1840 sixteen were written - nine of them between the Bishop and the Provincial. They always stayed on the right side of politeness - just. *'I am sorry that Your Lordship should be so much troubled'*. *'I entertain a sincere respect for yourself (Fr. Bird) and your Society'*. *'I have only ever spoken of you (Bishop Brown) in terms of great respect and in expressions of much personal regard'*.

The Bishop finished one letter with the words *'I am the last man in the world who would interfere with the rights of anyone'*. A gentle man, but a weak administrator, as one contemporary cleric described him, it is perhaps too easy to malign him in this confrontation.

The fact that letters in reply were often sent off within twenty-four hours of receipt is perhaps some indication of the underlying passion. Fr. Bird accused his opponents of *'treating us like a parcel of fools'*. Dr. Brown is quoted as saying that he was now *'determined to lay down my life rather than shrink from my duty'* on the Liverpool question. *'St. Anthony's would be ruined by the new church'*. Fr. Lythgoe complained to his superior that the bishop *'suffered from want of nerve - and was allowing himself to be pressured by his clergy'*. Brown and Bird clashed in particular over aspects of Canon Law, both of them appealing selectively to precedent and papal decrees, as it suited their arguments.

Some attempts were made to ease the tension by both sides. Rome was drawn deeper and deeper into the controversy. But by Christmas 1840 at the end of Round Two, after four more exchanges between Bird and Brown, there was the same intransigent stand-off that had characterized this dispute from the beginning.

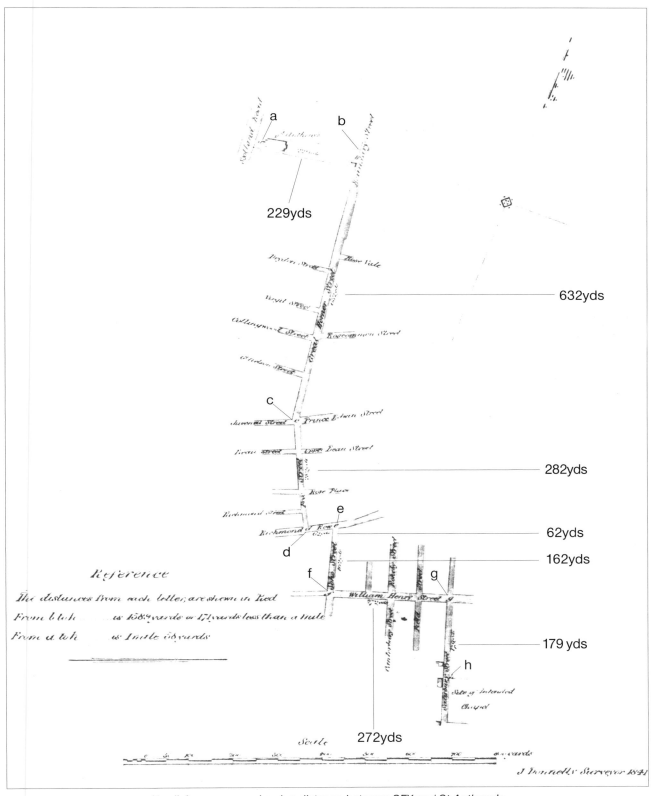

*'1 mile' survey map showing distance between SFX and St Anthony's*

**Round Three   January - August 1841**

# First Report of the Society of St. Francis Xavier

On the 24 January 1841 the Committee published its first annual report, in which it expressed its hopes for success in their endeavours in the near future. As red rags go, this was bright red indeed. In February Dr. Brown wrote to Fr. Bird, as Jesuit Provincial, complaining formally about the actions of Fr. Lythgoe and the Society of St. Francis Xavier. He regarded their behaviour as *'a grievous violation of respect and submission to authority'*. Not for the first time he demanded that their activities cease.

Dr. Brown also wrote the same month to Cardinal Fransoni at *Propaganda.* He ended this letter by saying that he would prefer to return to the tranquillity and obscurity of his former work, catechising the country folk of North Lancashire, than to have to continue much longer with his present problems with the Jesuits in Liverpool.

There was also a telling response from St. Anthony's to the Annual Report of the Society of St. Francis Xavier. A circular letter dated 10 February 1841 was distributed which dealt cogently with the origins of the parish, the probable impact of the new church of St. Francis Xavier, and the financial implications for a church already heavily in debt. Well argued and beautifully written this letter is reproduced in its entirety at Annex 4.

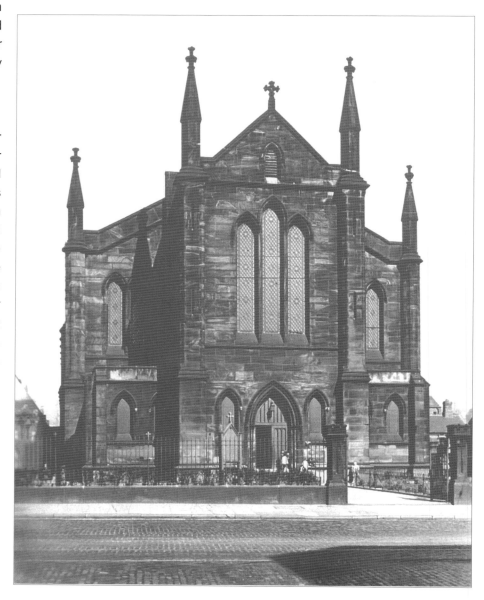

From April to November 1841 there were further exchanges of letters and even conciliatory meetings of the protagonists which went sour. Frs. Bird and Lythgoe both tried to pressurize Rome to force Dr. Brown to submit. The Society of St. Francis Xavier was becoming downcast and there are indications that they felt the fight was about to be lost.

Round Three had gone to the Bishop with a sense that an end was in sight which did not favour the Jesuits.

*St. Anthony's Church,*
*Scotland Road*

**Round Four   September 1841 - April 1842**

# Propaganda Decides

In September 1841 Fr. Randal Lythgoe was made Provincial. At almost the same time he received the welcome news from Rome that a decision would not be long delayed. And that the decision was now likely to support the Jesuit cause.

Probably as a result of this news, Lythgoe attempted further efforts at reconciliation in October, but he was rebuffed by Dr. Brown in no uncertain terms. The Bishop refused to see Lythgoe and left for Rome, determined *'to conquer or lay down my mitre'.*

Dr. Brown was in Rome from March to April 1842. It is clear from the letter of Dr. Brown to Liverpool dated April 22nd and published in full at Annex 2 that his mind was finally changed for him by no less an authority than Pope Gregory himself. On 17 April 1842 *Propaganda* issued a decree which favoured the Jesuits. It can be assumed that the support they had enlisted in the beginning from Monsignor Acton had been crucial.

Dr. Brown returned to England in a much more conciliatory mood.

Nonetheless the opposition were still not prepared to throw in the towel. As their solution to the problem, St. Anthony's, through Dr. Brown, submitted to *Propaganda* the proposal that the Jesuits should be empowered to open a school with a church attached for the scholars, and, by implication, with no rights to serve the local community. It is impossible to know whether this suggestion was made once Dr. Brown knew of the decision of *Propaganda* - both sides had their informers working for them in Rome. It is more likely that he knew that Cardinal Acton's Report, which *Propaganda* was about to consider, contained a detailed discussion of the idea of colleges being opened by the Jesuits in England. If so, then this could have been an attempt to twist the situation to their own advantage. The Jesuits themselves rejected the proposal as preposterous - *'illusory to the highest degree'.* (Extracts from the Report can be found at Annex 1)

Given the conditions, Round Four had ended with a victory on points for the Society of St. Francis Xavier. But it was not the knock-out they wanted,

# The Terms laid down by de Propaganda Fide

On 17 April 1842 *Propaganda* issued the decree addressed to the Jesuit General, Fr. Jan Roothaan. The Jesuits were to be allowed to build a church in Liverpool, but it was not to be opened for six years. In addition the church was to pay the Bishop £10 a year. It would not be authorized to carry out baptisms, marriages or funerals.

Of the possibility of a school no mention was made. But Professor Whitehead writes that Fr. Lythgoe was not slow in responding to Cardinal Acton's suggestion in his Report to *Propaganda*, that a Jesuit day-school should be opened in Liverpool. Unable to open a church in the town for six years, Lythgoe did not want to lose the opportunity of opening a house and a school which would allow educational work to begin; nor did he wish to delay further such an initiative, as the educational needs of the Anglican middle classes of Liverpool were now being met in the newly-founded Liverpool College, (later The Collegiate) then in the course of construction in Shaw Street, overlooking the very site of the proposed church of St. Francis Xavier.

The speed with which Fr. Lythgoe reacted may also have been connected with the fact that earlier the same week Dr. Brown had placed an advertisement for a new Catholic secondary school, the Catholic Institute, at St. Domingo House in Everton, not a mile from the SFX site, which later became St. Edward's College.

The delay of six years before the church could open seems to have been the instrumental factor in persuading Fr. Lythgoe to establish a foothold immediately by opening the new St. Francis Xavier's Preparatory, Classical and Commercial Day-School. The advertisement was placed, the School opened, and a modest start was made to the education of Catholic boys in Liverpool.

*The Architect's drawing for St. Francis Xavier's Church*

*Chapter 2*

# The College Premises

Since 1842 the College has taught its pupils in eight different sets of buildings.

| | |
|---|---|
| **1842 - 1843** | **36 Soho Street** |
| **1843 - 1845** | **43 St. Anne Street** |
| **1846 - 1856** | **6 Salisbury Street, sharing the Presbytery** |
| **1856 - 1877** | **Purpose-built College next to the Presbytery** |
| **1876 - 1877** | **13 Salisbury Street, 4 Salisbury Street and in rooms in the Presbytery, as the new College was being built** |
| **1877 - 1908** | **New College on site of 6 Salisbury Street** |
| **1908 - 1961** | **An addition built in space between the Presbytery and the 1877 school. The 1856 building was demolished.** |
| **1961 - 2001** | **Move to the new building in Woolton. Warner Building was added in 1995 to accommodate part of the Lower School, and the De la Mennais Sixth-Form Centre was built in 2000** |

The College started out in what were rather grand three-storey and four-storey town houses in Soho Street and St Anne Street. It had its first school with regular classrooms in the Presbytery at Number 8 Salisbury Street, which it shared with the Jesuit Community.

Its first purpose-built college came in 1856. Its second was built in 1877, the surviving red-brick pile still a familiar sight at the top of Islington. In 1908 the fine 1856 building was demolished and an extension was added in the space left between the Presbytery and the 1877 College.

In 1961 the College moved to lavish new premises in Woolton, where facilities have been since improved with major additional buildings .

Church                 *Presbytery  College  4 Salisbury St*

*Salisbury St. 1873*
*(NB The steeple was not added till 1883)*

**Part 1**

# The First Three College Premises

## Soho St., St Anne St., Salisbury St. 1842-1856

### 36 Soho Street

Fr. Francis Lythgoe was the first Rector of the new Community and the first Prefect of Studies at the College. He welcomed SFX's first pupils at Number 36 Soho Street on 27 October 1842. With only two pupils, accommodation was hardly a problem.

*Soho Street*

### 43 St Anne Street

A year later Fr. Lythgoe and his two Scholastics (priests-in-training) moved the College to 43 St. Anne Street - now with a dozen pupils on roll.

*St Anne Street*

## 6 Salisbury Street

In 1844 Fr. Johnson took over from Fr. Lythgoe, and in 1846 he transferred 24 pupils to the newly-opened presbytery at 6 Salisbury Street. Fr. Johnson remained in charge with a small staff till 1852.

Soho Street, St Anne Street and Salisbury Street were good residential streets in an attractive under-developed area. It was described by those who first broached the idea of a new church on this site as 'a respectable part of town'. Indeed this was one of the reasons the Bishop had objected in the first place, preferring the Jesuits to go to work in the tough slums along the docks. There were good views over the town from Salisbury Street and on clear days the Wirral and the Welsh hills could be seen. The Mayor had a cottage in Soho Street. The Prince Consort had lodged in St. Anne Street, and it counted as one of Liverpool's more fashionable districts.

*Map of Rural Everton. Map by William Swire 1824*

The street map of 1836 shows the Salisbury Street area still unbuilt with the rural stretches of Everton village just up the hill to the North. By 1845 houses of uniform design but of a superior class - according to Fr. Ryan in his book *St. Francis Xavier's Church: Centenary* - had been built in Salisbury St. itself and No. 8 had been bought to serve as Presbytery, Community House and College. The church on the corner of Salisbury St. and Langdale St. was consecrated in 1848.

No 4 at the corner of Salisbury Street and Carver Street, bought in 1852, was used by the College as its Commercial Department till its demolition in 1875. The Jesuits now owned the whole of the north side of the street between Langdale St. and Carver St.

Fr. Johnson and Fr. West with two scholastics ran the College between 1851 and 1853, teaching the twenty-four pupils in one of the two front rooms of the Presbytery. When the church was opened in 1848, the chapel at No 8 was divided by a partition to give two more classrooms, one for the juniors and one for the seniors. With this extra space, numbers began to increase slowly. An Academy Room was added later upstairs, capable of seating 400 people, where plays and exhibitions were staged.

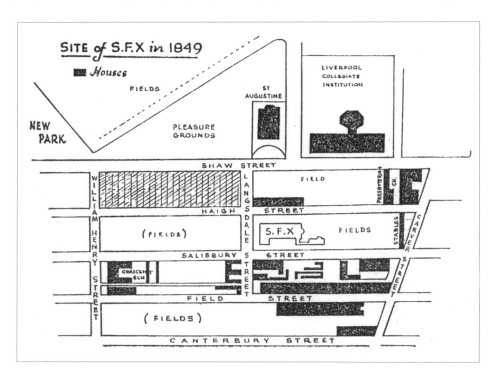

# Two Purpose-built Colleges - 1856 and 1877

### First College Building 1856

By 1855, with more than fifty pupils on roll, Father Collyns, the Rector, decided new premises were needed. The new College, described later by The Xaverian as 'a lovely Gothic construction', was built on the site of 6 Salisbury Street, next to The Presbytery at No.8. In this building the College Office and the Chapel followed the line of the street, but little is known of the internal arrangement. The College complex was made up with 4 Salisbury Street on the corner with Carver Street and 13 Salisbury Street opposite, both of which housed the Commercial School at one stage or another.

These new buildings served the community well for twenty years, but by 1870 with over 250 pupils, accommodation was hardly sufficient and Father Thomas Porter, the Rector, decided to retain the 1856 building, but to erect a new college alongside with classrooms for 500 pupils.

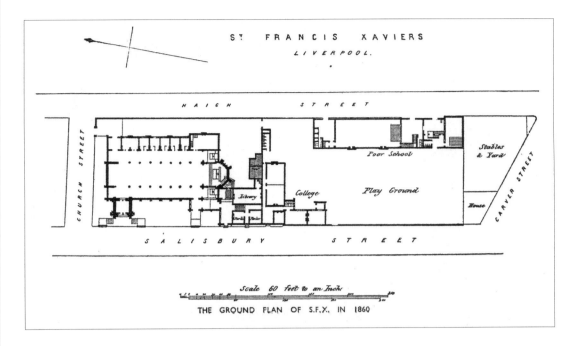

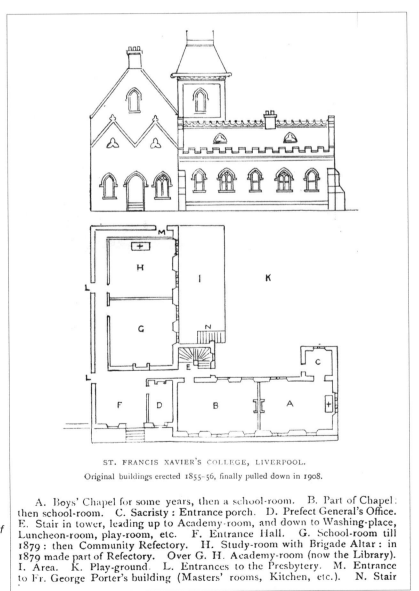

ST. FRANCIS XAVIER'S COLLEGE, LIVERPOOL.
Original buildings erected 1855-56, finally pulled down in 1908.

A. Boys' Chapel for some years, then a school-room.   B. Part of Chapel: then school-room.   C. Sacristy : Entrance porch.   D. Prefect General's Office. E. Stair in tower, leading up to Academy-room, and down to Washing-place, Luncheon-room, play-room, etc.   F. Entrance Hall.   G. School-room till 1879 : then Community Refectory.   H. Study-room with Brigade Altar : in 1879 made part of Refectory.   Over G. H. Academy-room (now the Library). I. Area.   K. Play-ground.   L. Entrances to the Presbytery.   M. Entrance to Fr. George Porter's building (Masters' rooms, Kitchen, etc.).   N. Stair

*Diagram of lay-out of 1856 College (Letters and Notices, Number 31, pp. 234-235)*

## Second College Building 1877 : Clutton's Magnificent Pile 1877

As early as 1867, as numbers increased, Father Weld, the Provincial, had decided to build a new College, but there were delays, partly owing to strikes, and the project never got under way.

By 1870 Fr. Harris' robust approach was having its effects - he had taken over as Prefect of Studies in 1865. It was now clear that the school numbers desperately demanded larger premises. In 1875, with 270 pupils, Thomas Porter, the Rector,  asked Father Richard Vaughan, a science teacher at the College, but hardly a professional architect, to draw a bold new plan for a single building in Salisbury Street. It was to accommodate 500 pupils; and the hall, seating 2000 people, was  to be a meeting place for the Catholics of the city. The choice of Fr. Vaughan was not that remarkable. He had previous architectural commissions to his name - including several important buildings in Glasgow and Edinburgh, and at the Jesuit schools of  Beaumont and Mount St Mary's. But his work was described as severely plain without any architectural effect: the sole aim was utility.

Clearing began in 1875. For two years the pupils were dotted around the district. 13 Salisbury Street in particular was used to bursting point. Then, as the foundations were being laid, doubts were expressed. Fr. Gallwey, The Provincial,  decided that the building proposed by Fr. Vaughan was not worthy of the Society. He recruited a new architect, Henry Clutton in September 1875. With a humility not found in every Jesuit, Fr. Vaughan co-operated with the new plans whole-heartedly.

*Fr. Vaughan's Rejected Plan ( a drawing based on the only surviving image in the Vatican)*

# Clutton's Designs for the New College

Henry Clutton was one of the foremost Catholic architects of the day, who built in his own idiosyncratic style. He had been appointed architect for the proposed Catholic Cathedral in Westminster, although this was eventually built to the designs of his pupil J.F. Bentley. For some Westminster's loss was SFX's gain.

Clutton was very interested in French domestic architecture of the fifteenth and sixteenth centuries and was the author of a very successful book *Domestic Architecture of France in the Middle Ages*. He was a master of early French Gothic and a leader of the Gothic revival in France. Everything he built reflected these concerns.

Clutton designed for SFX an 'amazingly vigorous' building in what is sometimes mistakenly referred to as 'a striking Queen Anne style'. Clutton and a friend, William Burges, travelled to France on a number of occasions, sketching as they went. It is clear from these sketches, some of which are reproduced here, that the new College is indebted not to Queen Anne, but to Hôtel de Ville. The dormers, the turrets and the horizontal repetitive line are Clutton trademarks and in the French tradition he espoused. His buildings were bold but never pretty. Utility, reality, space, scale, and mass were the chief principles of his designs, but his details were invariably French. He specifically argued against copying the French style; times and materials had changed. But he did advocate borrowing elements appropriately.

'It is quite possible to obtain many useful and valuable suggestions from a careful study of the composition of these (French) buildings and of their details.'

These 'valuable suggestions' he used to good effect at SFX.

Henry Clutton, Architect

*Clutton's sketches*

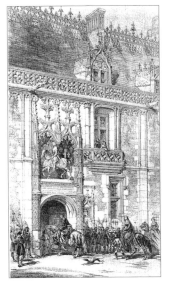

In the new College a number of features seen in his drawings stand out. The spectacularly flamboyant dormers, the triangular gables set in pierced tracery panels, and the whole rich silhouette which the school still presents to the West. For the sake of comparison a picture of another of his local designs is included here - the Church of Our Lady of Compassion in Formby; its solid round towers and buttresses again show French influence.

 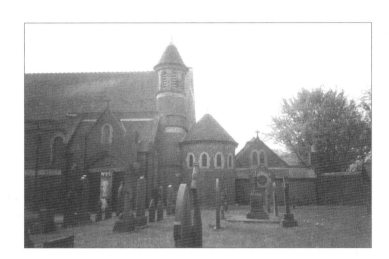

*'Our Lady of Compassion, Formby '*

Amongst the dozens of Anglican and Catholic churches Clutton designed, one in particular should be mentioned in passing - the Chapel of the Sacred Heart in the Church of the Immaculate Conception, the Jesuit headquarters in Farm Street in London. St. Michaels' in Widnes, originally a Jesuit church, is another fine example of his work.

By November 1875 it was decided that Vaughan's ground plan should be retained, but that Clutton would do a new elevation. This was ready and approved in a few weeks and building began on 29 November The architect's plan was printed in Building and Engineering News of May 1876. In the event no clock tower was built nor was the fleche, the arrow spire, intended for the central roof.

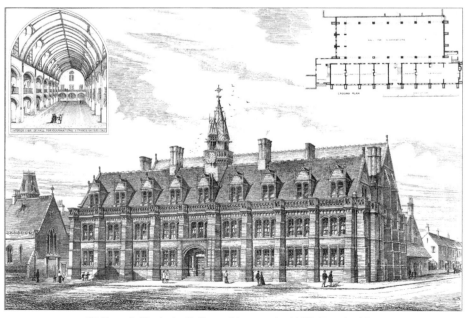

*St Francis Xavier's College, Liverpool.   H.Clutton Architect*

P S Hunting in a PhD. thesis for London University in 1979, 'The Life and Work of Henry Clutton', writes :

'SFX, a formidable building in Clutton's French Gothic style, incorporates many of the features of French Hôtel de Ville. Built of local red brick and terra cotta on an even design on a corner. The length of building is divided by ten buttresses giving nine bays of three light windows. Entrance is a small arched door and there is a highly pitched roof broken by distinctive dormer windows behind an open balustrade which unites the composition. Strict attention was paid to economy of design, giving the effect of stripped Gothic, but the obtrusive dormer windows and the Flèche add a peculiar fire to a simple plan.'

The new College was completed in the summer of 1877 at a cost of £30,000 and the Beadle's log dated 8 August 1877 is quoted in Letters and Notices No. 31. p. 301 :

'In 1877 the College was finished and Thomas Porter, the Rector, with Father Harris and the Masters met the boys for the first time in the large hall. The echo in the hall was so great that scarcely a word of what was intended to be pleasant and encouraging was heard. The students however seemed to know by a sort of boyish instinct what was meant and applauded vigorously, rightly guessing that they were to have extra play'.

The Great Hall came to be known as Vaughan's Folly.

INTERIOR VIEW OF HALL FOR EXAMINATIONS, ST FRANCIS XAVIER'S COLLEGE

THE ORIGINAL COLLEGE HALL

THE HALL, WHEN ST. FRANCIS XAVIER'S BILATERAL SCHOOL TOOK IT OVER, 1961

## Additions in 1884

In 1884 the Presbytery was enlarged. Letters and Notices of 1911 records 'The two gables of Fr. Collyn's 1856 College building were taken down, and the wall rebuilt to the height of the old house, the latter receiving a new front, with improved window light and six additional rooms. The door of old No. 8, for long the entrance to the Presbytery and the College, was removed and a window took its place.'

The same year the Singing Gallery was added - presumably in the hope that the abominable acoustics of Vaughan's Folly might be improved. They were not. But at least the Gallery gave some character to the vast space for the next hundred years.

*Church, Presbytery & College 1907*

In the November edition of the Xaverian in 1884 the building of the Gallery is recorded.

'Hitherto at Entertainments given in the College a large part of the audience towards the back of the Hall has always been seriously inconvenienced through not being able to see the stage. To remedy this defect, the seats, commencing about half way down the Hall, will be raised towards the back so that each person seated there will be able to see over the the heads of those in front. In addition to this, there will be a raised gallery supported on iron pillars, which will slope upwards as far back as the partition separating the present Sodality Chapel from the body of the Hall. This Gallery will seat nearly 400 persons and the slope is calculated to give to all a complete view of the stage.'

In 1906 Father Joseph Browne, The Rector, had the 1856 buildings demolished - with some recrimination for the loss of this small Gothic gem. A new wing, designed in the style of the original by the architect Mr. Honan, was built on the site between the Presbytery and the 1877 College. This only took ten months, even though excavations struck old quarry workings and digging had to go down forty feet before solid rock was reached.

*Extension to the College built in 1908 on the site of the demolished 1856 school*

No other major work took place till the College moved out to Woolton, although, for the record, there were some minor improvements. The Xaverian of 1885 praises the new Harris Memorial Organ, erected to the left of the stage. The organ was heard for the first time in December at the Christmas Proclamation. After its removal in 1909 the organ was installed in St. Mary's, Douglas, in the Isle of Man, where it still serves the church community there.

There were changes made to the Sodality Chapel to give two new schoolrooms. The Physics Laboratory was equipped in 1899, using money donated by Sir Joseph Walton, an Old Xaverian and eminent judge. In 1935 a new library and a chemistry laboratory were added. In 1937 the proscenium arch was installed with two classrooms built over the stage, which nevertheless remained capable of flying its scenery.

*Crucifix and Shrine, S.F.X. College, Liverpool.*

S.F.X. College, Liverpool.

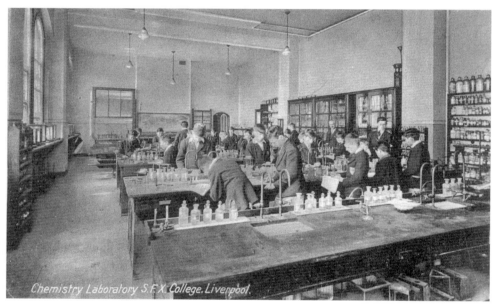

Chemistry Laboratory S.F.X. College, Liverpool.

St. Francis Xavier Church, Liverpool.

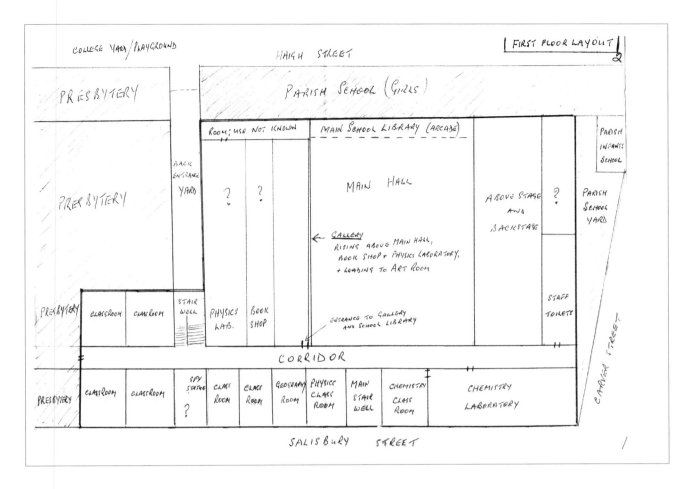

FIRST FLOOR LAYOUT 2

COLLEGE YARD / PLAYGROUND

HAIGH STREET

PRESBYTERY

PARISH SCHOOL (GIRLS)

PRESBYTERY

BACK ENTRANCE YARD

ROOM; USE NOT KNOWN

MAIN SCHOOL LIBRARY (ARCADE)

PARISH INFANTS SCHOOL

? ?

MAIN HALL

ABOVE STAGE AND BACKSTAGE

?

PARISH SCHOOL YARD

GALLERY
RISING ABOVE MAIN HALL, BOOK SHOP + PHYSICS LABORATORY, + LEADING TO ART ROOM

PRESBYTERY

CLASSROOM CLASSROOM

STAIR WELL

PHYSICS LAB.

BOOK SHOP

ENTRANCE TO GALLERY AND SCHOOL LIBRARY

STAFF TOILETS

CARVER STREET

CORRIDOR

PRESBYTERY

CLASSROOM CLASSROOM

SPY STATUE ?

CLASS ROOM

CLASS ROOM

GEOGRAPHY ROOM

PHYSICS CLASS ROOM

MAIN STAIR WELL

CHEMISTRY CLASS ROOM

CHEMISTRY LABORATORY

SALISBURY STREET

Based on the recollections of Mick O'Neill and Ted Walsh.
Others will remember differences in layout and use.

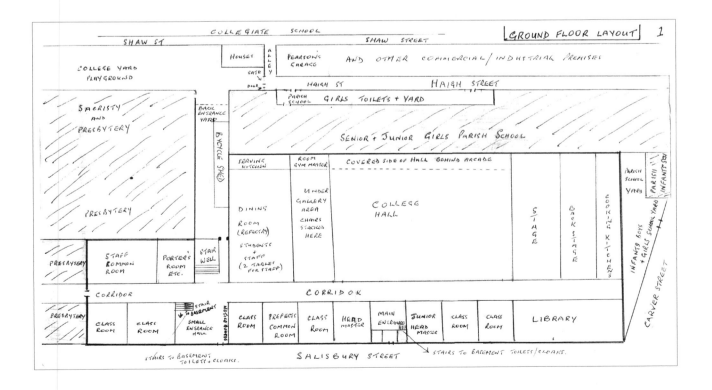

GROUND FLOOR LAYOUT 1

COLLEGIATE SCHOOL

SHAW ST

SHAW STREET

HOUSES

PEARSON'S GARAGE

AND OTHER COMMERCIAL / INDUSTRIAL PREMISES

COLLEGE YARD PLAYGROUND

GATE
DOOR

HAIGH ST

HAIGH STREET

SACRISTY AND PRESBYTERY

BACK ENTRANCE YARD

BICYCLE SHED

PARISH SCHOOL

GIRLS TOILETS + YARD

SENIOR + JUNIOR GIRLS PARISH SCHOOL

SERVING KITCHEN

ROOM GYM MASTER

COVERED SIDE OF HALL BEHIND ARCADE

PARISH SCHOOL YARDS

PARISH INFANTS SCH

PRESBYTERY

DINING ROOM (REFECTORY)

STUDENTS + STAFF (2 TABLES FOR STAFF)

UNDER GALLERY AREA
CHAIRS STACKED HERE

COLLEGE HALL

S T A G E

B A C K S T A G E

C O O K I N G   K I T C H E N S

PRESBYTERY

STAFF COMMON ROOM

PORTER'S ROOM ETC.

STAIR WELL

INFANTS BOYS + GIRLS SCHOOL YARD

CARVER STREET

CORRIDOR

CORRIDOR

PRESBYTERY

CLASS ROOM

CLASS ROOM

STAIR TO BASEMENT
SMALL ENTRANCE HALL

CLASS ROOM

PREFECTS COMMON ROOM

CLASS ROOM

HEAD MASTER

MAIN ENTRANCE

JUNIOR HEAD MASTER

CLASS ROOM

CLASS ROOM

LIBRARY

STAIRS TO BASEMENT TOILETS + CLOAKS.

SALISBURY STREET

STAIRS TO BASEMENT TOILETS / CLOAKS.

# Salisbury Street Vacated : Woolton Era Begins

In the 1960s, after SFX moved to Woolton, the architects Weightman and Bullen re-designed the old school for Liverpool Education Authority and it re-opened as SFX Bilateral School, closing at the time of re-organization in 1974. The building was put to various uses in the 1980s and came close to demolition in 1991.

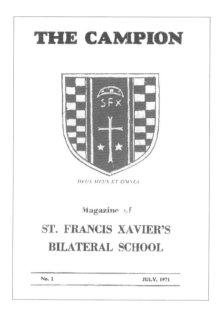

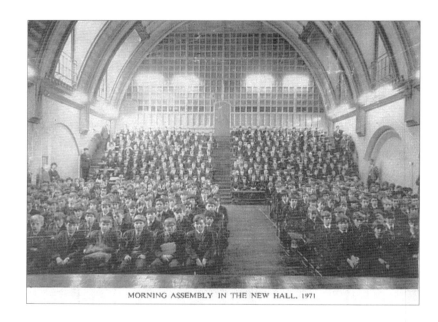

MORNING ASSEMBLY IN THE NEW HALL, 1971

'During the re-building the body of a woman thought to have been dead 600 years was found in the cellars of the school. The police are looking for a 650 year-old caretaker to help them with their enquiries.'

The building has now been spectacularly re-designed by the Manchester architects downs and variava (sic) under the direction of Mr William Hodge, and it has risen like a phoenix as the downtown campus of Hope University. The renovations, both internal and external, have been sensitively conceived and imaginatively carried out. They reflect great credit on the architects and their clients, Hope University.

*Hope University at Everton*

**Part 2**

# Woolton Site

Fred Devereux, teacher and governor, is the best person to describe the new College:-

Clutton's building in Salisbury Street was always more impressive than its surrounding area, which over the years became increasingly derelict. *"Never very inspiring, even in its most prosperous days,"* wrote Dr Grace in 1942, *"the district began to assume an appearance that was positively depressing."* The acquisition of the High Lee estate, 22.3 acres bought from Mrs. Burman and Mrs Rubinstein for £18,500 in 1941, determined that the future of the College would be at Woolton. In contrast to the situation at Salisbury Street, most people have come to agree that at High Lee it has been the site rather than the building that has impressed the visitor. On the occasion of the opening of the new College in 1961, Fr. Adamson observed that

> 'when Fr. Neylan bought the estate at Woolton, it was no casual choice. . . . . he looked round the city and decided Woolton was the ideal choice, an eminently attractive area, surrounded on the map by a mass of green . . . High Lee is one of the highest spots in Liverpool. From the top classrooms the Mersey gleams in the evening sun and on the skyline runs the silhouette of the Clwydian hills, just concealing the next Jesuit stronghold of St. Beunos.'

On the architectural merits of the new building he remained silent.

*Aerial Views of Woolton Site*

*Ground View of High Lee*

# New College at Woolton

**W**ork on the building of the new College began in August 1959, when the first sod was cut by Fr. Taunton, the Rector of SFX. The architects were Weightman and Bullen, and the building contract went to Tysons, the long-established Liverpool firm. At that time there was no capital grant from public funds. The cost of approximately £275,000 had to come from money raised from a weekly lottery launched by the Building Development Society, which had been set up in 1957. This was supplemented by payment out of Jesuit salaries. Despite these efforts it was necessary to raise a loan of £120,000 from the Midland Bank; and the fund-raising to service and pay off the debt continued for some years

*Chapel and Classrooms*

On 26th May 1960, a large gathering of clergy, staff, parents and guests assembled at High Lee on the occasion of the laying of the foundation stone of the new College by Archbishop Heenan. "I doubt", the Archbishop remarked, "if there will be any finer Jesuit College in the country than the new St. Francis Xavier's College."

During the extended summer holiday in 1961 the enormous task of transferring the contents of the old building in Salisbury Street to Woolton was accomplished, much to the credit of Fr. Warner. It was, recorded Les Bailey at the time, "all the more astonishing when it is recalled that he suffered from a grave illness during a great part of the year."

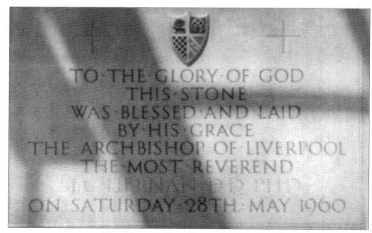

TO THE GLORY OF GOD
THIS STONE
WAS BLESSED AND LAID
BY HIS GRACE
THE ARCHBISHOP OF LIVERPOOL
THE MOST REVEREND
ON SATURDAY 28TH MAY 1960

*The Foundation Stone Laid in 1960*

## Pre-1961 Buildings at High Lee

The High Lee estate is typical of the many Victorian estates to be found on the South side of Liverpool. Unfortunately, little remains of the original house which was situated near to the sandstone coach-house, which still stands. High Lee House was demolished when it was discovered to be seriously affected with dry rot, perhaps an unnecessary step as many similar sandstone mansions in the locality, including the adjacent Abbots Lea, have been successfully preserved and restored.

There were two entrances to the estate, one of which on Beaconsfield Road is still in use. Another entrance to the house was from Druids Cross Road by way of a path across what is now the first eleven pitch. The remains of this entrance can still be seen beyond the far corner of the pitch. With the High Lee estate the College acquired the cottage situated at the main entrance on Beaconsfield Road and two adjoining houses on Woolton Hill Road within the sandstone perimeter wall. None of these dates from the time of the original house. The only building on the site of real interest was the sandstone coach-house of the original mansion, which had been situated adjacent to it.

*Beaconsfield Road - Entrance and Gatehouse*

*The Coach House*

Made of local sandstone, this building is of early Victorian origin and consists of two storeys. At the time of the transfer of school games to High Lee in 1950, when the old sports grounds at Melwood were sold to Liverpool F. C., the coach-house was brought into use as a sports pavilion. The cost of the conversion was £2,500, which at the time was an appreciable sum. Although some thought that this was an excessive expenditure on such a building and it was sometimes referred to as Neylan's Folly, it should be remembered that at the time wartime restrictions on building still applied, and while a permit might be granted to restore an existing building, it could not be obtained for a new pavilion, which would not be considered essential.

A new pavilion was eventually built as part of the overall building programme for the new college in 1961. However, the wheel has now turned full circle, for the 'new' pavilion is dilapidated and due for demolition, while the old coach-house is to be restored as a sports pavilion. The irony of this would not have been lost on Fr. Neylan.

*The Gables*

It is necessary to make a brief departure from High Lee but not from Woolton. At the time of the acquisition of the High Lee estate, the SFX Preparatory School was accommodated within the main building at Salisbury Street. However in 1946 the school was transferred to its own premises at The Gables, a large sandstone house situated on Menlove Avenue near the Junction with Beaconsfield Road and so within easy reach of High Lee. It was formally opened on 29th October 1946 with Fr. Fishwick in charge assisted by Miss Horner and Mr Petry SJ. The Gables can claim, therefore, to have been the first building in Woolton to accommodate SFX pupils. There were 53 of them in 1946.

## Main College Building

At the time of the purchase of the High Lee estate it was assumed that the building that would arise on it would possess architectural distinction comparable with that of Henry Clutton's building of 1877. In his inimitable style Dr Grace expressed his vision of the new College: *"As yet no plans have been prepared for the imposing edifice in which, we may anticipate, dignity, restraint, elegance and utility will be united amidst surroundings worthy of the building itself."* Such a vision was not to be realised. Inevitably, on grounds of cost alone, the main building which rose at High Lee was typical of school buildings of the time - it was a teaching-block where visitors often had difficulty finding the main entrance. However, it was better finished than most, with such refinements as wood-block floors and polished wood banisters. The entrance area, where one is still greeted by St. Francis Xavier in his niche, is attractive, as is the College chapel, although, since it opens off the dining room, its use is restricted.

For a building of its time, the assembly hall, with its side gallery and splendid views across the playing fields, is considered by many to be especially impressive. It has been used for any number of memorable occasions over the years, and remains the most fitting venue for functions such as Proclamations and Prizegivings and gatherings, both formal and informal, which are enhanced by a setting of distinction. The war memorials to be found there give the hall an added dignity and provide a link with the past.

*Entrance Hall*

*College Chapel*

*Assembly Hall*

The swimming pool in the new building was not typical of its time. At 75 feet long by 30 feet wide it is bigger than most school swimming pools. To allow for diving it was necessary to have a depth of three feet to eight and a half feet. Diving was subsequently discontinued, but to allow for it in the first place the pool was built with a very steep gradient - by no means ideal for teaching purposes. Younger boys find themselves out of their depth within a few paces. However, faced with the option of sinking or swimming, most tend to make rapid progress, and no drownings have been recorded.

*Swimming Pool*

The library at High Lee was another feature superior to most to be found in buildings of the time. Although it could not match the splendour of the library at Salisbury Street with its odour of scholarship, it had about it an ambience conducive to study and learning. Whether by design or accident, the views from the windows across the lawn, lent it an atmosphere of calm and quietness - especially during school holidays. These reflections are written in the past tense for the library is no more. It has been converted into a Learning Resources Centre. The bookshelves which were designed and fitted by Tysons in keeping with the design of the original building, have been discarded and replaced with shoddy, movable metal shelving; the polished wood-block floor has been covered with carpet tiles; the lighting has been incorporated into a lowered ceiling; the room has been increased in length and has consequently lost its fine proportions.

*Sixth Form Library*

The house for the Jesuit community was built at the same time as the school building. It is a commodious residence with its principal rooms facing south overlooking a fine lawn stretching down to the boundary wall on Beaconsfield Road. At the time of its construction, culminating in its copper roof, a lay member of staff naively asked Fr. Sermin, a Jesuit colleague, who was about to enjoy the comforts of the new accommodation, how he managed to square such luxury with his vow of poverty. "Poverty", he replied like a true Jesuit, "does not mean squalor."

*Community House*

## Cardinal Newman Building ( Queen's Drive Childwall )

A brief departure must again be made from High Lee. In the scheme of Comprehensive reorganisation in 1983, SFX College amalgamated with Cardinal Newman Secondary School, situated at Queen's Drive, Childwall, and Our Lady of the Assumption (OLA) Secondary School, Gateacre. The accommodation at High Lee was quite inadequate to provide for the vastly increased school population resulting from the amalgamation. SFX was by far the biggest and strongest constituent and It was decided that ultimately the whole new school would be housed at High Lee. However, as this would involve a costly and extensive building programme, it was necessary to use the Cardinal Newman building as a

*Lower School (previously Cardinal Newman School)*

Lower School which would accommodate the first three years. After three years pupils would transfer to High Lee. This temporary solution was to last for eighteen years.

The buildings on the Cardinal Newman site at Childwall - almost two miles distant from High Lee - were in a state of extreme dilapidation and disrepair; so much so that the governors of SFX refused to accept them until the local council carried out the most essential repairs and maintenance. Depressing in appearance and grossly overcrowded, the Lower School never recovered from its bad start. Over the years the condition of the buildings deteriorated further till they became unfit for use. While the troubles of the Cardinal Newman site must be primarily attributed to bad design and structural faults, it must be added that the uncertainty surrounding its future added greatly to the problem. There was always a reluctance to spend money on a building when departure was always thought to be imminent. In time people seemed to become acclimatised to poor conditions until they became accepted as the norm. Much that was unsightly, not least to the general public on Queens Drive, had nothing to do with design and structural faults and could have been remedied at little expense. Some improvement in the daily life at the Lower School was admitted by all but the incurably defeatist when 200 pupils were transferred to High Lee in 1995 on the completion of the Warner Building. All pupils will be accommodated at High Lee in 2002. The Cardinal Newman Building will be demolished and SFX will at last be a single-site school.

## Old Xaverians' Sports and Social Club - 1987

The years following the move to High Lee in 1961 were a period of consolidation, and it was not until 1984 that a further building project was started. This took the form of the Old Xaverians' Club, launched to mark the centenary of the founding of the Association in 1884. Much of the credit must go to Brother Francis for initiating and seeing through this undertaking. The first phase, consisting of a social area, four squash courts and related facilities, was completed by December 1987, and the official opening by Bishop O'Connor OX took place soon afterwards. The club building is situated near the entrance to High Lee from Woolton Hill Road. Good relations have been forged with local residents to whom the club's facilities have been made available.

*Views of Old Xaverians' Club*

## Technology Block - 1990

Visitors to High Lee would now have difficulty in finding this building, for it has been swallowed up, as it were, by the Warner Building and the De La Mennais Centre, the former to the south of it and the latter to the north. A corridor above the Technology Block connects these two later buildings. The building deserves mention since it was the first significant development of school accommodation at Woolton since the transfer from Salisbury Street in 1961. By providing specialist accommodation for technology and art in the Upper School it greatly reduced the need for inter-site travel. The building was officially opened in June 1990 by Angela Rumbold, Education Minister, and it marked the first development at High Lee during the College's period of grant-maintained status.

## The Warner Building - 1995

The opening of a third-form block at High Lee in 1995 marked the first major step towards single-site accommodation. Unfortunately it had to be completed in two stages. It began life as a two-storey building with a temporary roof, and a third storey was added five years later. The designation of this new accommodation as the Warner Building was particularly appropriate as a recognition of Fr. Warner's work in achieving the transfer of the College from Salisbury Street to Woolton. The Warner Building is of regular proportions and has some architectural merit, although it is now

*The Warner Building*

dwarfed by the De La Mennais Centre. The editor of the College Magazine at the time recorded that "unusually for a modern building mere functionalism has not been allowed to dominate. Externally it blends in well with existing buildings, while internally it is bright and commodious."

## The De La Mennais Centre - 2000

The completion of the De La Mennais Centre in 2000 transformed the appearance of the College at High Lee in much the same way, one imagines, as Henry Clutton's did in Salisbury Street in 1877. Built on the site of the former tennis courts, it presents a line of development from the Warner Building on the west side of the main drive which runs through the school site from Beaconsfield Road to Aldbourne Close. The Centre provides the most up-to-date facilities for the curricular and social needs of a Sixth Form at the beginning of the twenty-first century, and it can accommodate as many as 250 students. The exodus of the Sixth Form from the main building has released the classroom space needed for the transfer of pupils from the Lower School. When complemented by the provision of necessary specialist rooms, which is the next and final stage of development at High Lee, St. Francis Xavier's College will at last be totally settled in Woolton.

Although inevitably an example of modern design and construction methods, with no distinct or monumental features, such as are to be found in the buildings of Henry Clutton's time, the De La Mennais Centre with its pleasing brickwork and its magnificent views across to North Wales has won much favourable comment, not least from those who assembled for the official opening by Brother Jean Petillon, Assistant Superior General of the De La Mennais Order, on 3rd December 2000, the Feast of St. Francis Xavier.

Xaverians whose years at the College fell before 1961 will always retain an understandable attachment for the old College at Salisbury Street. Indeed, there are some who still find difficulty in convincing themselves that the school has ever moved from there. We must, however, come to realise that the College has developed more in terms of its buildings in the years since 1961 than in all its preceding years. The High Lee estate has long been recognised as the most attractive school site in Liverpool. It now possesses buildings worthy of it, which have been erected with no encroachment on its extensive playing

*The De La Mennais Centre*

fields. From the heights of Woolton it might, however, be salutary to be brought down to earth by no less a person than the Reverend W J Neylan SJ, the Headmaster responsible for the purchase of the High Lee estate in 1941. On being informed of all the magnificent facilities at the new College, he retorted characteristically that " it is the men and not the walls that make the city". Fred Devereux.

*Some of those attending the Old Xaverians' Mass on December 2 2001*

*Chapter 3*

# The College, The Government and The Law 1842 - 1918

In the one hundred and fifty nine years of its existence the College has enjoyed different kinds of close and not-so-close relationships with Town Hall and Westminster. It remained a purely private establishment for most of the nineteenth century. It entered into a lukewarm arrangement with Government in the first half of the twentieth century. It can now claim recognition as a valued and trusted partner in the task of educating the nation's children in the twenty first century.

## Influential Headmasters

| | | |
|---|---|---|
| 1865 - 1874 | Fr. Harris | Prefect of Studies |
| 1898 - 1909 | Fr. McHale | Prefect of Studies |
| 1919 - 1937 | Fr. Woodlock | Prefect of Studies |
| 1939 - 1953 | Fr. Neylan | Headmaster |
| 1953 - 1961 | Fr. Warner | Headmaster |
| 1979 - | Brother Francis | Headmaster |

## Institutional Status of the College

| | |
|---|---|
| 1842 | College founded by Fr. Lythgoe as a private fee-paying school |
| 1902 | Municipal non-provided secondary school in receipt of direct grant |
| 1944 | Direct Grant College - a centrally-funded school |
| 1983 | Comprehensive School - St. Francis Xavier's High School ( Voluntary-Aided) |
| 1990 | Grant-maintained - St. Francis Xavier's College |
| 1999 | Foundation School |

## Landmark Dates in the History of the College

| | |
|---|---|
| 1842 | College opened in Soho Street |
| 1877 | Salisbury Street building opened |
| 1921 | Melwood playing fields opened as Melwood Bridge in West Derby |
| 1925 | Senior and Junior Shields both won two years running |
| -26 | (Football Shields competed for annually by Liverpool Grammar Schools) |
| 1939 | Evacuation to St Asaph |
| 1941 | Woolton property bought |
| 1942 | Centenary year |
| 1961 | College opened at Woolton |
| 1974 | Brothers of Christian Instruction in charge. Jesuits withdrew |
| 1980 | Five Old Boys gained 'firsts' at Oxford and Cambridge |
| 1983 | Split-site Voluntary Aided Comprehensive. |
| 1987 | Ten places awarded at Oxford to SFX pupils - College record |
| 1990 | Grant-maintained status |
| 1998 | Foundation status |
| 2001 | Seven Merseyside football trophies won including Senior Shield |

# Stage One : 1842- 1884

Two Catholic events in 1842 may have prompted Fr. Lythgoe to open St Francis Xavier's College when he did. First of all and most importantly, in a report to the Vatican in January 1842, Cardinal Acton had advocated the foundation of a Jesuit college in Liverpool. Hence Lythgoe in a pre-emptive bid opened SFX in October 1842. Secondly - and perhaps as a reaction to Acton's reference - Bishop Brown had announced the opening of an establishment in Everton at St Domingo House - a seminary and a secondary school, called St Edward's and it duly opened its doors in January 1843.

*Liverpool Institute for Boys*

Father Lythgoe had more respectable incentives. Several successful day-schools had been opened in the city since 1835. Such schools, subsequently called 'Proprietary' schools by the Bryce Commission on Secondary Education in 1885, were mostly a phenomenon of the nineteenth century. They were typically founded by the churches, as was SFX, or by a local group of high-minded individuals, as were Liverpool Institute for Boys and Liverpool Institute for Girls ( Blackburne House). Liverpool Collegiate was founded in association with the Church of England.

These founders, acting out of public-spiritedness or commitment to the community, were prompted by a desire to offer a secondary education to those for whom there was no adequate provision. In some cases altruism may not have been the only motive. As local businessmen, they were interested in employing 15 and 16 year-olds with literacy and accountancy skills as clerks in their offices. All three boys' schools kept complaining that pupils left for clerical jobs in the city far too early.

*Liverpool Institute for Girls*

The three boys' schools started out with a Commercial School alongside the Classical School, in order to recruit boys from more vocationally orientated families. These were two departments of the same school rather than separate schools, although they had separate curricula and the Commercial School fees were lower.

*The Liverpool Collegiate*

The History of St. Francis Xavier's College, Liverpool, 1842-2001

It did not escape the notice of those who later came to inspect the College that the two departments served two different social classes. SFX kept its Commercial School till 1908, when under pressure from His Majesty's Inspectors the two sections were amalgamated.

The Liverpool Echo in November 1892 reporting the fiftieth anniversary of the foundation of the College commented:

> 'The students in the Classical course study Latin and Greek; while French and German, the different branches of mathematics, chemistry, natural philosophy, shorthand, drawing and typing are common to both the classical and commercial departments'.

The seminary, called St. Edward's and founded in 1843 by Bishop Brown, should not be confused with The Catholic Institute (later St Edward's) which opened in 1853.

St Edward's College was opened by Bishop Brown in St Domingo House in Everton in 1843 as a boarding school and junior seminary - a source of secular priests for the Diocese. It also took day-pupils in the 1880s.

The Catholic Institute was founded by Monsignor Nugent in Hope Street in 1853 - possibly as a rival to SFX, since it had both Classical and Commercial sections. By 1900 the CI - as it was commonly referred to - was failing. It closed In 1901. Archbishop Whiteside asked the Irish Christian Brothers to take it over. They re-established it with almost immediate success.

In 1919, St Edward's, by now entirely a Junior Seminary, moved out of Everton to the diocesan seminary at Upholland and became part of St Joseph's College. The Christian Brothers moved the CI into St Domingo House. For the sake of continuity they changed the name to St Edward's. In 1937 St Edward's moved to Sandfield Park, West Derby, in what was then the outskirts of Liverpool.

*St Edward's College, St Domingo House, Everton 1843*

# Survival in the first forty years

As a private school, St Francis Xavier's depended almost entirely on fees to keep it running during its first 40 years. It was helped to some small degree by fund-raising and by donations from wealthier individuals, usually Old Boys.

The Holder Bursaries were typical of a number of contributions made to the College between 1850 and 1900, which helped to stem the problem of early-leaving, as the money was usually directed towards boys in the upper forms. Fees at the time were about £8 a quarter.

### The Holder Bursaries

The Mayor donated £10 in 1884 and again in 1885 for £5
bursaries to 'the two best boys in the third form in the ensuing
year, who are returning for the Oxford Local Examinations'.
'An example of Protestant generosity', said the Rector, 'well
worthy of imitation by Catholics.'   (Xaverian August 1885)

A new college building had been constructed in 1855 and the second new school, built in 1877, had cost £30,000. There were continuing maintenance and capital costs. Large annual deficits had to be met from the central funds of the Jesuit Order - £100 in its very first year, £8000 by 1900. In 1902 interest of £400 per annum was still being paid on the sum borrowed to build the 1877 school.

By the 1860s things began to change. Many Irish immigrants had improved themselves socially and were looking for a secondary education for their sons. A dramatic increase in pupil numbers followed the appointment of Fr. Harris in 1865 as Prefect of Studies. His contribution to the success of the College was considerable. The year before he arrived there were 84 pupils, and the year after he left in 1884 there were 400. Such a healthy enrolment must have considerably lightened the financial problems  of the College, and much of it was down to the energetic Harris.

During his term of office the staff, mostly Jesuits, increased threefold. In 1867 all the staff were Jesuits and therein lies another of the College's lifelines. Although they had to be housed and fed, perhaps rather frugally, these teachers did not have to be paid. If the Jesuits had had to meet a large salary bill, it is unlikely that the College would have survived in its original form.

# Stage 2 : 1884-1902

## The College Establishes Itself

The Jesuits began to publish a monthly journal in 1884 which detailed the activities in the parish. The Xaverian, as it was called, included each month a section devoted to the affairs of the College. This valuable source for this history had the entry below in its first edition of April 1884.

### The College Entry in The Xaverian April 1884

#### College Notices.

St. Francis Xavier's College offers, at a moderate expense, a liberal Education to Boys preparing for the Learned Professions or for Business.

##### CLASSICAL COURSE.

The Classes in the Classical Course are entirely under the charge of Members of the Society of Jesus.

The Course of Study comprises the Latin, Greek, French, and English Languages ; History and Geography ; Writing, Arithmetic, Algebra and Geometry ; Natural Philosophy and Chemistry. The Boys of the Senior Classes are prepared for the Oxford Local and London Matriculation Examinations. Special attention is also given to Commercial subjects.

**TERMS PER ANNUM PAYABLE—QUARTERLY IN ADVANCE.**

£8 10s.

Books and Stationery Extra.

————:o:————

##### COMMERCIAL COURSE.

The Classes in the Commercial Course are conducted by competent Masters under the direction of the Vice-President and Prefect of Studies.

The Course of Instruction comprises English, French, Geography, History, Writing, Arithmetic and Chemistry ; the Elements of Algebra and Geometry.

**TERMS PER ANNUM.**

Each Pupil ... ... ... ... ... ... £4 10 0

Books and Stationery Extra.

————:o:————

##### PREPARATORY COURSE.

For Boys under Eight. The Preparatory Course is taught by a Father of the Society of Jesus. All Boys are expected to be able to Read and Write on entrance.

**TERMS PER ANNUM—PAYABLE AS ABOVE.**

Each Pupil ... ... ... ... ... ... £4 10 0

Books and Stationery Extra.

#### College Notices—continued.

##### COLLEGE REGULATIONS.

1. Boys are expected to be present at the College Mass at 8 30 every morning. Special arrangements will be made for those who live at a distance.

2. No Student must be absent without permission, cases of illness excepted.

3. A Quarter's Notice required before Removal of a Pupil. No allowance can be made for Absence, except in cases of infectious illness.

4. No Holidays are permitted except those granted by the College Authorities.

5. The Authorities will at once resign the charge of any Boy for whose correction the ordinary means are found to be in-effectual.

6. Cards of Conduct and Application are issued every week to the Boys, and the Parents are earnestly requested to insist on these being regularly shown to them.

Applications for Admission to be made to the Rev. William Burns. S.J., Vice-President, at the Office of the College, Salisbury Street. Office Hours :—Daily (except Thursdays and Sundays) from 10 till 12 30, and 2 till 4.

————•◦•————

The Easter Proclamation of Certificates, Marks of Distinction, &c., obtained by the Students at the 3rd Term Examination, will take place in the College Hall on the Evening of Thursday, 24th April.

The 4th Term will commence on Wednesday, 16th April, on which day the Students will assemble as usual for the College Mass at 8-30.

Parents intending to place their sons at the College are advised to enter them, if possible, on the first day of the new Term.

A Meeting to choose a Committee for the **Harris Memorial Fund** will be held on Wednesday, 2nd April, at 4-15 p.m., at the Office of Mr. Joseph Walton, 13 Harrington Street.

The College's financial situation began to improve a little in the 1880s. The new school built in 1877 was an impressive landmark at the top of Islington. Pupils began to do exceptionally well in the Oxford Local Examinations - the GCSE and A-Levels of the day.

From 1884 a third and much smaller source of revenue came from contributions from the Old Xaverians' Association, which had been formed in that year. Books for the library and instruments for the physics department were two of the items covered by such donations. Old Boys also donated money for scholarships to cover the fees of needy pupils. A rather quaint form of self-help came from an unexpected source. In 1895, at the suggestion of the Association, the pupils in Form Four put on a performance of *The Hidden Gem*, a play written by Cardinal Wiseman. They charged for admission and used the proceeds to help provide scholarships to be competed for by the boys in their own class.

The Xaverian of December 1895 reported 'Our friends will be glad to hear that the proceeds have been amply sufficient to provide for this object'. Given the abominable acoustics in the Hall it was remarkable that 'the very careful enunciation and management of voice on the part of all the actors ensured that they were heard in every part of the Hall.'

The curriculum broadened to include physics and chemistry. Small grants were made to the College by the City Council and by the Science and Art Department of the Education Department. In 1893 a capitation grant and a science grant brought in £350. In 1892 two new typewriters were bought for the Commercial School and the purchase attracted considerable publicity. Success bred success. Pupil numbers were maintained and income from fees increased.

In 1892 the College celebrated its Golden Jubilee. This was duly written up in the press. With newspaper articles praising the academic, social, moral and religious achievements of the College, its reputation was now assured.

**The Advent of Government Support for Secondary Schools**

Successive Governments were beginning to realize that a national system of schools would have to be established. The Forster Education Act of 1870 established elementary schools run by locally elected School Boards. The Elementary Act of 1891 made elementary education free and compulsory. The Voluntary Schools Act of 1897 gave unconditional capitation grants 'of five shillings per scholar' to voluntary elementary schools, freed them from payment of rates, and also removed the 17s. 6d limit per child; this limit had been introduced by Lord Sandon in his Act of 1876, above which the schools had had to provide matching funds from local contributions in fees and subscriptions.

However the Voluntary Schools Act of 1897 was not well-received by the Catholic hierarchy. Cardinal Vaughan said :

> 'We must get rid of the reproach that our schools are charity schools, dependent upon casual alms; we want to have done with the sorry and degrading business which makes the salaries of teachers in denominational schools hang upon the success of this or that grinning comedian or upon the pious audacity of some fraudulent bazaar'.

Strong words !

In the short term none of this affected SFX directly, since these Acts did not apply to secondary schools. But it did mean less of a demand on the pockets of Catholics in supporting their own schools. In the long-term it also meant that the College would able to draw upon a larger and better-educated population.

By the 1890s two pieces of legislation were introduced which gave positive assistance to secondary schools and gave the College direct access to public funds.

**The Technical Instruction Act 1889**

The Government had become concerned that Britain was being left behind by foreign competition in science and in 1889 passed The Technical Instruction Act.

This enabled the Department of Arts and Sciences, a branch of the Education Department, to pay money to schools for 'instruction in the principles of science and art applicable to industries......including modern languages and commercial and agricultural subjects.' The College had already established strong teaching courses in physics and chemistry and it was now in a position to bid for funds to equip laboratories to an improved standard. SFX's contribution to the development of the teaching of science in the city was considerable. Much of the credit for this must go Fr. Vaughan, on the staff from 1877 to 1899, who was a tireless and energetic science enthusiast. He was ably supported by two Prefects of Studies, Fr. Gerard and Fr. Donnelly.

One of the first science grants came from the City in 1891, recorded in The Xaverian of September 1891.

> The Liverpool Corporation has allotted to St. Francis Xavier's College the sum of £150, out of money granted by the Government for promoting Technical Education, for the purchase of Educational appliances for the Science and Art classes of the College.

## The Local Taxation (Customs and Excise) Act 1890

A second piece of legislation - the Local Taxation (Customs and Excise) Act of 1890 - injected much-needed vigour into local support for technical instruction and indirectly for secondary schools. In 1890 the Government set out to reduce the number of public houses and an extra tax on spirits had been intended to compensate publicans, who had surrendered their licences. Temperance interests persuaded Parliament to give surplus tax receipts (£800,000 in the first year) to County Councils to help with technical education. Thereafter it became a permanent grant. In 1898-9 Liverpool received £800 as its share. This 'whisky money', as it was known, was used for grants to schools to encourage the teaching of technical instruction, and the College was one of the recipients.

Then by an Act of 1899 the Board of Education paid £7 per head for any school adopting a complete School of Science course. Physics, Chemistry, Woodwork and Drawing were included in this course and the school had to pass an inspection before payments were made. SFX secured this approval in 1900 together with the very acceptable per-capita grant.

While government finance was now helping, it was offset to a certain extent by the cost of the improvements that were required, and the deficits in the College budget towards the end of the century remained between £500 and £800.

# Stage Three : 1902-1918

## The Education Act 1902 and the Sadler Report

The Education Act of 1902 for the first time made public money available systematically to secondary schools and SFX was a potential beneficiary.

At the end of the century, with exports declining and steel production lagging behind our competitors, the Government was forced to acknowledge that the country's future depended as much on 'school power' as on 'sea power.' Yet the nation's secondary school system was hopelessly inadequate. The voluntary elementary schools - educating more than half the nation's children - were financially exhausted and incapable of taking on any further burdens. The haphazard doles and hand-outs of the last twenty-five years were no longer a satisfactory method of administering the system - if indeed they ever had been. Robert Morant, the civil servant in charge at the Board of Education, and Balfour, the Prime Minister designate, set about drafting a bill that would drag schools into the twentieth century and form the basis of a national system of education

There were two administrative and organizational provisions of the Act that were destined to be very important. First, the Board of Education was given authority over public education in England. Hitherto this authority was shared by the Charity Commissioners, various arms of government and by religious groups - mainly the Anglican Church. Second and of equal importance, Local Education Authorities were established to manage public education in their areas in place of the School Boards of the 1870 Act. This led to a great reduction in the number of bodies with financial powers. The general proliferation of authorities with rate-raising powers that had prevailed in the nineteenth century bordered on the farcical. One 200 acre farm in Gloucestershire, the classic case that is commonly mentioned, was in 12 parishes, paying 50 different rates.

The imminent passing of the Bill presented the College - and other Catholic secondary schools - with a dilemma. Under the Act the proprietary schools potentially stood to gain a good deal, and the possibility of regular state support would remove a great burden from the shoulders of the Jesuits at SFX. But to surrender even some of their control over their own affairs and to open the College to external inspection seemed at the time too high a price to pay. With sectarianism growing in Liverpool there was a real fear of interference in the religious nature of the College. The issues were discussed in public and in private by the whole of the Catholic establishment with much agonizing over whether the Government's offers should be accepted or not.

After 59 days of debate the Bill was passed. SFX accepted and became a municipal non-provided school. Of the other Jesuit colleges, St. Michael's' Leeds, St. Ignatius, London, and Preston Catholic College also accepted, but Wimbledon, Beaumont and Mount St. Mary's Sheffield, remained outside the system.

Although the 1902 Act has had a good press, often being credited with taking the first steps towards establishing a national system of secondary education, questions can be asked. In some ways it put the clock back.

Regrettably, it laid firmer foundations for education's sectarian structure in formalising the Dual System with its municipal and non-municipal separate schools. It also failed to grasp the opportunity to promote a new curriculum. Whilst the Germans and the Americans were introducing science widely into the schools along with a broadly-based curriculum, the English schools promoted under the terms of the 1902 Act kept Latin and Greek firmly in the centre and in control; this remained so till after the 1944 Education Act.

## Conference of Prefects of Studies 1909

A few years later in 1909 the Prefects of Studies met on April 14th and 15th at SFX to discuss how the relationship with central and local government had worked. Fr. McHale, Prefect of Studies at the College, spoke first. Not only were the 'present relations satisfactory', but he felt that the College 'owed much to central and local government.' Regretfully the minutes do not go into details beyond saying 'this is shown in a comparison of staff before and after the change.' It is not clear whether he was referring to quality, quantity, or some other characteristic.

He comments that 'the Board's inspections of 1901, 1904, and 1908 made it clear that SFX was superior to non-Catholic schools in the city, which had enabled the Bishop to regulate against Catholic attendance at non-Catholic schools.' Perhaps the apprehension about opening up the Colleges to external inspection was misplaced from the outset, since Jesuit Colleges had always been subject to an exhaustive annual inspection by the Provincial. From the comments in the HMI Reports it is obvious that SFX operated at a level of efficiency in almost every department which would guarantee 'efficient status', as did the Institute and The Collegiate.

Other Prefects of Studies added their support. 'Inspections had proved..very helpful... a great encouragement to teachers'. 'The free-place scholars had been found to be satisfactory.' This against all expectations. 'The authorities' requirements in relation to the courses of studies were seen as reasonable'; and 'the wisdom of excluding the under-15s from public examinations' was now seen to have been well-judged, although one or two members had reservations. Again there had been apprehension over the required minimum standards in the curriculum, but SFX could claim to be teaching an adequate curriculum in most departments. These curriculum standards had to do with clearly defined and continuous courses in English and Mathematics, a Physics and Chemistry course supported by adequate laboratories and equipment, the teaching of a modern language and a classical language, and the physical well-being and development of the boys by an organized programme of physical training and games.

Support was not unanimous. The restrictions on external examinations have been mentioned. Some thought that there were still dangers to the freedom to locate religious education in the curriculum as they would wish. This was connected with the possibility of an increase in the number of Local Education Authority governors and what might flow from such an increase. One head complained that there were no mechanisms for getting rid of an objectionable or inactive governor - such a bare comment makes one wish for the details that prompted it.

The Act had laid down terms for the compulsory training of teachers and there was a feeling that too much had been ceded to the Board over the inspection of 'our arrangements for the training of teachers.' It is difficult to understand what was at issue in this last point, since the Jesuits had been involved in some hard bargaining with the Board and had succeeded in getting their teacher-training arrangements at St Mary's Hall Stonyhurst accepted as a suitable qualification.

Given the course a Jesuit followed before he was ordained, the new requirements for qualified teacher registration were going to be impossible to meet as they stood originally. There followed a series of meetings between the Jesuits and the Board of Education which resolved the problem to the satisfaction of both sides. The training of the Scholastics (priests-in-training) was accepted with minor adjustments as teacher-training within the meaning of the Regulations, and the course at St Mary's Stonyhurst was specifically designated as such.

In a wide-ranging discussion, unspecified difficulties with the LEA at Leeds were contrasted by one head with the helpfulness in Liverpool. There was a worry that more free places would be required of them, which in fact turned out to be the case - without any disastrous consequences. It was thought that in the appointments agreements there were special dangers that incompetent masters might be placed in charge of lower forms.

In the minutes of the same meeting there is a rather strange reference to the Jesuits themselves. 'Objections are sometimes made that the Jesuits are working for their own advantage in the school and neglecting the cause of Catholic education in general. We must beware not to give an appearance of a selfish policy.' One would guess that this is an intra-Catholic matter, unrelated to the LEA.

There were also middle-ground statements made. 'Not enthusiastic for the gains from the relationship. But acceptance of LEA conditions is unavoidable, if we are to continue our educational work. Education is now a recognized function of the state and we have a duty to our generation and to poorer Catholics to take part.'

But 'the esteem amongst outsiders for our schools' is probably the comment that best characterizes the feelings of the meeting. From these minutes one must conclude that the relationship was working well.

## The Conditions of the 1902 Act
(as they applied to SFX)

**Inspection by HMIs**
**Certain minimum standards in the curriculum**
**LEA right to appoint one third of the governors**
**Two thirds appointed by (Jesuits)**
**Compulsory training of teachers before registration**
**College as a permanent and essential part of national provision**
**Aid automatically adjusted to changing costs**
**The Authority responsible for 'fair wear and tear' maintenance**
**The College responsible for the provision and up-keep of buildings**
**The College retained the right to appoint and dismiss teachers**
**The Authority to pay the travelling cost of pupils**
**Scholarships for students whether resident in the area or outside**

In retrospect the price being demanded was not excessive, although it was more the principle and the fears of the thin end of the wedge that stood in the way of acceptance. These fears seem to be confirmed with the Liberal landslide of 1906. Bills came before Parliament that would have ruled out religious education in rate-supported secondary schools. These bills in 1906 and 1908 were only defeated by the combined efforts of the Catholic and Anglican hierarchies and the crucial support of the House of Lords. Such proposals were not revived in that form again.

### Liverpool Education Committee

What could SFX expect from this new relationship with Liverpool Education Committee? At the end of the century it was acknowledged generally that Liverpool ran one of the best elementary school systems and that it had one of the best universities in the country - not to mention its reputation for other forms of social provision; Liverpool was the first city to appoint its own Public Health Officer.

This makes it all the more strange that its secondary-school system was just about the worst in the country.

Since the 1870 Act Liverpool had built up a reputation as the best School Board in the country. Its School Board was the first in the country to be elected - in place a few months after the Act was passed. The manner of its selection showed an unusual degree of co-operation. There were 15 places to be filled. The Anglicans, the Catholics and the Non-Conformists came to an arrangement, which today would give rise to charges of gerrymandering. The Anglicans were to have 7 seats, the Catholics 4 and the Non-Conformists 4. On the day nominations closed all the other candidates by agreement withdrew their names and the Board was returned unopposed. Hardly democratic, but nonetheless very effective.

## The Sadler Report on Liverpool's Secondary Schools 1904

After the passing of the Technical Instruction Act of 1888 Liverpool Council set up a Technical Instruction Committee to advise it on its responsibilities under the Act. In 1901 the Committee was asked to submit a memorandum on the current state of secondary education. Its report was highly critical.

> The position of secondary education is altogether
> unworthy of the City.
> The provision of secondary education is inadequate
> to the wants of the City.
> Things are going backwards...worse than they were in the 1880s".

It pointed out that The Royal Institution, which had had 100 pupils in 1881, had closed in 1892. The Catholic Institute, with 96 pupils in 1881, had closed in 1901. The Liverpool Institute had only half of its 1881 roll, and SFX had a quarter of its 1881 roll. Only The Collegiate had improved its intake - from 592 in 1881 to 808 in 1901. No explanation is offered for these figures. Significantly 21% of the pupils attending the city's secondary schools in 1901 lived outside its borders. Elsewhere in the report SFX, the Collegiate and the Institute were being praised for the quality of the education they were providing, but this report left the city Fathers in no doubt that far too few of its sons were benefiting.

To the Council's credit, it immediately commissioned Professor Michael Sadler of Victoria University Manchester to investigate the state of secondary schooling in the city. Sadler had been an eminent civil servant at the Education Department in Whitehall and was one of Europe's most respected authorities on the subject of comparative education. He reported in 1904.

Although couched in more elegant language, his findings were more devastating than those of the Technical Instruction Committee. He began by drawing attention to the city's acknowledged achievements in elementary and university education.

> 'For many years before the compulsory requirements of the Elementary Act of 1870, Liverpool made voluntary efforts, unsurpassed elsewhere in England, to grapple with the educational destitution of the masses of her people..progressive improvements in their primary schools....variety of methods and ideals....regular scientific and manual training in the elementary schools. Liverpool has been in the van of progress.'

In 1884 one Catholic primary school, St Peter's Seel St., had a Newspaper Club. Seventy pupils paid a half-penny per week each for the privilege of meeting at the end of the school-day to read and discuss the newspapers.

> The crown of the educational effort of the City is the University..liberally aided by the City and by private benefactors ..incorporated in 1881...given its charter as Liverpool University in 1903...the work of the Liverpool School of Tropical Medicine known and valued all over the world..the readiness of a great municipality like Liverpool to give liberal aid to the University...'

Sadler also called attention with approval to the Teacher Training Colleges in the city, the School for the Blind, the School for the Deaf and Dumb, the Evening Continuation Schools, the Nautical College, the Domestic Science College, the School of Art, the School of Commerce and the School of Hygiene. That Liverpool should have such a range of provision made a deep impression on him. He went on to add to the list the Free Public Library, the Walker Art Gallery, the Museum, the parks and recreation grounds and the swimming baths.

When he came to comment on the secondary system things could hardly have been more different.

> ...grave concern at the present state of much of the secondary education.
> ...its defects are serious and threaten the vital interests of the city.
> ...intellectual resources run to waste....promising boys and girls at a growing disadvantage in the struggle of life.
> ...the indifference with which the majority of businessmen regard the needs of the secondary schools of Liverpool.

One statistic Sadler used several times was the number of pupils per thousand of the population in secondary education. In 1903, New York had 24 per thousand of elementary pupils passing on to secondary education. Liverpool had 3 per thousand. He went on to compare Liverpool's secondary school population unfavourably with many cities of similar size in Europe and America. His target was not schools like SFX, the Collegiate and the Institute. It was the city's businessmen who got the blame for the very low proportion of children receiving any secondary education at all. 'Liverpool businessmen had little or no interest in the continuing education of the boys and girls in the city', he said. They were responsible for the deplorable trend amongst parents to terminate schooling as soon as a position in the city was offered. This remained a constant cri de coeur well into the twentieth century. Pupils left school for employment far too soon - to their detriment, to the detriment of the schools, and, according to Sadler, to the detriment of the business, commercial and cultural life of Liverpool.

The three schools - SFX, the Collegiate and the Institute - did not escape criticism - low salaries, early leavers, under-staffing, low admission standards, and undue attention to Oxford Local Exams. Sadler recognized that SFX 'has long enjoyed a high repute for the carefulness with which it carries out its educational aims. The value of its work (for the city) calls for hearty acknowledgement'.

Overall, the College seems to have benefited from its decision to join the public system. Sadler used the term 'public non-provided secondary schools' to describe schools in the City like SFX. and praised the supportive system of capitation grants. The College went on to take many of its pupils from the elementary schools, receiving state funding for them. But it was firmly non-municipal ; it did not, as did the Institute and the Collegiate, pass into the ownership and direction of the City Education Department.

**Further Beneficial Regulations**

In 1907 under Article 20 of the Regulations of Secondary Schools, grammar schools such as SFX were given £7 extra per pupil for any boy transferring from a public elementary school at the age of 11, if such pupils represented  25% of the intake. Presumably the College benefited from this increase, since the proportion of such pupils at SFX reached the required 25%.

There was one important historical provision in the aftermath of the Act. Schools like SFX were given a choice in the methods of funding. They could receive all their funds from the Local Education Authority or choose to receive some directly from Central Government. Thus the principle of a school receiving some of its grant directly from Whitehall was established, although not officially formalised till the Education Act of 1944. SFX was amongst the schools that opted for direct funding at this stage and later in 1944 was one of 165 schools formally accorded Direct Grant status.

With increasing government funding, the College continued to operate successfully, in spite of the vicissitudes of the First World War, with a steady, if reduced, intake, and with a changing and transient staff, as teachers joined the war effort. Fr Woodlock, Prefect of Studies from 1919 to 1937, had served as Chaplain in the trenches and experienced enemy shell-fire on several occasions. Frank Checkland had distinguished himself when, at risk to himself, he turned off valves on gas cylinders whose contents were blowing back on our own troops. From 1920 onwards Fr. Woodlock enlisted more and more Old Xaverians to teach at the College - devoted teachers like Frank Checkland, Les Bailey, Putty Grace, Charlie Birmingham, Natty Lucas, Willy Crook and F.X. Bradshaw. This cohort of lay staff were to stay with the College from the 1920s till the 1950s supporting and supported by some equally devoted Jesuit teachers.

Over 150 Old Xaverians died in action in the First World War. Over 75 honours were awarded to Old Xaverians in all three services.

1 V.C., 1 K.B.E.,4 D.S.O.,1 D.F.C., 1 A.F.C., 2 D.S.C., 26 M.C., 1 M.C. and Bar, 1 M.C. and two Bars, 3 D.C.M., 1 M.S.M., 11 M.M., 1 M.M. and Bar, 4 Croix de Guerre, 1 Albert Medal, 1 Medal of St George, 15 mentions in despatches.

*College Memorial*

Number of Pupils on Roll 1842 - 2001

No complete record survives. These figures are taken from issues of The Xaverian, the College Magazine, and the files at Farm Street, which occasionally contradict each other.

The College roll reached 200 in 1868. 'Fr Rector gave a banquet to the community in celebration of the number of scholars having passed 200. Rich soup, collop and fried eggs, cutlets, four prairie fowl, sweet omelette, flat apple tart, rhubarb tart, special dessert, grapes etc.' Xaverian. The boys had extra recreation. There were similar celebrations in 1884 when Athelstan Keane enroled as the first 400th pupil.

| 1842 | 2 | 1905 | 325 |
|------|-----|------|-----|
| 1843 | 11 | 1906 | 357 |
| 1846 | 24 | 1910 | 383 |
| 1856 | 60 | 1913 | 364 |
| 1858 | 61 | 1915 | 367 |
| 1866 | 83 | | |
| 1867 | 144 | | |
| 1868 | 200 | 1930 | 680 |
| 1875 | 270 | 1939 | 560 |
| 1884 | 400 | 1941 | 426 |
| 1888 | 304 | | |

Pupil numbers remained in the 400s during the war, went up to 500-600 in the 50s and 60s, and doubled to over 1000 when the College went comprehensive in 1983. There are now 1300 girls and boys at the College in 2001, with a Sixth Form of over 240.

ST. FRANCIS XAVIER'S COLLEGE MAGAZINE.

## Distinctions Gained
### By Old Boys of St. Francis Xavier's College during the War.

**Victoria Cross**
Captain G. Coury.

**Distinguished Service Order**
Lieut.-Col. W. Dodd    Capt. C. W. McFeeley
Major G. J. Keane    ,, F. H. Lawless

**Distinguished Flying Cross**
Lieut. A. Reeves.

**Distinguished Service Cross**
Capt. J. Flynn    Lieut. A. E. McNab
,, J. Meria

**Military Cross**
Rev. W. Fitzmaurice,    Capt. J. C. Derlien
   S.J., C.F.    ,, G. Horner
,, M. Cullen, S.J., C.F.    ,, A. E. Morton
Major P. Cottle    Lt. A. Inglis
Capt. B. N. Murphy    ,, B. McDermott
,, J. L. Whitty    ,, T. Farmer
,, F. St. George-Yorke    ,, P. W. Lace
,, C. W. McFeeley    ,, J. A. Parle
   (and Bar)    ,, A. Heyes
,, H. Foster    ,, F. McKeown
Major J. Rafter    ,, J. F. Crilly
Capt. J. Howie    ,, A. B. Lythgoe
,, F. H. Lawless    ,, J. Mercer
,, N. Burgan (and Bar)
,, C. Balmforth

**Air Force Cross**
Captain W. Bruce.

**Knight of the British Empire**
Sir F. W. Scott-Stokes

**Distinguished Conduct Medal**
2nd Lieut. J. Cowley    Corp. E. Furniss
Co.-Sgt.-Major H. D. Whitford

**Meritorious Service Medal**
Co.- Sgt.-Major V. Bullen.

**Military Medal**
2nd Lt. J. Cowley    Signaller J. J. Gobbi
,, J. Dunn    Lce.-Corp. L. Walker
,, J. Jones    Private J. Carty
Sgt. A. Redmond    ,, J. Hanlon
   (and Bar)    ,, J. Longton
,, J. Corless    ,, A. Turner

**Order of the British Empire.**
Major P. Cottle    John A. Sullivan

**Albert Medal**
Engineer J. Connolly.

**Croix de Guerre**
Major P. Cottle    Lt. H. Stirrup
Lt. Arnold E. NcMab    T. H. Formby

**Medal of St. George** (Russian Decoration).
2nd Lieut. J. Cowley.

**Commended for Distinguished Service**
2nd Lieut. A. P. Crawley.

**Mentioned in Despatches**
Brig.-Gen. Paul A.
   Kenna, V.C.    Lt. R. Hodson
Lt.-Col. W. Dodd    ,, S. J. Baker
Major P. Cottle    2nd Lt. A.P.Crawley
Capt. E. Murphy    ,, H. P. O'Donoghue
,, J. A. Whitty    S.Maj. W. H. Wallace
,, A. E. Morton    C.S.M. H.D.Whitford
Rev. J Parsons, SJ., CF.    Corporal E. Furniss
Lt. A. E. McNab    Rev. W. Fitzmaurice
,, R. Whitty    S.J., C.F.
Capt. W. McFeeley.    Pmstr. F. Stewart, R.N.R.

ROLL OF HONOUR

*Chapter Four*

# The College, The Government and The Law : 1918 - 2001

## Part One :Three Significant Education Acts

Between 1918 and 1944 Parliament passed three major pieces of educational legislation. The 1944 Act had a direct impact on the College, whilst the other two were more significant for the general Catholic community in Liverpool.

**The Education Act of 1918** placed the onus on Catholics for providing schools for their own increasing secondary population. Under this Act, the Fisher Act, secondary education was made compulsory and the school-leaving age was raised to 14. As a result, the secondary school system was greatly expanded.

**The Education Act of 1936** was a significant national event which brought Liverpool and its schools to the attention of the nation.

The Act gave assistance to Catholics to help them in building new secondary schools. It was an attempt to adjust denominational commitments to contemporary conditions. Or, to put it another way, there were thousands of Catholic as well as Anglican children for whom secondary education could only be provided if the Government stepped in with substantial aid. LEAs were empowered to make grants up to 75% of the cost.

However sectarian controversy in Liverpool led to the refusal by the City Council to apply the Act. It should be said in Liverpool's favour that the city had the largest number of prospective pupils in the country - 12,000 in the dockside area alone. Implementation by Liverpool would have cost the city a rate increase twice as high as any other Authority.

But the Law was the Law. The President of the Board of Education withheld £15,000 from Liverpool's monthly grant for non-compliance. This concentrated minds and a compromise was reached. In 1939 a special Act was passed - The Senior Public Elementary Schools (Liverpool) Act 1939. Instead of a grant to the Catholic community to build its own schools as per the 1936 Act, the Authority was empowered to build the schools and then lease them to the denominational managers. This seemed to satisfy the considerable egos involved and the Catholic community got its senior schools, the forerunners of the post-war secondary modern schools.

For the College, this period came to an end with the retirement of the Head, Fr. Woodlock, in 1937, two years under Fr. Brinkworth and the arrival of Fr. Neylan in 1939.

**The Education Act 1944** was bitterly contested by the Catholic community, faced with the prospect of either losing autonomy or of incurring heavy financial burdens. The College had reason to be apprehensive on two counts. As it was about to move to Woolton, it was anxious as to how the finances would add up if the government did not share the building costs equitably. Secondly, it was concerned about new administrative arrangements that might lead to Local Authority control.

In the event the architect of the Act, the Conservative Minister, Rab Butler, won great credit for the compromises he persuaded Anglicans, Catholics and Non-Conformists to accept. Butler recognized the two categories of schools which already existed - the fully-provided council schools under the Local Education Authority, and the voluntary-aided schools under their providing bodies. The terms that applied to the voluntary aided schools now applied largely to SFX as a voluntary-aided direct grant school.

## Features of the 1944 Act as applied to SFX

**Two-thirds of the governors to be appointed by the Jesuits**
**One-third appointed by the Local Authority**
**Governors responsible for capital costs and external alterations**
**Government to pay half the costs of building repairs and alterations**
**(contribution raised to 75% in 1959, 80% in 1967, & 90% from 2002)**
**Local Education Authority responsible for College's running costs**
**(This included salaries, interior repairs, playgrounds and playing-fields, and for buildings used for school health and meals services.)**
**No fees in LEA schools, but direct grant school retained fee-paying**
**( LEA a right to 25% free-places with an option on a further 25%. Fees of free-place pupils paid for by LEA)**
**Residual places kept for governors to admit fee-payers.**

Butler justified the retention of fee-paying against considerable opposition by saying that 'one of the fundamental principles of the Act is that there shall be a variety of schools'.

# Part Two : Major Institutional Changes : 1945 - 2001

### Direct Grant Status

In 1944, SFX was a direct grant school, which meant that it received its funds directly from central government. Voluntary-aided schools were financed through the local authority.

The Act of 1902 had established that, if a voluntary school observed certain standards and undertook a definite responsibility in the public educational field, it could secure grants from the central government and from the local authority. In 1926, all grant-aided schools not under an LEA had to choose to get their finance by one route or the other, not both. This ruling in Board of Education Circular 1381(1926) effectively established the direct grant list. 250 schools opted to receive their capitation grant from Central Government. SFX was on this list.

In 1945, the 231 direct grant schools still on the list had to apply to become direct grant schools on new terms. 35 decided to become independent. 160 applied and were accepted. 36 were rejected. When the applications were in, there was a particular problem with Liverpool and on Oct 18 1945 a meeting was held at the Ministry of Education, attended by senior civil servants and representative Heads from Liverpool. Its purpose was to discuss the allocation of Direct Grant status amongst the Liverpool Catholic Schools.

Fr. Neylan, the Headmaster of SFX, and Monsignor Traynor, the Diocesan representative, led the Liverpool delegation. The Ministry spokesman began with a description of the problem. It was intended that only 150 of the 231 eligible schools in the country, should continue as Direct Grant schools. There were seven applications from Liverpool Catholic schools - SFX, St Edward's, Bellerive, Broughton Hall, Notre Dame Everton Valley, La Sagesse, and Notre Dame Mount Pleasant - and they could not all succeed. In addition, three Anglican girls' schools had applied - Liverpool College for Girls Grove Street, Belvedere, and St Edmund's.

The Ministry had a number of concerns. Would the two boys' schools be able to cope with the number of Catholic boys passing the 11+, if they did not became voluntary-aided and hence get help with building costs? More immediately, a way had to be found to reduce the number of girls' schools applying. Protests were already being voiced about the possible favourable treatment of Catholic schools in the final decision.

Fr. Neylan asserted that an intake of 45-50 pupils was about right for SFX, if the boys were to profit from the academic curriculum offered. He based this on his opinion of the abilities of the previous year's intake. He proposed that SFX could take 45, St. Edward's 45 and St. Elizabeth's, a voluntary-aided school, could take 60. The Ministry spokesman took this as an acceptable solution for the boys' schools and suggested that - rather than someone at the Ministry wielding the axe - Monsignor Traynor should go back to Liverpool and persuade the girls' schools to agree to the same arrangement - two Direct Grant schools and the rest voluntary-aided.

There was local opposition - especially to SFX's application. The Liverpool Daily Post ran an article on 7th of July 1945 in which members of the City Council accused the College of snobbery.

> 'Inclusion in the new Direct Grant list would enable the
> school to continue to charge fees, to preserve their
> preparatory schools, and to remain free from Burnham
> (salary) scales. The Authority felt strongly that social
> stratification amongst schools that were dependent on
> public funds is undesirable.'

Eventually SFX was included in the list, as were St. Edward's, Notre Dame Everton Valley, and Bellerive. St. Edmund's and The Belvedere were the Anglican schools included.

There does not seem to have been any triumphalism, but it needs no great leap of the imagination to conjure up what must have been an almost palpable feeling of relief in the College. Subjectively, Fr. Neylan may or may not have felt personally relieved. Objectively, it is difficult to imagine a man of his nature surviving in a culture dominated by the LEA. He was not well suited to arguing a weak case from a position of subordination.

After 1945, Direct Grant status was regarded as a mark of excellence - at least amongst those who possessed it. It granted a degree of independence, which was not only jealously guarded but also boasted of, as these remarks which Fr. Doyle left for his successor in 1974 illustrate:

Notes left by Fr. Doyle on retiring in 1974 for his successor, Brother Power

> The virtue of a direct grant system is its relative
> independence - and the school is really independent.

> It is important that all relations with the Department of Education and
> Science be maintained at a happy and efficient level, and every
> communication has to be dealt with carefully.

> Control is exercised through H.M. Inspector who comes rarely
> and should mainly be concerned with academic matters. He
> should always be treated with great courtesy and attention,
> but tell him only the minimum. Occasionally you get one who
> is a nuisance - fussy over detail.

Do not be tempted to let masters complete the actual registers. They make a mess of them and cause appalling work at the end of the year.

Ensure that 3rd Year Sixth-Formers entering for Oxford stay till March 1st. Otherwise they cost the College £163 in grant. Least upset if you tell them they must stay till end of Easter term. The present College system is the fruit of experience.

*Salisbury Street*

MISS EDNA H. LEWIS
Secretary to the College 1927-1970

## Application to go Voluntary-Aided

The next forty years saw decisions taken that would alter life at the College considerably. Some proposals, like the suggestion to change to Voluntary-Aided status, came to nothing. Others had a decided effect on the way the College was conducted. Amongst these were the withdrawal of the Jesuits, the arrival of the Brothers of Christian Instruction, the move to a comprehensive system and the application to become grant-maintained.

Direct Grant virtues notwithstanding, in February 1956 Fr. Warner raised the question of Voluntary-Aided status. He argued that the extra freedom a Direct Grant School had over an aided school was diminishing and that it was not worth the struggle for so little extra. It involved, he thought, a waste of the Society's money, and in his opinion Aided status was inevitable.

Fr. Warner then made an informal approach to a member of the Authority and received a positive response. In May he met with Brother Oswald, the Headmaster of De La Salle, a Voluntary-Aided school. He was assured that the LEA's touch was very light and more than acceptable, that a good deal more finance for books, stationery, etc was available from the relationship, and the only problem might be staff qualifications. Fr. Warner was reassured. Discussions took place in utmost secrecy with the Rector, the Archbishop, and the Provincial. Permission from Rome would be necessary and this was duly applied for and received. In June the Authority had been approached officially and things were set for a change of status for the year 1957-58.

But in October 1956 Fr. Warner had a complete change of heart. Maybe it was because the direct grant had been increased significantly. Government attitude to Direct Grant schools was said to have changed for the better. Old Xaverian Governors spoke of dismay in the city. Probably the thing that was most influential was Fr. Warner's rather belated realization that as a Voluntary-Aided school the new College would be built at Woolton at the city's expense, but that it would go to the bottom of the queue. This was likely to mean no new school for at least five years.

The application was dropped and Fr. Warner set about re-organizing the finances to allow building at Woolton to start right away. But not without some tart remarks from the Provincial as to how what had been inevitable and highly beneficial one week could suddenly become unacceptable and out of the question the next. Building at Woolton was completed in 1961 when the move from Salisbury Street took place.

## The Withdrawal of the Jesuits 1974

In the late 60s the Jesuits were faced with staffing problems, as their numbers declined. Some sort of rationalization was required which was bound to involve reducing their commitments and SFX was one of the Colleges it was decided to sacrifice.

## Timetable

| | |
|---|---|
| May 1969 | Issue raised and Fr. Doyle's objections overruled<br>First date for withdrawal considered - July 1971 |
| July 1970 | Possibilities considered:- hand over to the Archdiocese or close |
| Dec 1970 | Meeting between Fr. Provincial and Brother Provincial of De La Mennais Brothers |

May 1972      Approval of Archbishop

Oct 1972      Appointment of lay deputy

1972 -1973  Staffing and financial issues arranged
                   Decision to leave before change to comprehensive

Apr 1974      Announcement made to Governors and Staff

Apr 1974      Brother Power Headmaster-Designate and took over from Fr. Doyle in July 1974

                   Announcement in a letter to Parents

## The Course of Events

In May 1969, when the issue was first raised, Fr. Doyle made a case for remaining in Liverpool, suggesting that four Jesuits on staff represented an adequate Jesuit presence. He failed to convince and he was left with the task of managing the withdrawal. Fr. Doyle combined the roles of Rector and Headmaster from 1969. Just possibly, this could have been seen as a hint to the discerning that there might be a non-Jesuit future for the College.

In July 1969 the possibility of handing the College over to the Archdiocese was discussed, but went no further. Closure was considered and rejected. In December 1970 a meeting took place between the Jesuit Provincial and Brother Patrick, the Brother Superior of the De La Mennais Brothers of Christian Instruction. An agreement was reached in principle and negotiations began. There were problems over finance, since the Brothers would have to close their preparatory school in Woolton before they could take on the cost of the move to the College. There were staffing problems. There was some doubt about the ability of the Order to provide the necessary minimum of six  brothers. The delay in deciding who would be the new Headmaster also made for some anxious exchanges between Farm Street and the Brother Provincial in Southampton.

Archbishop Beck was informed of the proposals. In September 1971 the two Jesuits remaining on staff at SFX were told that, because of manpower problems and the shrinking and top-heavy age profile, negotiations for a withdrawal had begun; they were told that under no circumstances should the lay staff be informed. The dangers of premature announcement were thought to be very real.

In April 1974 the public announcement was made and the reaction was predictable. Old Xaverians wrote letters to the Provincial in London and 2,500 of them signed a petition organized by the Parents' Association.

Constantly recurring sentiments were expressed:

'Sense of grief...Jesuit capital, skill, labour and endeavour on which the College had been founded.' 'Distress at the news...the contribution the Society has made to Catholic education in Liverpool cannot be over-estimated.' 'We can ill afford to lose the influence of the Society from the local educational scene in Liverpool.'

In addition there was open antipathy towards the De La Mennais Brothers. The more extreme opponents registered their feelings in harsh terms.

'An obscure congregation of lay brothers...' 'the inexperience of the Brothers in running a school.' 'An unsuitable body of men to run SFX'. Fr. Doyle, who was renowned for his inability to delegate anything to anybody, even to another Jesuit, had second thoughts: 'perhaps we should not be handing over to the Brothers.' More to the point, the Order had for many years run successful schools all over the world, as the section at the end of this chapter notes. St. Mary's College in Southampton was founded in 1922 and is currently a flourishing flagship for the Order.

But none of these fairly emotive outbursts represented a reasoned or coherent argument for a change of policy. Yet there was a cogent and ethical case against withdrawal to be made and it was left to the Jesuits to make it - but only amongst themselves. Parents had chosen SFX in the expectation that their sons would be educated by the Jesuits for at least five years. It could have been powerfully argued that the Order was morally at fault if it failed to keep its side of the bargain; furthermore, if the move had been known at the time of selection, many parents might well have opted for St Edward's or other secondary schools. But none of the objectors thought to argue along these lines.

It might have been simpler to announce in 1969 that the Jesuits would be withdrawing in five years time - which is exactly what happened. The time scale would have softened the blow. Current parents would not have seen their interests threatened. Future parents would have had the leisure to make their choices as they saw fit. Banner headlines might well have been avoided.

Conversely, it can be argued that a concern to avoid uncertainty - rather than an obsession with secrecy - was justification in itself for proceeding as the authorities did. Rumour and counter rumour, negotiations started and broken off, agreements made and not kept - in the light of such possibilities the wiser course in the interests of stability may have been to tread with caution.

In the light of what passed, the De La Mennais Brothers, the Governors and the Staff, who have run the College since 1974, must look with some satisfaction on the highly successful reputation the College enjoys in 2001.

The decision was finally announced at a staff meeting in Spring 1974 and in July 1974 Brother Power succeeded Fr. Doyle as Headmaster and the Brothers of Christian Instruction took charge.

Some lay staff saw the College in rather different terms by 1970 and for them the withdrawal of the Jesuits did not represent any great disaster. No one wanted to belittle the contribution of the Jesuits since 1842 nor the efforts the Brothers were making to promote the development of the College. Some thought that Fr. Doyle, who had no teaching role, had an exaggerated idea of his own influence, although this

*The New College at Woolton 2001*

should not detract from his established reputation as a Latin teacher. For some years many pupils had passed through the College without being taught by a Jesuit. No Jesuit had run a Department for some time. By 1974 it was certainly legitimate to question the sense in which SFX might still be regarded as a Jesuit College.

The Jesuits themselves addressed this problem at a conference in Rome in 1980, where an attempt was made to identify and describe Jesuit education. In a pregnant phrase Fr. Arrupe, the Superior General, suggested that 'the education which our students receive should give them a 'certain Ignacianidad'. The mark of St Ignatius. A booklet, 'Characteristics of Jesuit Education', published in Dublin in 1987, was the results of the conference and this will be referred to in Chapter 6 where Religious Education at the College is treated separately.

In the end, 1974 heralded an evolution, not a revolution. The important thing was not the change, but the continuity. The departure of the Jesuits in itself was not considered of great significance by many closely involved with the College. There was a well-established and successful staff. All Heads of Departments were laymen. That the change took place so smoothly is to the credit of all those who worked there in 1974 and who continued to promote the success of the College in the years after.

## Comprehensive Status 1983-1990

Since the war, SFX with its Direct Grant status had enjoyed the autonomy to run its own affairs with only the lightest touch from Whitehall. For Catholics outside the College things also improved in the 60s when the Wilson Government decided that voluntary schools would receive 80% of capital costs. But for Fr. Doyle, a zealot where Direct Grant Schools were concerned, another of Labour's policies loomed as a distinct cloud on the horizon. The Labour Government was determined to press ahead with comprehensive schools.

In 1955 Liverpool City Council had resolved that immediate steps should be taken to establish comprehensive schools in the city, and that the Director should be instructed to prepare a scheme in which the first of these schools schools would open in 1956. Progress was slow and it was the mid-seventies before plans for a general system of comprehensive schools were implemented.

From the comparative safety of Woolton, Catholic SFX must have watched anxiously as Church of England Collegiate, its stronger rival on Shaw St., was included in the list in 1963. However, the Collegiate escaped and remained selective, its conversion to a comprehensive having been turned down by the Ministry of Education. Then a proposal for it to become a non-local comprehensive was tabled in 1972. It finally changed in 1975 and closed down in 1985. Had it moved to West Derby in 1961, as the Governors proposed, or indeed if it had moved to Sandfield Park in 1935, when costs, site and permissions had all been obtained - anticipating St Edward's migration - it may well have survived to prosper like SFX. With The Liverpool Institute for Boys and Blackburne House for Girls closed in this last exercise, SFX was the sole survivor of Liverpool's four pre-1850s secondary schools.

With the future of the county schools settled it was now the turn of the voluntary schools to be considered for reorganization. Fred Devereux, Deputy Head till 1995 and a Governor since then, is one of the best persons to describe these years.

He writes:

"After the withdrawal of the Jesuits in 1974, SFX remained a Direct Grant selective grammar school. Some places continued to be reserved for fee-payers, who took the Governors' entrance examination, but the majority of pupils, who were not exclusively from Liverpool, gained admission on the basis of their eleven-plus performances.

During this period, both major political parties had expressed support for a comprehensive system of secondary education and an end to selection. It had become clear that SFX would have to become part of a scheme of local re-organization of Catholic schools along comprehensive lines or else choose to become a completely independent fee-paying establishment. The Trustees believed that Catholic education would be best served if SFX were to become part of the diocesan proposals. A decision was taken to co-operate with the working party appointed to draw up plans for the re-organization of Catholic secondary schools. After prolonged negotiations, a scheme was produced. This was found to be unacceptable to St Edward's and its governors decided to withdraw and become fee-paying and independent with a heavy reliance on the assisted-places scheme. The archdiocesan working party had to begin again from scratch. With some delay a new scheme was produced and implemented in 1983.

The changes brought about in 1983 marked a turning-point in the history of SFX. At once the school doubled in size; and in theory at least it was meant to be a new school. Some schools were prepared to register this with a change of name. Notre Dame became St Julie's and Cardinal Allen became Cardinal Heenan. Those who exercised influence at SFX were determined to resist any unnecessary change and to preserve all that was best from the past. The traditions and reputation of SFX were seen as assets not to be abandoned lightly. Thus the name was retained, although slightly altered to St. Francis Xavier's High School. When the school became grant-maintained in 1990, the name was restored.

Although there was much continuity after 1983, the changes brought about were fundamental. Most, but not all, of the staff were appointed to the 'new' school. There was an influx of staff mainly from Cardinal Newman. SFX, a selective school with an annual admission of 90 boys, became an all-ability comprehensive school with an annual intake of 180 pupils in six forms. An amalgamation of three schools - SFX, Cardinal Newman and Our Lady of the Assumption - provided the initial school population. The new Upper School was accommodated at High Lee, Woolton, and the Lower School on the Cardinal Newman site in Childwall. SFX was clearly the dominant constituent in the amalgamation, made evident not only in the retention of the name of the patronal saint, but in numerous other ways, from the composition of the governing body and the trustee status of the Brothers of Christian Instruction to the keeping of the maroon blazer. Schools under the trusteeship of a religious order had reserved Headships. Brother Francis therefore retained his post and this further re-inforced the fact that the 'new' SFX was a continuation of the old school.

By the re-organization of 1983, SFX was allocated feeder schools - Catholic primary schools whose boys would have the automatic right of admission to the College. This arrangement remains in force to the present day, and, since the boys in these schools cannot have an application rejected, there can be no question of academic selection. The effect has been that since 1983 the intake of pupils has been academically and socially comprehensive. It depends on the social and economic profile of the feeder parishes. These are Christ the King, St. Paschal Baylon, St. Mary's (Woolton), St. Clare's, St. Gregory's, Our Lady of Good Help, Our Lady of the Annunciation (Bishop Eton), Our Lady of the Assumption, Holy Family, St. Andrew's, and St. Mark's. In practice, the intake from these schools varies considerably. Any places remaining when priority has been given to feeder schools are offered to applicants from other parishes.

After 1983, SFX experienced seven difficult and sometimes turbulent years as a voluntary-aided school under the LEA. Local politics took an extreme turn when the city council was dominated by the group known as the Militant Tendency. A series of financial crises followed. Education services were badly affected. There was a great deal of political involvement in the administration of the services, and professionals in local government were pushed aside. A climax was reached when the Council voted to issue redundancy notices to all its employees - including teachers. Although the staff at SFX were at this time paid by the local authority, they were in fact employed by the school governors. This distinction was ignored by the Council and taxis delivered notices to High Lee. Despite threats the Governors decided not to serve the notices on the staff. The Council eventually backed down, but the whole episode marked a particularly turbulent time for the College. SFX suffered material neglect and stagnation when building maintenance ceased and the upkeep of the playing fields passed to the local parks and gardens department, which was itself a victim of the Council's policies. Against this background it is not surprising that the Governors showed interest when Central Government presented schools with the means of opting out of local control by applying for grant-maintained status. This opportunity was made possible by the Education Reform Bill which received royal assent in the summer of 1988."

An account of one of the more unusual confrontations with the Local Authority during this period, which came to be known as ' The Case of Derek Hatton's Sandwiches', was written up in the College Magazine of 1984 Vol XXII No. 104.

September 14, 1983 **REGIONAL**

# School lunches storm

### by Alan Qualtrough

A ROW was simmering last night over a private school meals service at a Liverpool college.

Yesterday hundreds of packed lunches were wasted when they were dumped outside the St Francis Xavier's College in Beaconsfield Road, Woolton.

The school refused the meals provided by Liverpool education department and preferred instead to continue a contract with a private catering company.

Angry Labour councillors met with college headmaster Brother Francis yesterday to demand that the contract with caterers Gardner Merchant be terminated.

The college board of governors and solicitors met last night to discuss the row but refused to comment.

At the beginning of the new term on September 2 the Roman Catholic college switched to become a voluntary aided school.

Formerly it had been a direct grant establishment outside the control of the local authority.

Last night Liverpool education director Kenneth Antcliffe said the headmaster had been warned on several occasions that the city's Labour-controlled council would not agree to private companies serving school meals.

Deputy education chairman Councillor Julie Lyon-Taylor added that discussions between the city council and the college had continued through the summer holidays and the headmaster had no right to sign a contract with a private company.

SFX headmaster Brother Francis last night said he would not comment on the dispute while talks with the education department were in progress.

*Dumped — hundreds of packed lunches outside the college.*

*School Lunches Storm*

'During the early weeks of the term the school attracted an unexpected degree of attention from the outside world. The refusal of the City Council to purchase the kitchen and dining room at High Lee in order to fulfil its obligation of providing school meals led to events best described as Gilbertian. For several days, the authority delivered packed lunches to the school as a token of discharging its obligations. School meals were still being provided, as previously, by private caterers, and the meals delivered by the authority were at first left on the steps of the kitchen while the local press was invited to photograph the scene. On subsequent days the packed lunches were returned to their place of origin. The farce was eventually abandoned, but not before it had attracted wide coverage in the press and on television. The general view was that the ensuing publicity was much to the school's advantage. What ought to be made known is that ultimately the issue, which was referred to the Department of Education and Science, was decided in the school's favour, and the local authority has since fulfilled its obligation of purchasing the kitchen and dining room.'

Still more earth shattering changes were now in the pipe-line, as the Government introduced the idea of the grant-maintained school. The Headmaster, Brother Francis, and the Governors had felt themselves unduly restricted since their return to local authority control in 1983. The unsettled political situation in Liverpool only added to the frustration of those who were trying to run the College, but the Governors' readiness to apply for grant-maintained status under the 1988 legislation provoked violent opposition from both the Local Authority and from the Archdiocese.

## Grant-maintained Status.

Again, the best placed person to comment on this period is Fred Devereux :

"The Governors were not unanimous in deciding to seek grant-maintained status. Local Council representatives and those Governors nominated by the Archdiocese did not support the proposal. The majority of Governors who were in favour therefore passed a resolution to proceed to ballot the parents in accordance with the provisions of the new legislation. A further resolution recommending grant-maintained status to the parents was also passed. It was also made known that the headmaster and the senior staff were unreservedly in favour of the proposal.

The school magazine reported in one issue : 'There followed a heated campaign, and coverage in the local and national media confirmed the rest of the country in the belief that in Liverpool they do things differently. The opposition campaign brought together an alliance of interests united only in the wish to keep the school under local government control for reasons that were hardly educational.'

Chief among the opponents was the National Union of Teachers. During the weeks leading up to the parental ballot there were meetings which at times ended in disorder, notices appeared in the local press, and accusations were made against the Governors in general and the Headmaster in particular. Because the opposition was for the most part politically motivated, the significance of opting out for grant-maintained status was inflated out of all proportion. The dire warnings, including the allegation that SFX would cease to be a comprehensive school, failed to make much impression on the parents. When the result of the ballot was declared by the Electoral Reform Society on 27th February 1989, 60% of voters were in favour of the proposal. This was acted upon at once and an application to opt out of local control under certain specific terms and regulations was submitted to the Department of Education and Science.

Hopes of a successful response were raised when it was learnt at Easter 1989 that the London Oratory School had become the first Catholic school to achieve grant-maintained status. Unfortunately a decision in the case of SFX was delayed for a term while objections from the Archdiocese were considered. These were rejected, and on 25th August 1989 the Chairman of Governors was informed that our application was successful, taking effect from January 1990. The delay caused by the objections of the Archdiocese meant that the change of status did not come into effect till the beginning of the new academic year. It is notable that in the proposals for grant-maintained status the name of St Francis Xavier's College was re-instated, and in a subsequent amendment to the admissions' procedures it was agreed that girls could be admitted to the sixth form. In all other respects the school remained as it had been previously with regard to admissions. SFX continued as a non-selective comprehensive with a commitment to pupils of the same feeder schools as before. This exposed the extent of the misinformation disseminated by some of the more unscrupulous opponents of the change. It is worth recording that during the stormy years from 1983 to 1990 SFX continued to maintain a high level of academic and other successes. Indeed it was in 1987 that the College's record of gaining ten places at Oxford University was achieved.

The benefits of grant-maintained status were felt immediately by the whole College community. The school was funded directly from central government for two years, and thereafter by the Funding Agency for Schools set up for this purpose; Brother Francis was invited by the Secretary of State to serve on the Board of this new Funding Agency. In effect it meant that the College received extra funding to administer all the services, previously the responsibility of the Local Authority, although it could buy in some of these services if it so wished. Capital expenditure also came under Central Government, bids being made through the Funding Agency in competition with other grant-maintained schools. These were soon to be numbered in hundreds, including some in Liverpool which had followed the lead of SFX. The main capital development at High Lee was the Warner Building which was completed in 1995 and enabled 200 pupils to move up from the former Cardinal Newman site.

Numerous other advantages were made during this period. The buildings were regularly maintained and repaired and ground staff were employed again. Extra teachers and ancillary staff were added, including a librarian for each site. A library budget was re-introduced and resources were increased in all departments. Direct ordering from suppliers eliminated delay and inefficiency, which had been the norm before 1990. Towards the end of the period of grant-maintained status the College was successful in its bid for major capital-development money for the new De La Mennais Sixth Form Centre, which has now been completed and which dominates the Woolton grounds. This has released accommodation for younger pupils in the existing buildings at High Lee. It is expected that this development and a final building phase will accommodate the whole school at High Lee some time in 2002."

Grant-maintained status meant considerable independence for a school and Brother Francis was not the only headmaster to find himself at logger-heads with his local Archbishop. The Archbishop presumably was arguing that the SFX governors were acting in an isolated, asocial and selfish manner. He appears to have considered them to be preoccupied with their private good, no longer recognizing an obligation to pursue the common interest.

Their answer would surely be that they do expect to play their part in working for the common good. It is just that they are not prepared to accept the Establishment's limited prescription of what that is and how that should be obtained. From Plato to Marx, appeals to the common good have too often been associated with oppression. Our governors were clearly not accepting the experts' superior ability to judge on their behalf. A mis-reading it might be, but the Authority and the Archdiocese gave the impression of being mainly interested in exercising power: an educational version of 'Trust me. I'm a doctor.'

A separate point was made, when the matter came before the courts. A governor is appointed to work in the interests of the school. It is not immediately obvious, the courts said, that, where these clash with the interests of the wider community, he or she should give way.

In the event the College has succeeded where failure was forecast, and neither the LEA nor the Catholic education system of Liverpool can be seen to have suffered any mortal blows from the stance the Governors took.

Something of the bitterness with which the case was fought can be seen in the pages of the Liverpool press. The Council paid £15,000 for an advertisement opposing the application. Brother Francis responded in the same style and format, which he distributed to the all the parents.

The second extract is a newspaper debate between Brother Francis and Councillor Scott, the Chairman of the Education Committee.

# CITY of LIVERPOOL
## CHANGING FOR THE BETTER

IMPROVING EDUCATION

## An open letter from Liverpool City Council to all parents of boys attending S.F.X. or due to attend in the future

Dear Parent,

The Education Reform Act now in force allows, under certain conditions, governing bodies of schools to ballot parents on the question of Grant Maintained Status (GMS). GMS effectively means going outside the 'umbrella' of the Local Education Authority (LEA) and, in the case of religious schools, the Church, and receiving funds directly from the Government.

You will now know that the Governing Body has decided to instruct the Electoral Reform Society to issue ballot papers on the question of S.F.X. acquiring GMS status from September 1989.

The City Council is taking the unusual step of addressing parents and all other interested parties through the 'Liverpool Echo' because of our deep concern over this major issue, and our strong feelings about the need for full information to be available.

Some of the *facts* are as follows:

1. Grant Maintained status will *not* give any school more resources than it will get anyway. This has been stated categorically by the Secretary of State.
2. If the School becomes GMS, it is an irrevocable step. A GMS school *cannot* opt back into the system.
3. There are no guarantees, after five years, that the School would remain the same. For example, it could become co-educational, lose its religious character, or have formal entrance examinations.
4. No school has yet become GMS, and no one has any certain knowledge of how it will work or, indeed, if it will work at all.
5. The School will lose all the benefits of participation in centrally provided services like training, financial and legal advice, school meals, etc.
6. Under the Education Reform Act the Governing Body will, in any case, be responsible for 90% of the School's finances, but with the advantage of the support of the services referred to above.

WHO CAN VOTE? All parents of boys *presently* attending the School, including those in the final few months of their schooling. However, many parents will be sending their sons to S.F.X. this September and in future. They will have NO SAY WHATSOEVER in this vote on the School's future. All parents who do have a vote should consider the issue of future school pupils very carefully.

It is essential that all those entitled to vote do so. You do have three weeks to consider all the arguments. We consider that the LEA and Archdiocesan views have not, as yet, been fully brought to the attention of parents. We would, therefore, strongly recommend that all parents should be in possession of all the facts before they vote.

We would particularly ask that you attend the meeting for all parents with Liverpool City Council at the Upper School, Childwall Comprehensive School, at 7.30 p.m. this Wednesday, 8th February, 1989. Please do not vote until you have heard all the arguments.

Councillor Ian Scott, *(Chair, Education Committee)*
Councillor Keva Coombes, *(Leader of the Council)*
Councillor Paul Clark, *(Leader of the Opposition)*
Councillor Mike Storey, *(Deputy Leader of the Opposition and Opposition Education Spokesperson)*

---

# St. Francis Xavier's School
## CHANGING FOR THE BETTER

IMPROVING EDUCATION

## An open letter from Bro. Francis, Senior Staff to all parents of boys attending S.F.X. or due to attend in the future

Dear Parent,

The Education Reform Act now in force allows, under certain conditions, governing bodies of schools to ballot their parents on the question of Grant Maintained Status (G.M.S.) G.M.S. effectively means going outside the 'umbrella' of the Local Education Authority (L.E.A.) and, in the case of a Catholic school remaining within the Archdiocesan provision, although receiving funds directly from the Government.

You will now know that the Governing Body has decided to support a petition of parents to request G.M.S. and to instruct the Electoral Reform Society to issue ballot papers on the issue of S.F.X. acquiring G.M.S. from September 1989.

School Management is taking the unusual step of addressing parents and all other interested parties through the 'Liverpool Echo' because of our deep concern for the future of our children and for that of children in our feeder parish schools.

Some of the facts are as follows:-

1. Grant Maintained status will ensure the resources come direct to the school. This will mean better financial management – the pound will go farther.
2. If the school becomes G.M.S. it will not wish to opt back into the L.E.A.
3. It is guaranteed to keep the character of the school the same for the future. No entrance examinations could be set. It would always remain a Catholic school.
4. The Education Reform Act 1988 spells out how a G.M.S. school will operate. The idea is not entirely new. S.F.X. has 141yrs. operating outside the L.E.A. It knows that G.M.S. will work.
5. The school will be able to buy in all the benefits of services like training, financial and legal advice, school meals, in-service etc.
6. Under the Education Reform Act the Governing Body will, in any case, be responsible for 90% of the school's finances but only after the L.E.A. has retained a portion as deemed necessary for central expenditure.

WHO CAN VOTE? All parents of boys who presently attend the School, including those in the final months of their schooling. However those parents from feeder parish schools presently listed are guaranteed places next September. They will be first to contribute to the bright future of S.F.X.

All parents who do have a vote should consider the issue of the school's future very carefully. It will have no future under an L.E.A. which holds back essential funds for books and equipment and fails to maintain the buildings.

It is essential that all those entitled to vote do so. All interested parties have flooded your home with information or called meetings to ensure you are informed.

ALL VOTERS ARE URGED TO VOTE FOR THE FUTURE OF THEIR CHILDREN AND NOT LISTEN TO THE POWER STRUGGLE FOR S.F.X. FROM OUTSIDE FORCES.

**ENSURE A FUTURE FOR S.F.X.**

**VOTE IN FAVOUR OF OPTING OUT**

The Headmaster & Senior Staff.

**8**     Liverpool Echo, Monday February 13, 1989

# WAR OF WORDS

SPECIAL REPORT BY KEITH KENDRICK

PARENTS of pupils at Saint Francis Xavier's RC School, Woolton, are now voting on the most crucial education issue in Liverpool for years.

To opt out or not: that is the question.

The ballot papers are out and the battle lines are drawn for what is becoming one of the most vicious fights ever.

In the blue corner are SFX headmaster Brother Francis, his board of governors and a group of concerned parents.

They say opting out will free the school to secure a brighter future for the children.

In the red corner are both Labour and Liberal councillors, the National Union of Teachers and parents of pupils now attending SFX's feeder schools.

They say opting out is an experiment in which the people that matter — the pupils — will be used as guinea pigs.

And in the middle are the undecided

Tonight the Echo steps into the ring to act as referee in the battle for SFX.

Headmaster, Brother Francis

Councillor Ian Scott

SO FAR the battle has been fought on general grounds — principles rather than specifics.

Brother Francis argues that life under Liverpool City Council control since 1983 has been intolerable and "very damaging".

Unleashed from their reins, the headmaster says the governors would be able to provide a better education for the children.

His opponents say applying for grant maintained status would turn SFX into an elitist school which could collapse because of a lack of funds.

We decided to probe deeper by asking Brother Francis to detail his grievances against the city council and to offer his own solutions.

Then we put his complaints to Cllr Ian Scott, chairman of the city council's education committee.

Here we reproduce their war of words:

**Francis:** "There has been no interior decorating of any part of the main school at Woolton while under local authority control."

**Scott:** "The LEA has a rolling programme for interior decorating ... ... ...: Schools should be decorated every seven years. There are many schools that have not been decorated, but also many that have. Those that have not are due in the near future.

"But even if SFX has not been decorated this is no reason to opt out of LEA control as by 1993 all schools' governors, under the Education Reform Act, will be able to manage 93 per cent of its own budget and will be able to do what it likes with that money, be it decorating, buying books or paying for sports equipment."

**Francis:** "On two occasions, in summer 1988 and November 1988, the Examining Board had refused to release GCSE certificates to our boys because the city council had not paid the fees."

**Scott:** "This was an adminstrative hiccup. In any organisation hiccups occur and every effort will be made to ensure it doesn't happen again."

**Francis:** "There is clear evidence that SFX and other denominational schools in Liverpool have discriminated against in resourcing.

"This evidence is produced in a league table of schools in Liverpool detailing how much money each establishment receives per year for each pupil.

"The majority of RC schools appear at the bottom of the table, whereas the county schools are at the top.

A comparison can be drawn between SFX, which has 1,010 pupils, and Breckfield Comprehensive, which had 987.

SFX is 25th on the list; Breckfield is 7th."

**Scott:** "This can be easily answered. The voluntary aided schools, such as SFX, do not pay rates; the county schools do. These rates are paid by the council on behalf of the school and that figure is included in the final cost-per-pupil figure.

For example, in the case of SFX and Breckfield, Breckfield pays £46,367 rates and SFX pays a nominal sum of £11,000 for rent, which means the city council has to pay £30,000 more on Breckfield's behalf than for SFX.

"It is nonsense to suggest that we discriminate against church schools."

**Francis:** "There has been a regular failure to advertise staff responsibilities without long delay.

"One example was of a resignation in May last year. The LEA did not advertise the post until last month."

**Scott:** "On many occasions in the past the governing body of the school has placed its own advertisements and we have done nothing to hinder them.

"But we do expect voluntary aided schools to observe council procedures. Occasionally the process leads to a temporary delay but temporary staff have always been available from the support services."

**Francis:** "There has been a refusal by council to accept responsibility for any repairs to furniture or fittings on the school's upper site.

"Because of this I have had to employ a joiner at the trustees' expense. He costs us several hundred pounds a term."

**Scott:** "In a letter to the council from the Department of Education and Science said in June 1985 the responsibility of furniture and equipment at schools such as SFX 'rested with the promoters'— that is the school governors.

"In this, the DES is saying quite clearly that it is up to the governors to provide furniture and equipment and that the council could even be held to be unlawful if it was to provide these things from its own budget."

**Francis:** "There has been a failure to keep the conditions of the licence under which the LEA maintains the playing fields. This has resulted in deteriorating playing pitches.

"There was even a period when I had to go and cut the grass myself."

**Scott:** "Increasing costs and a lack of extra government resources have made it difficult to keep fields in good condition. However, this situation will hopefully soon be rectified.

"If the school does opt out then it will be the governors' total responsibility for the maintenance of the fields."

**Francis:** "The council has failed to remove asbestos from all areas affected in the lower school due to an alleged lack of funds.

"The council identified 24 classrooms as having asbestos content in the ceilings. We were promised in July 1988 that this would be dealt with during the summer holiday.

"The money was approved from council funds to do this, but on the first day the contractor who got the job walked off the site.

"The next highest tender was £10,000 higher and therefore the city council had to cut back and they said they could only afford to do seven of the 24 ceilings."

**Scott:** "Once we were alerted about the asbestos emergency we combed through the city council's accounts very carefully to see where we could find the £30,000 needed to pay for this work.

"Eventually we found the money, but initially the governors were not happy that the work had been done.

"The director of maintenance and building work visited the school and several of the rooms were then re-done."

**In conclusion:—**

**Francis:** "We felt that the level of provision from the local authority has been inadequate even to cover basic needs.

"Far too much of our time has been taken up with repairing and maintaining the school when we should be concentrating on teaching the children.

"Under grant-maintained status the school would enter into its own contracts for maintenance and repairs and pay directly.

"We would determine our own league table of needs and budget according to those needs."

**Scott:** "By 1993 all governing bodies of schools will be responsible for 93% of their own budget.

"The 7% that the local authority keeps will provide services such as supply and cover staff, it will provide a safety net for emergencies such as the asbestos scare.

"Inspectors, legal and personnel expertise will be readily available, and the provision of school meals and other needs that are essential to a coordinated education service will also be available.

"I doubt if a grant-maintained status school could provide all the back up services we have referred to from within that seven per cent."

# Opt out bid by SFX sparks angry debate

80

## Foundation Status

The Labour Government, elected in 1997, finally abolished grant-maintained status in 1998. Brother Francis and the Governors were now faced with a decision that would provoke another confrontation with the Archdiocese.

Fred Devereux writes:

"The Labour victory in the general election of 1997 was of constitutional significance for SFX. The Party had opposed grant-maintained legislation in 1988 and had pledged to repeal it after the election. Although it had committed itself to repeal, its views on the grant-maintained arrangements had modified considerably since 1990 and senior members of the party were aware of a shift in public opinion. Hundreds of GM schools were among the most successful in the country. Many Labour members favoured them. The new School Standards and Framework Act of 1998 was consequently something of a compromise. Grant-maintained schools were given the choice of becoming Voluntary-Aided or Foundation schools - a new name if not a new category.

There was national opposition to Foundation status for Catholic schools from the Conference of Catholic Bishops. In Liverpool there were strong objections to Foundation status for SFX from the Archdiocesan authority, but none of any significance from the Council, which was no longer under Labour control. Fortunately the opposition, though again relying on misinformation, had little effect. Particularly misleading was the assertion that the College could cease to be a Catholic school. Such an alteration of the denominational status of a school was expressly forbidden under the Act. Again there were claims that selection would be introduced. But selection procedures remained the same. The College continued to accept its pupils from its designated feeder schools.

The governors told parents in November 1999 that, if a sufficient number so wished, a vote would be held on the decision. Despite an appeal from the Archbishop in a letter to all parents urging them to oppose, the response amounted to no more than a few inquiries to the College office. Foundation status was subsequently granted to take effect from September 1999. The College was and is (January 2002) the only Foundation school in the country with a religious character.

The main effect of this change was that the College was able to preserve much of the independence which it had enjoyed under the grant-maintained scheme. In particular it would continue to receive 100% funding from Central Government for any successful bid for capital development. The new legislation abolished the Funding Agency and transferred the responsibilities to the Local Authority. This has proved to be very satisfactory and recent bids for capital funding have been given full support by the LEA, whose officers work in close collaboration with the governing body. Despite the differences of opinion over the decision, relations with the Archdiocese remain cordial and positive."

**ARCHBISHOP'S HOUSE**
**LOWOOD**
**CARNATIC ROAD   MOSSLEY HILL   LIVERPOOL   L18 8BY**
Tel: 0151 724 6398
Fax: 0151 724 6405

30th September 1998

Dear Governor,

## Choice of new Category for your School

You are about to take a very important decision affecting the future of your school. Your governing body must decide whether to accept the allocation of your school to the voluntary aided category in accordance with schedule 2 of the School Standards and Framework Act 1998, or to make a decision which will lead to the Secretary of State considering whether to allocate your school to either the voluntary controlled or foundation categories.

I strongly urge you to accept the school's allocation as a voluntary aided school. Your school has been given the indicative allocation of voluntary aided because, as a self-governing school provided by a voluntary body, that is the category into which it most naturally fits.

Like voluntary controlled and foundation schools, voluntary aided schools will continue to be self-governing schools funded by the LEA. Like foundation schools, voluntary aided schools will continue to be employers and admissions authorities. Unlike voluntary controlled or foundation schools, voluntary aided schools will continue to receive captial funding centrally, rather than through the LEA. Voluntary aided schools also have a smaller provision for local authority governors than other types of school.

However, it is the effect which your decision will have on the Catholic character of your school which is my greatest concern and, I hope, will be yours as well. By law, Catholic schools must be governed in accordance with the trust deed which applies to them. In accordance with section 579 (1) of the Education Act 1996, the trust deed of your school defines a Catholic school as "one which is under the control of the competent ecclesiastical authority or of a public ecclesiastical juridical person (e.g. a religious order), or one which in a written document is acknowledged as Catholic by the ecclesiastical authority". Your school currently satisfies this requirement because a majority of the governing body are appointed by the De La Mennais Brothers.

If the school were to become a voluntary controlled or foundation school, the Christian De La Mennais Brothers would not be able to appoint more than one quarter of the governing body. It would then fall to me, as the competent ecclesiastical authority, to decide whether exceptional circumstances existed to justify declaring that the school remained a Catholic school despite the loss of Church control.

In order to make such a declaration, I would have to be satisfied that sufficient legal safeguards were in place to ensure the continued Catholicity of the school, particularly in important areas such as staffing and religious education.

In voluntary controlled and foundation schools, the law prohibits a governing body, however well intentioned, from requiring a Catholic as head teacher, deputy head teacher or for most other teaching staff. The only teachers that the governing body may require to be Catholics are "reserved teachers" which are those teachers specifically appointed to teach Catholic RE. The head teacher and at least 80% of the staff may not be reserved teachers. In practice, reserved teachers would constitute only part of the RE department of the school.

Voluntary controlled and foundation schools are obliged to teach RE according to the agreed syllabus of the local education authority (i.e. religious education which, contrary to the school's trust deed, is not Catholic in its content). Even if individual parents request RE which is Catholic in content, the school will generally be prohibited from teaching RE to the extent required by the Church.

If, therefore your school were to end up in a category other than voluntary aided, it is unlikely that I would be able to declare that the school remained a Catholic school. That being the case, the school would cease to be a Catholic school on 1st September 1999 as a result of the loss of the foundation majority on the governing body. It would no longer have the right to call itself a Catholic school, and would cease to be part of Catholic education in this diocese.

Catholic schools exist because of the sacrifices made by generations of Catholics. I am sure you take seriously the trust which the Catholic community has placed in you as the governor of a Catholic school. For reasons I have given I therefore urge you once again to ensure your governing body accepts the school's indicative allocation as a voluntary aided school thus safeguarding the school's Catholic character, not just for the present generation of pupils but for future generations as well.

May I take this opportunity to thank you for your continued and valuable hard work on behalf of your school and of Catholic education.

Yours sincerely,

Archbishop of Liverpool

To all Members of Governing Body,
St.Francis Xavier's College,
Beaconsfield Road,
Liverpool 25.

*Letter from the Archbishop of Liverpool to Governors re Foundation Status*

## De La Mennais Brothers of Christian Instruction

In 1964 Brother Durkin and Brother Melody, the first members of the Order to teach at the College, joined the staff. Brother Melody stayed three years working in the Craft Department; Brother Durkin taught English for two years, being replaced by Brother Mahon in 1966. For the next five years other demands were made on the Order and no Brothers were assigned to teach at the College.

But in 1974 the Order took over the direction of the College with Brother (now Father) Power as the new Headmaster, and in the mid-seventies the De La Mennais Brothers were a major presence. The seven Brothers on the staff in 1975 together with the Chaplain, Fr. O'Leary, made up nearly 20% of the teaching body, which meant that there were now more Religious teaching at the school than at any time since 1967. Brothers Augustine (Chemistry), Bradley (Head of Middle School) and Malcolm (RE), were joined at different times by Brothers Cullen, Slattery, and Thomas with Fr. O'Leary teaching Religious Studies. Brother Francis was appointed Headmaster in 1979 and this heralded over twenty years of important institutional developments. As with all religious orders since, vocations have dwindled, but till 1990 there were always four Brothers on the staff. Currently Brother Edmund in the Maths Department and Brother James in the Music Department hold the fort for the Order along with Brother Francis.

The Order of the Brothers of Christian Instruction was founded in 1817 by Jean-Marie de la Mennais, committed to the task of teaching the poor children of Brittany. Such was the success of the Congregation of Brothers that they were soon in demand not only throughout France but also in the French colonies and in England. In 1850s young Englishmen were educated by Fr. de la Mennais at the request of the Vicar Apostolic of London, the future Cardinal Wiseman. These men formed a separate Congregation in England and were responsible for establishing St Mary's, the original men's Catholic teacher training college at Strawberry Hill in Twickenham. They also opened schools in London and Liverpool in the 1850s, which did not survive.

An English District of the Order was eventually founded in 1922 with the opening of St Mary's College in Southampton, which has been a successful school in southern England ever since. The Brothers returned to Liverpool in 1962, when they opened a Preparatory School at the Gables. Then in 1969 negotiations began for the move to SFX.

The Order is engaged in the work of education internationally in a surprising number of different institutions. Orphanages, technical schools, agricultural colleges, naval schools, university colleges, grammar and comprehensive schools from Rome to Buenos Aires, from Tokyo to the Seychelles. In these schools, as at SFX, the Brothers remain committed to an education grounded in Christian principles and to a desire 'to make known Jesus Christ'.

*Chapter 5*

# The Curriculum : Drama

In the main, successive headmasters have seen to it that the curriculum at the College has kept up with the current developments. When appropriate, new areas of study have been readily introduced without sacrificing traditional subjects.

The College was founded with a Commercial Course which held its place alongside the Classical Course for sixty years. With the introduction of chemistry and the natural sciences in 1875, SFX was ahead of most schools in the area. The title of School of Science was granted by the Board of Education in 1900. Woodwork and geography were taught before they were generally included in timetables. The present headmaster, Brother Francis, has seen to it that Computing and Information Technology Departments have not only been supported but equipped to a high standard. The range of sporting options open to pupils in the year 2001 makes impressive reading.

Instead of taking a roll call of the subjects introduced at the College over the centuries, it is more interesting to examine in detail some of the areas of the curriculum in detail to see how they fitted into the overall concept of Jesuit education and how this concept was capable of moving with the times.

## Drama

In the Spring of 1949 the members of the Sixth-Form Drama class staged *"Caesar's Friend"*. Given that drama had played an important role both in Jesuit education down through the centuries and at SFX since 1850, why was this the first full-length play performed at the College for thirteen years? In this sense the play is something of a land-mark, and it deserves to be given some prominence here. A very full review was printed in the College Magazine of 1949 - some indication of how seriously drama was taken at the College - at least by some staff.

*The School Hall*

**Shrovetide Play - Caesar's Friend**

On Shrove Monday and Tuesday, 28th February and Ist March, the members of the Sixth Form Drama Class presented *Caesar's Friend*, a Passion Play by Campbell Dixon and Dermot Morrah, in the College Hall.

The cast was as follows :

Caiphas, High Priest of Israel ............................. J. P. SULLIVAN
Judas.................................................................. T.J.GRISEWOOD
Malchus, servant to Caiphas................................ G. W. CHANTRY
Annas................................................ ... ... ... ................. J. F. McGLASHAN
Gamaliel, a Pharisee      .................................... F. J. SWIFT
Joseph of Arimathaea     .................................... A. J. MAWDSLEY
A Roman Soldier  ...      ...      ......................... T. F. CARNEY
A Roman Sentry   ...      .................................... F. C. OAKLEY
Decurion      ...      ...      .................................... J. A. WORRALL
Peter, a fisherman............................................. L. P. MURPHY
A Blind Man ...      ........................................... G. U. KELLY
Sextus Pontius Pilate ....................................... G.F. FITZGIBBON
Marcus Horatius Balbus ................................. P. L. O'KEEFFE
Damon. servant to Pilate ................................ E. J. BUSHELL
Mary of Magdala ... ......................................... J. F. FITZGIBBON
Claudia Procula, Pilate's wife.......................... D. P. BURKE
Marcella, her niece ......................................... P. D. SWEENEY
Lucius Licinius Cotta........................................ A. R. GALEA
      Jews...............................P. V. GAUGHAN; P. J. RUANE;
                  F. P. QUINN ; J. L. SCARISBRICK.

Some extracts from the review are worth recording.

First there is a general disclaimer - or is it an apology - for the more cutting remarks the writer goes on to make.

> 'Dramatic criticism, especially of school productions, is a sphere into which even angels might fear to tread - an occupation only one degree less dangerous than the adjudication of a baby competition. Such criticism as is made here is offered in no carping spirit, but from the conviction that acting can be a most satisfying means of self-expression, and that the satisfaction is increased in proportion to the degree of perfection attained by the actor.'

Then there follows a sally in the direction of those who did not learn their lines.

> 'Too many actors, having neglected to learn their lines even by the dress rehearsal, make what they deem to be a heroic effort for the first night, at which, with disconcerting pauses and mute appeals to the prompter, they stumble through their part : and then they lay the flattering unction to their souls that they have done all that may reasonably be demanded of them. Much is forgiven them, not from any feeling that they have done well, but from relief that they have not proved even worse'.

Then there were those who had learned their lines, but failed to deliver.

> 'Audibility is the first requirement in an actor, and the inaudible actor, unless he is an expert in mime, might as well not be on the stage at all.'

Of individual performances, the portrayal of Caiphas, by J. P. Sullivan, was the most highly praised.

> 'Sullivan appeared perfectly at ease, dominating the scene, passing smoothly from mood to mood, suave, ironic, persuasive, menacing in turn with a voice rich and expressive.'

There is a touch of damning with faint praise about some of the other comments.

> 'J. F. McGlashan, as Annas, was a good foil to him in appearance, manner and, when audible, in voice.' T. J. Grisewood, who played Judas, 'opened shakily, but gradually gained strength. But he gained in confidence, and his later exchanges with Caiphas and Pilate were one of the highlights of the play'.

G. F. FitzGibbon played Pilate with

> 'a quiet dignity and confident bearing, but the scene in Pilate's villa lacked variety of pace and mood and character' And 'D. P. Burke, as Claudia Procula, appeared to have the cares of the whole world upon him, and his voice lacked volume, tone and interest.'

This is interesting, since Burke went on to play both West End and Broadway leads.

> 'A. R. Galea, as Lucius Cotta, having entered unobtrusively, seemed possessed by one desire - to make what speed he could to be gone...splendidly costumed, handsomely made-up, elegantly coiffured..to the eye a delight..but the ear could not assimilate the volley of words he discharged.'

One is tempted to think that this is the director's fault, not Galea's, and likewise for the criticism of Damon (E. J. Bushell) for his *monotonous delivery*. P. L. O'Keeffe, as Balbus, was noted *for a distracting and uncontrolled right hand and for not living up to his swashbuckling reputation*. (Whether this reputation is as O'Keeffe or as Balbus is not made clear.)

A. J. Mawdsley gets some very back-handed compliments.

> 'He gave a sympathetic portrayal of Joseph of Arimathaea, and his voice was well-modulated and clear, except when he spoke with his back to the audience. Few actors have a back so expressive that they can retain the interest of the audience when facing straight upstage.'

The review ends with the remarks that

> 'While the soldiers would not have qualified for the Tenth Legion, the "crowd" by contrast achieved a fair measure of success. Nonetheless in the scene before the Praetorium, Balbus found himself compelled to enjoin "Silence!" upon a momentarily mute and docile crowd'.

The scenery, Mr Vandeput, and his helpers get full marks.

> 'The richness of Caiphas' house, the solidity of Jerusalem's walls, the grandeur of the Praetorium, the distance of the hill of Calvary, the most ordinary furnishings transformed by a touch of paint, all bespoke the hand of the master.'

Such a review, whilst it bears the marks of the midnight oil, was careful and thorough, and did the boys the honour of treating them as actors, not pupils. If no allowances were made and no quarter given, this does seem in keeping with the demands in a Jesuit school that, whatever the activity, only the highest standards would do - a failing, perhaps, as well as a virtue.

*The College Stage*

## Other College Performances

Prior to *Caesar's Friend* in 1949 the last full-length play performed at the College was *The Ten Minute Alibi* in 1936. This was typical of the short farces put on in the late Twenties and Thirties. Others were *The Safety Match* and *The Admirable Crichton* and *The Baby Elephant.*

" THE BABY ELEPHANT."

Ebenezer Spikes (C. Hughes).       Bartholomew Rakes (W. McHugh).
James (A. McAllister).                              John (V. Donnelly).
*College Magazine 1932 Vol VII No 39)*

*The Ten Minute Alibi. 1936*
*John Doyle, Bill McGrath, Wilfrid Larkin, Frank Hart, Liam Burke*
*front row Raymond Parkes, Ray Mullins, Colin Campbell, W.Sneade, Adrian Mitchell*

A hugely successful *Macbeth* in January 1923 seems to have been the last substantial play at the College, and in view of this success the lack of serious drama since is all the more surprising. After all, the dramatic tradition in Jesuit Colleges from the seventeenth century onwards had been very strong, and the enthusiasm for the stage at SFX in its first eighty years was remarkable.

This performance of *Macbeth* was so popular that the play was repeated in February and all the secondary schools of Liverpool were invited. F. McDowd, who played Macbeth, received such rave reviews that one hopes that his talents were usefully deployed later, if not on the stage, at least at the Bar or in the Lecture Hall. Nearly two thousand sixth formers crammed into the Hall - the play was the exam text for that year - and it made such an impression that it was credited with the establishment of drama departments in several Liverpool schools. At the Northern England Educational Conference the performance was described as 'epoch-making' and it was recommended as a model for all schools to copy.

*The Safety Match (1929)*
*Kevin Reade, a teacher at the College in the 1950s and 1960s plays the female lead.*

2nd Witch—J. LEYLAND.        1st Witch—J. ALCOCK.        3rd Witch—C. DODDS

90

## The Importance of Drama in the Jesuit Curriculum

'And plays are not to be neglected, for poetry perishes when drama disappears' .
Ratio 1591. Provincial's Rule 84.

It will perhaps come as a surprise to some to learn that drama - or the theatre, as it was known - has held an important place in the curriculum of Jesuit schools from the very beginning of the Order in the sixteenth century.

St Ignatius, the founder of the Order, had written a memorandum to his secretary in 1555, the year he died. He had sketched out some ideas for oral work in schools, and it is possible to see this note as a starting-point for those who went on to write the Ratio Studiorum.

'Boys from all walks of life should be accepted. To make theory more interesting for them and to afford them and their parents pleasure, at times during the year orations should be delivered and verses and dialogues recited. This will also add prestige to the school'.
(McCabe 1983 p.11)

Then, when the Ratio et Institutio Studiorum was drafted in 1586 and published in 1599, containing the general educational policy for Jesuit colleges, it laid down the rules to be followed in the conduct and administration of schools - including theatre - in an attempt to harmonise the mediaeval scholasticism with the new humanism.

At the time the Ratio was written, utilitarian and humanitarian arguments were being advanced in England for the place of school plays in Protestant schools. Drama had been an accepted part of the curriculum in many schools since the Tudor period, but the acting of plays in the classroom was considered useful only in teaching decorum, self-confidence, good delivery and an appreciation of dramatic literature and theatre.

The Jesuits, in the Ratio, acknowledged these advantages. They recognized that drama developed *'Latin eloquence, speaking in public and declaiming well, and that the theatre gave grace of gesture and fluency, and a blend of assurance and modesty'.* Whether or not drama had its origins in St Ignatius' note, one section of the Ratio went on to deal with the role and practice of drama in colleges. It was felt that: 'the theatre could be a forceful agent for stirring pupils'

'interests in learning, a strategy in an educational programme of self-help and development of talent, and an aid to the study of the humanities or a tactic at least for enlivening instruction in grammar and rhetoric.'                                        (McCabe, 1983 p. v)

'From the beginning the Jesuits recognized all the benefit which they would derive from the use of drama by the students of the colleges which they had just founded. They adopted then the practice, which became general in the sixteenth century, of giving dramatic representations in their educational institutions'. (Motter 1929 p.298)

It will be clear from the foregoing, then, that the dramatics described here were not just seen as a help to the academic study of the text - still less were they meant simply as entertainments.

# RATIO, ATQVE
## INSTITVTIO
## STVDIORVM
### SOCIETATIS IESV.

IHS

ROMÆ,
In Collegio Romano eiuſdem Societatis.
Anno Domini. M.DC.XVI.

SVPERIORVM PERMISSV.

*Ratio atque Institutio Studiorum*

## Drama and the Teaching of Morals

To the humanist aim of producing Latin plays as a means of teaching language skills and cultivating poise and rhetorical flourish, the Jesuits added religious and moral instruction as a formative influence on the student's whole person.

Thus in addition to the training aspects found in Protestant schools, the Jesuits on the Continent were also advancing a moral appeal, if at times on a rather exalted plane. One Prologue to a seventeenth century tragedy written by a Jesuit reads :

> 'Perhaps one day, when they all have grown up, these young people will be fired with the desire of equalling these virtues and will be in their turn ambitious for a good death. They would  like perhaps actually to imitate those whose actions they represent today, and to carry off similar victories. Thus, even as we play, it is necessary to  direct morals toward piety, to conduct through great images to great deeds, and to  plant in their hearts the love of Christ'.
> (Motter 1929 p. 298)

Wider public motives, some suggest, were at work also. Simultaneously with the beginning of their educational work, the Jesuits started a system of theatrical activity:

> 'in order that the human love of spectacular effects which showed  signs of breaking away from the Church with the advent of humanism might be gratified and at the same time maintained in the spirit of the Catholic religion.'
> (McCabe 1983 Chap. 2)

Or to put it more strongly, the Jesuits found themselves forced to organise a

> 'theatrical counter-revolution' in response to the ' violent and  polemical tendencies of a humanistic and Protestant drama school which developed first of all in Genoa and later in England'.
> (Fulop-Miller p.420)

## Jesuit Conditions for Acceptable Drama

In the early days strict conditions were laid down by the Jesuits. It was stipulated that the plays should be in Latin and that they should be on sacred subjects. Any interludes between acts should also be 'in Latin and decorous.' It added: 'Let no feminine character or costume be introduced.'
(Schwickerath,R. SJ 1929 pp. 165-167)

But the Ratio of 1591 Rule 84 did allow female dress. 'If it cannot be avoided, let it be decorous and dignified'. And 'The pieces shall be examined before being represented; and it is absolutely forbidden to play them in the church.' Drunkenness and swearing were specifically mentioned as targets for Jesuit playwrights, and to this end plays were often written with a moral purpose.    (McCabe 1983 p. 14)

The stories from the Greek tragedies were forbidden, specifically *The Medea, Oedipus* and *Eumenides.* Instead ancient history, the history of the Church, the  Old Testament, and scenes of contemporary history were the subjects prescribed or authorized, and the chief pieces of the repertory were almost always taken from these sources. It was suggested that 'eclogues, scenes and dialogues should be composed by the boys themselves'.

## The Rapid Development of Drama in Jesuit colleges

Drama, then, in the Jesuit curriculum, belongs in a long tradition, and its place at SFX can be traced back through Stonyhurst College and thence to the Jesuit colleges on the Continent. The English-speaking world is almost completely unaware that for two centuries (1550- 1773) in hundreds of European towns the Jesuit academic theatre produced thousands of plays before eager audiences drawn from populations in the surrounding towns and villages.                                            (McCabe 1983 p.17)

An article printed in the College Magazine (1929 pp. 448-451)  called ' Jesuit School Plays' will come as a surprise to many, since in most people's minds the Jesuits are not immediately associated with amateur dramatics - still less with the writing and performing of plays to a highly professional standard for the general public. But to quote from the article:

> 'During the latter half of the sixteenth century the whole of the seventeenth and the greater part of the eighteenth the Jesuits were literally world-famous as masters in every branch of the theatrical art.'

Where in modern times would we find a single performance of a school play attended by 8,000 people, as happened at a Jesuit College in Prague in 1560? Some authorities claim that the famous *Passion Play* at Oberammergau is an off-shoot of the Munich Jesuit Drama. We can do no better than reprint the article in full.

### Jesuit School Plays by Dr. W. F. F. Grace

Seeing that a certain number of articles have lately appeared in the local Press on the subject of Drama in the Schools, perhaps the following notes on the history of Jesuit School Plays may not be without interest.

It is a matter of sober historical fact that, during the latter half of the sixteenth century, the whole of the seventeenth and the greater part of the eighteenth, the Jesuits were literally world-famous as masters in every branch of Theatrical Art.

This does not mean that the Society controlled or conducted theatres in the commercial sense: nor that the playbills announced that Father X or Mr. Y would delight the crowds twice nightly. Theatres were not conducted on those lines during the sixteenth century. To understand exactly how and why the Society came to gain such a reputation, one has merely to recall one's knowledge of some of the then existing social conditions.

It was an age of pageantry, when even the everyday clothing of men was bright with a variety of colours. It was the accepted thing to celebrate any great event by a pageant, or by the performance in the court or public theatre of some great dramatic spectacle. Cities were smaller in those days, and it was quite possible to approach to something like a family spirit in these rejoicings. Particularly was this the case in the independent German principalities, each of which had its capital and its court, its burgomaster and stout burgesses, and its mob of tradesfolk and apprentices. The Court would have special performances in its private theatre, the municipality celebrated these occasions in the public theatre, while the trades guilds also performed various plays in their guild halls, much in the same way as their forefathers had been responsible for the production of the Mystery plays. It was but a step from the guilds to the schools, and it was considered quite a part of school life to provide dramatic entertainments on the greater festivals.

When the Jesuits made their first appearance in the educational world, they found one serious fault in this practice of getting up school theatricals. The pieces played were in many cases by no means fit for reading - to say nothing of committing to memory - by the young. The first thing to do was to provide suitable plays. Then the effort to raise the standard must be backed by a marked superiority in all other departments - acting, scenery, costume - over the schools of lower ideals. In a very short time they had eclipsed not only the other schools but also the guilds, the municipalities and even the court performers themselves. Eventually the plays at the Jesuit Colleges became the most prominent feature of all these festive occasions.

At first the libretti were written by laymen, but it was soon found that the Jesuit members of the College staffs could produce work far superior to any that lay assistance could provide; and gradually there sprang up a race of Jesuit playwrights whose work grew so rapidly, and was of so high an order, that competent literary critics regard it as forming by itself a separate branch of literature. A random selection of names of authors from the long list may give some idea of the universal nature of the vogue of the school play among the Jesuits. De Cruz - a Portuguese; Benci - an Italian; Pontanus a Bohemian; Malapert - a Belgian; Biedermann - a Swabian; Surin-a Frenchman; Avancinus - an Austrian.

Patavius, a Frenchman, was perhaps the most famous of all, but Fr. Porrée ranks almost on a level with him. Carparni, an Italian, flourished in Rome; Spirelli was a Neopolitan, Neumaier a German, and Edmund Campion (if I remember rightly) wrote a drama of some kind during his stay abroad before returning to England to commence his missionary career. The dates of these authors range from the middle of the sixteenth to the close of the eighteenth centuries.

Originally, following the general custom of the schools, the plays were entirely in Latin. Later, when the popular knowledge of that language became rather 'foggy', it was found necessary to print on the programmes an account of the plot and its chief 'situations' in the vernacular. Eventually - the change occurring about A.D. 1700 - Latin was abandoned entirely and the audiences were able to listen to plays in their native tongue.

The actors were exclusively boys in the College. It seems that there was a tendency for masters of some histrionic ability to be included occasionally in the cast, but this practice was prohibited by Superiors even though the parts played were those of ecclesiastics.

But it is not the fact that plays were produced, nor that they were the work of Jesuit authors, that causes one surprise : what is really beyond words astonishing is the unparalleled magnificence, the brilliance and the gigantic proportions of these performances. Let me give a few examples. The Jesuit College at Munich was perhaps the most renowned of all the colleges for its Dramatic work. There in 1574 on one of the great feasts of the year a tragedy, entitled *Constantine* was produced. Some idea may be gained from old descriptions of this play of the splendour of costume and scenery and of the immense scale on which these pageants were carried out. When Constantine made his entry into the city after the defeat of Maxentius he rode in a superb triumphal chariot. Those who are familiar with Durer's etching *Maximilian's Car* will be able to form some idea of what this may have meant. But this was not all. Glittering in all the 'splendid panoply of war' there rode with the Emperor a bodyguard of horsemen 400 strong! Nor had the Jesuits hired the local cavalry for the occasion. None but the boys of the school were allowed to take part. If this was but one item of the performance, we are not surprised to learn that the entire cast worked out at a thousand.

Three years later they produced *Esther.* For this performance the Duke of Bavaria, whose court was at Munich, placed the whole of his treasury at their disposal. The dresses were supplied from the ducal wardrobe and the jewels, plate, coronets and crowns were all genuine and lent by the same munificent friend. For the great banquet of King Assuerus he provided no less than one hundred and sixty dishes of gold and silver, each one probably an art treasure in itself. It does not need much imagination to picture the competition there must have been among the boys to keep in the good books of the master getting up the play. Had he not at his disposal such glorious parts as ' Guest at the Banquet '? The only qualification needed for these was the ability to consume the choicest viands with decorum before a vast and admiring - and possibly envious - audience.

In 1560 the Comedy *Euripus* was presented at Prague. It took place in the great public square before a crowd of more than 8,000 people. So immense was its success that three successive performances were given at the request of the entire city. A fourth was asked for, but the Rector had to intervene and request the people not to press the matter as 'after all it was not the primary function of the College to exhibit comedies.'

It is interesting to note that Trautmann, in his 'Ober-Ammergau und sein Passions spiel', lays it down authoritatively that the famous *Passion Play* is ' an off-shoot of the Munich Jesuit Drama.'

The French Colleges were hardly less famous than the German for their dramatic productions. In 1614 the great Jesuit College of La Flèche was the scene of a spectacle which even modern times might find it difficult to rival. The King, Louis XIII, the Queen mother, the Countess of Soissons, the Duke of Guise, the Archbishop of Rheims, the entire court and a host of stars of lesser note composed the audience. First there came a mythological representation of the reception of royal personages into Olympus. The King himself was welcomed by the muses in addresses of no less than seventeen different languages. Following this the class of 'Rhetoric' presented in the great Theatre of the College a tragedy, *Godfrey de Bouillon*. Lastly the audience gathered on one of the immense lawns of the College grounds to witness a comedy, *Glorinda*, acted by the class of 'Poetry.'

At the College of Ste. Barbe in 1682, in the presence of Louis XIV, the court, and all the highest ecclesiastics of the kingdom, there was a display which exceeded even this in splendour. In the mythological prelude, gods and goddesses floated through the air; triumphal arches, forests of trees and vast rockeries made a superb garden of delights.

Orpheus entered. The strains of his music stole through the air. One by one the trees uprooted themselves, the rocks broke away from their foundations and followed in charmed rhythm the bidding of the heavenly musician What fun to have been the boy cast as the moving spirit of a 'stately oak', a 'young beech', or even of a 'lumbering rock'. There must have been some aching sides among the young actors when the curtain fell and some regretful thoughts when they woke next morning to realise with boyish grief that it was 'all over' and that there were many months to wait before the next festival would come round. Other performances followed, and between each as an entracte came the ballet. The King's Maître de Ballet trained the boys for this. It was so highly esteemed that only the sons of the greatest families in the land could manage to become members of the 'corps.' Fr. Porrée, the playwright, objected to the ballet and refused to write the libretto. The omission of the ballet would have created such indignation that the Rector had to order the good Father to compose the libretto each year. At the time of the performance just described Ste. Barbe numbered 500 boarders and 2,000 day boys.

It is interesting to note how near to the time of St. Ignatius was the period of greatest splendour in the plays of the German Colleges of the Society. St. Ignatius died in 1556. *Euripus* was played at Prague in 1560 ; 'Judith' at Munich in 1565 ; *Esther* in 1577. So early did the tradition take root in the Society. The standard of performance had not deteriorated in the 18th century. Goethe himself, no mean critic in dramatic matters, bears witness. After witnessing a play given in 1786 at Ratisbon, where the traditions of the Jesuit schools were kept up after the suppression of the Order, he writes : 'This public performance has convinced me anew of the cleverness of the Jesuits. They rejected nothing that could be of any conceivable service to them, and knew how to wield their instruments with devotion and dexterity. This is not cleverness of the merely abstract order: it is a real enjoyment of the thing itself, an absorbing interest, which springs from the practical use of life. Just as this great spiritual Society has its organ builders, its sculptors and its gilders, so there seem to be some who, by nature and inclination, take to the drama . . . . . . . these prudent men have seized on the sensibility of the world by a decent theatre.'

## The Impact of Jesuit Drama

What is not clear from this article is the extent to which Jesuit drama influenced developments in France and Spain. Several authorities credit the Jesuits with launching the national theatres in those countries. Writers such as Molière, Corneille, Calderon and Lope de Vega attended Jesuit schools and were thus exposed to an embryonic theatrical tradition. Costumes, scenery and stagecraft were often on a lavish scale and performances of Jesuit plays were very popular in their local communities.

'It evolved from simple student exercises in delivering dialogue and presenting single scenes to the mounting of elaborate and ostentatious stage-productions that rivalled contemporary court and public theatres. Within a brief period of time the world-wide network of Jesuit scholastic establishments was supplemented by a similar system of Jesuit theatres. From a platform in a hall to purpose-built theatres. Pupils made up the entire cast, and performances lasted for from 2-7 hours and even days on occasions. The audiences were often distinguished members of court. In 1653 one performance at Louis-le-Grand Collège was attended by Louis XIV, Cardinal Mazzarin and the exiled KIng of England, Charles II'.

(Macabe p.42)

Sometimes royal weddings were celebrated with a play performed by the Jesuit pupils. At one performance in Vienna the police had to be called to keep back the crowds. By 1700 there were 586 Jesuit colleges world-wide, putting on thousands of plays each year and

'It is perhaps safe to say that in no schools has the powerful educational value of the drama been so accurately gauged and so consistently employed as in the Jesuit establishments throughout the world.' (Motter 1929 p.228)

The impact went way beyond the school, the performances often being repeated for the general public.

'For two centuries Jesuit academic drama in France charmed numerous generations, and prepared them to appreciate and admire all that was beautiful and noble in the secular stage of the grand siècle. As a result the great classical drama of France of the 1700s, which in turn influenced subsequent English drama, owed an incalculable debt to Jesuit academic drama.' (Motter 1929 p.297 &299)

## Drama at SFX in the Nineteenth Century

Father Richard Sumner - Rector 1853-1860

Father Sumner was appointed Rector at St Francis Xavier's Church in 1853 and, with a short break in the middle, stayed there till 1860. He had a reputation as a Shakespearean scholar, writing and lecturing on the subject, and he is credited with establishing drama and fostering performances at the College. He was a larger-than-life character involved in larger-than-life events. When the Holy Hand of Blessed Arrowsmith was applied to a diseased polypus on his nose, the polypus disappeared and a miracle was declared. (Letters and Notices 1879)

His obituary pays tribute to him as a preacher of some style. His sermons 'abounded in exclamations, apostrophes, abrupt transitions, vivid word painting, and picturesque and scenic details'. For histrionics he would sometimes kneel down in the aisle and abjure the congregation to mend their ways. (Letters and Notices 1879)

A rival Liverpool school, the newly-founded Catholic Institute, started to put on plays as part of its school curriculum in 1853. This prompted Fr. Sumner to introduce drama at SFX and for twenty years a well-regarded tradition was built up. Fr. Sumner produced the plays himself and trained his pupils in elocution. His pupils, it was remarked, reached a high degree of perfection in acting and speaking, and he was long remembered by them for the dramatic training to which he subjected them.

> 'By his instructions in elocution to the boys of SFX he bore a chief share in forming a tradition of good speaking which has been perpetuated in that College since his time'.
> (Xaverian 1879)

He was said to take immense pains in polishing and perfecting those who were to appear

> 'So particular and exacting was he in requiring the proper distinctness, tone and emphasis that not infrequently the budding actor would come away in tears from his room.'
> (Xaverian June 1893)

The plays were performed in the 1850s, first in the vaults of the church, and then in the Chapel where the audience were said to be 'cribbed, cabined and confined.' (Xaverian April 1892 p.57). The earliest recorded play was 'In the Wrong Box' put on in 1855 - (Xaverian June 1893)

Another pupil who was there in the 1840s writes in 1892 :

> 'Theatricals! What a wretched contrast between our poor affair and the present. We had neither stage nor scenery. Some blue and white check curtains did duty for everything. The costumes were something wonderfully grotesque'. Before 1856 there was no place to serve as a Green Room. 'The boys dressed at home and had to walk through the streets to the College in their costumes'.
> (Xaverian 1892)

A new Academy Room had been opened in 1856 and this was used till 1876. Then in 1877 the new hall was built and was used thereafter, though its acoustics were generally considered to be abominable.

Clearly drama was seen by Fr. Sumner and some of his successors as an important aspect of the education the College provided. They would have been aware of its provenance and history as an educational activity in Jesuit colleges, and they would have wanted their pupils to profit from their engagement with it. One of Fr. Sumner's successors, writing in 1915, is quoted as saying :

> 'The Jesuits have always attached great importance to the stage as an educational instrument. It is one of the points which all critics of our methods combine to praise.' (Xaverian 1915 Feb)

## Decline and Revival of Drama at the College 1860 -1880

After Jesuit education had returned to England at Stonyhurst in 1793 and at SFX in 1842, things began to change. Comments appeared in Provincials' Reports like 'It is regrettable that theatre has been introduced. Try at least to cut down on it, if it cannot be suppressed entirely.' There was a complaint about French Jesuit colleges in 1870. There was a call to 'put an end to objectionable love scenes and vulgar gesturing'. 'Plays were being performed whose themes were chosen not for sacred antiquity, but from modern, not to say unseemly, shallowness.' Subjects and treatments had travelled too far from early prescriptions. Warnings began to be issued and a reaction set in from 1860 onwards.

When Fr. Harris became Prefect of Studies in 1865, drama ceased to be favoured and to some extent the subject died away. It revived somewhat in the late 1870s, and even flowered in the thirty years before the outbreak of the First World War.

In spite of this discouragement from the authorities between 1884 and 1900, things changed. Individual Jesuits joined the College staff who were not only interested, but gifted in matters theatrical. During the 1880s there was a young scholastic on the staff who was a talented composer, Richard Ratcliffe. He and his brother, also a scholastic at the College, wrote words and music for performances by the boys. *The Naughty Nephews, The Baby Elephant* and *The Prince and the Page* were three of their compositions put on in 1888 - 1889, and repeated a number of times in the next twenty years.

The annual prizegiving ceremony - the Proclamation - became an important date in the College calendar and increasingly was presented not only as a celebration of pupils' academic achievements, but of their talents in fields such as music and drama.

In 1885 the Third Form Classical was praised for the talent shown in putting on *The Hidden Gem* by Cardinal Wiseman. This was an immense success - with repeat performances in and out of College. The money raised went to help pay the fees of needy pupils in their own class.

> 'The College authorities and the parents of the boys are equally interested in promoting the success of the undertaking (ie. *The Hidden Gem*).' ' Impressed by the easy and manly way in which the boys themselves took the matter up.' 'The actors were determined to succeed.'
>
> (Xaverian 1885)

A watershed was reached in 1888 when the newly-constituted Old Xaverians' Association was asked to make a donation to help with the cost of scholarships for the sons of the more indigent parents. The Association pointed to a recent event at a neighbouring Catholic girls' school which had put on plays at the school, charging parents and well-wishers for admission. They recommended that SFX do the same. This then became a small but regular source of income.

Throughout the 1890s Gilbert and Sullivan operettas were produced. Extracts from *Iolanthe, Patience, Pirates of Penzance* and *Trial by Jury* were performed at the Proclamation ceremony. These helped to make the occasion very popular, and one night in 1886 with 400 boys at the College 3,000 people squeezed into the College hall. The offering was *The Infant Prodigy* - a very clever adaptation of *The Mikado*. The critic in the Liverpool Review wrote

> ' too much praise cannot be given to the boys in the chorus of 35. The singing was perfect and it would put to blush many of our professional choirs'.

## Performances 1900 - 1920

The new century got underway with drama at the College seemingly in fine fettle. Up to the outbreak of war, regular performances continued to be hailed with successful reviews in the Xaverian and in the local press. *The Cornish Buccaneer* made the princely sum of £19 as a contribution to equip the physics laboratory.

In 1905 *Aladdin* lasted all of three hours and in 1906 a comic opera - *Barcelona, King of Spain* - with 64 actors played to a full house and was repeated on several occasions. The Old Xaverians formed their own dramatic society in 1906, putting on shows at the school and donating the proceeds to college funds.

A fine accolade came from a visiting critic. Sixty performers staged *The Cornish Buccaneer* in 1915 and the critic commented on the boy in the lead - *'the most effective boy actor it has been my pleasure to see'.*

Fortunately we have a retrospective article from the College Magazine in 1928 which detailed many of the performances given during the nineteenth century.

### College Dramatics - A Retrospect. by Dr. W. F. F. Grace

'I was one day in the room of the Prefect of Studies when, rising from his chair, he reverently opened a drawer and handed to me an old worn scrap-book - dust-laden, its leaves yellowing and crumbling with age. Reluctantly, as though he deemed it almost a sacrilege to let any but the holiest fingers touch it, he handed it to me. I sat me down and began to browse. And then, indeed, the reason for his reverential awe became apparent to me; then, indeed, I began to feel the glamour of the past steal over me ; then I in my turn knelt down and worshipped at the shrine of the Fathers of the College. I began to appreciate as I had never appreciated before the store set by the Ancients on Ancestor Worship. For the precious scrap-book was a collection of the Programmes of Speech Days, Exhibitions and Plays dating from the year 1851. And because this book is so frail and so precious everyone cannot dip as they will into this treasure house of the past, it has seemed good to gather together a few of its pearls of great price that all who will may admire.

The first Programme seems to be incomplete, one half of it being torn away. As far as we can judge it is a Proclamation of some sort. One would dearly like to know what *Heaven* by Master G. Hartell dealt with. Nor would it be less interesting to hazard a guess at what Masters P. White and J. Adamson of the first class knew of *The Marriage of a Daughter.*

It is not, however, with these ordinary Proclamations that we are at present concerned, but rather with the Dramatic Tradition of the College. In these days when every school, practically, has its annual Dramatic Entertainment, it is interesting to note that *The Admirable Crichton*, produced this year (1928), was the 70th Annual Dramatic effort of the College boys.

The first attempt was on December 22nd, 1857, when at the Christmas Exhibition and Prize Distribution scenes from Molière's *L'Avare* were presented. Nor can we pass on without paying a debt of justice due to these protagonists of College acting. For one feels that their names should be rescued from that dusty obscurity wherein they now reside. Where, we may ask, is there a memorial to M. Doyle, who took the part of Harpagon? On what brazen tablet do we find mention of T. Waring's interpretation of Maître Jacques ? Why struts not, on some portrait, M. Kirwan in the Continental finery of Le Commisaire ?

Where is the song made to commemorate the glories of N. Furry in his spirited portrayal of Valere? Nowhere, alas, are these fine monuments, unless in the hearts of those who love the College and its acting traditions. It is gratifying to note that the honour to which they were born did not lead the youthful actors astray. For we find that N. Furry is cited on the programme to hold forth on Greek Grammar, and also N. Kirwan gave a recitation or discussion – which is not indicated - of the *Fables of Phaedrus*. The lure of the boards evidently did not lessen their devotion to study. Let us across the years thank these four reverently for the good work they set in hand.

The College authorities, fired by this success, produced a few months later *Gibson v. Palmerston, or Peace And War : a Drama of ye present time* composed by the Academicians of the First Class. (What has happened to the dramatised version of *Treasure Island*, produced last year by the Query Club?). The actors in this case were F. Davis and T. Mackarell.

And so for some years we find at the Christmas Prize Distributions that there is at least one dramatic item. Sometimes recourse was had to the French dramatists, at other times to the Latin or Greek, and, as is to be expected, to Shakespeare. And it was not until 1863, on June 23rd, that a complete play was presented, viz, *Le Bourgeois Gentilhomme* of Molière. It may be of interest to quote this programme in its entirety:

---

**COMEDIE  FRANCAISE**
**LE BOURGEOIS GENTILHOMME,**
**(adaptation de Molière).**

Personnages et Acteurs :

| | |
|---|---|
| M. Jourdain -Bourgeois | T. HUGHES. |
| M. Jourdain (père) ..................| J. LOMAX. |
| Cléonte (aimant de Lucille, fille de | |
| M. Jourdain) | J. LAWLER. |
| Covielle  (ami de Cléonte) | W. SPARROW. |
| Un maître de Musique | T. McMULLIN. |
| Un maître à danser | T. McMULLIN. |
| Un maître de Philosophie | F. PITT. |
| Un maître Tailleur | J. KAVANAGH. |
| M. le Comte Darimon | T. McMULLIN. |

Laquais - Dervis - Choeur de Musique.

La scène est à Paris dans la maison de M. Jourdain.

Le Bourgeois Gentilhomme sera représenté selon l'adaptation ci-dessus à L'Externat de St. Francis Xavier à Liverpool par les élèves de la première classe, à la clôture de l'année Scholastique, le 23 juin à 7 heures du soir.

**L. D. S.**

---

Whether this venture was a success or no, we cannot say. But the fact remains that no other complete play was acted until January 2nd, 1866, when *Monsieur Tonson* was produced, followed by *A Fish out of Water*. Even after this there is not a constant succession of complete plays. The College was content for some years with excerpts. We say "content" but not in any spirit of self-laudatory criticism. How could we, in view of the Programme for June 23rd, 1879, when Specimens of the Comedy of various nations were given? In this programme we find English, French, Latin and Greek Comedy exemplified. English was represented by a scene from *Midsummer Night's Dream,* French by a scene from Molière's *Scapin,* Latin by an extract from the *Miles Gloriosus* of Plautus, and Greek by an excerpt from *The Frogs* of Aristophanes. To discuss this effort of the heroes of old would be an impertinence. Let us humbly admire.

This attainment was the herald of the bright day. And on April 13th, 1882, the full dawn burst forth with *Chrononhotontologos ; or a Model Kingdom* (Scene : Queer-Roumania; Time-historians not agreed; Plot founded on fact stranger than fiction). The sun of College Acting had arisen clear and beauteous, a sun which we hope has not even yet attained its noonday splendour. This play, by the little boys, was followed two months later by the *Pirates of Penzance.* And since that day never a year has passed in which some drama or another has not been played. As we turn over the leaves of the old scrapbook, we find such plays as *Rob Roy, H.M.S. Pinafore, The Hidden Gem, The Blind Beggars, Married and Buried, Paul Pry, Guy Mannering, The Courier of Lyons,* and a host of others.

But, unfortunately, the record stops short in 1902. The last programme is for July 21st of that year, when an Operetta, *Robin Hood* was performed. The record is taken up again in 1919, when the College Magazine was produced; but the seventeen odd years in between are a blank in our dramatic records.
(NB. Plays are reported in these seventeen years by the Xaverian. P. H.)

These are but some of the interesting gleanings to be garnered from this old scrapbook. But there is many another side-show in this old-time fair. Thus there is an interesting note in some long-forgotten hand - a certain H.B.S.J. - on the programme for the Christmas Exhibition for 1892. "This Proclamation is historical owing to the presence of our Very Rev. Father General, Fr. Martin. His Paternity distributed the Certificates." And one of a still earlier date, February 20th, 1878, "Leo XIII elected to-day. News reached us while assembling for the first time in the Great Hall. J.G." Or, in view of our present efforts to re-start the College Orchestra, it is of interest to note that on December 23rd, 1897 the College Orchestra made its first appearance with Watson's *Pizzicato* - and there is a note *Encore* - and with *Martel's Gavotte in D.*

Or perhaps we like to hark back to the schooldays of those who have become famous and to look for signs of future greatness even in those early years. We can follow up such names as those of William Madden who, later in life, became such a light at the bar and who rose to be Recorder of Blackburn. We may remember his last appearance on the College stage, at the Prize Distribution some three years ago. But it was by no means his first appearance. In these old programmes we can follow his career on the stage. Starting in humble wise on March 18th, 1863, as Smith the Weaver in *Henry VI,* he was promoted a few months later to be the Second Gravedigger in 'Hamlet', and thence to Corporal Pistol, and finally entered the Land of Promise, of which these other parts were his Pisgah, by playing the lead in the first complete English play produced at the College.

Or we may discover the seeds of future greatness in Joseph Walton's leading a debate in 1861 on the *Causes of England's Greatness*, at which Proclamation he also gave extracts from the *de Corona* of Demosthenes. Surely an omen! Many of these past actors have gone to their rest, having played the part written for them from Eternity by the Divine Dramatist Himself.

And so, having let our minds roam over the past glories of our stage, we close the book with a sigh of regret, but at the same time with a strong and sturdy faith in the ability of the present generation to live up to the old traditions of the past.'

## Drama at the College in the Twentieth Century

In trying to describe the place of drama in the life of the College one is tempted to use expressions like 'fits and starts', 'ups and downs', 'highs and lows'. Much depended on the attitude of the different headmasters, the responsible heads of departments and interested members of staff. To describe the position of the practising arts subjects at the College as peripheral would be unjust. But certainly they have never consistently enjoyed the favours of succeeding headmasters. On occasions drama, elocution or music gathered strength and fought its way into the mainstream, as the choral side of music has done in recent years.

Drama was considered an important educational instrument at the College in the nineteenth century and then again in the 'twenties. Later it came to be neglected. By 1945 the situation changed for the better. Plays were staged irregularly at first; then we have a flourish of productions of different kinds in the 50s and 60s. Teachers like Peter Beardwood and Kevin Reade (once referred to as SFX's Richard Burton) played a part in this revival. In the last thirty years dramatic activity has not been strong; the explosion in leisure time choices may account for this.

In the 'twenties and 'thirties elocution became a major activity and it elbowed out staged dramatic productions. The Elocution Competition was revived in 1920, and seventy five pupils (out of 300 c.) entered. The finals took place on two Sundays in March with three sets - Junior, Middle and Senior.

T. Matthews won the Junior with *Edinburgh after Flodden* - 'a dramatic rendering with voice, face and gesture all to a fine perfection'. The Senior was won by Gaffney of the Upper VI - with the last speech from Marlow's *Dr Faustus*. He is reported to have 'managed the fear and the pity with a powerful rendering that was almost painful to the hearers'.

Indeed, in the twenties and thirties under the direction of Miss St. George Yorke, the teaching of elocution and the annual Elocution Competition loomed large at the College. Dramatic performances were not common.

The College was first inspected by the officials of the Board of Education in 1902. In the Inspectors' Report then, and in almost every inspection since, comments were made - and defences mounted - about the excessive concentration on examination results in the mainstream subjects such as Latin, Maths, English and History to the neglect of activities such as drama. Proclamations were occasions to celebrate awards and places won to colleges and universities, and those who had passed A Levels and GCSEs or their equivalents of the day were called to the stage to be applauded. Musical, choral, dramatic and rhetorical items served as a backdrop only.

*School Play 1947: Henry IV Part I  Act II Scenes 2 & 4*
*Seated, left to right: B. O'Keeffe, G. Fitzgibbon, J. P. Sullivan, B. Checkland, T. McCourt, E.S. Walton,*
*Standing: P. Ruane, P. Heery, C. McDonnell*

After the war dramatic activity revived, even if not on the scale sometimes attempted in the past. In 1954, working from a back room in the Physics Lab, Eric Frane, Joe Morrissey, Tony Deus and Phil Fanning built sets and constructed a lighting and an electrical system that brought the stage system up to a very high technical standard. Performances went under different headings - The Christmas Entertainment, The Shrovetide Play, the Preface to Proclamation and eventually The Pantomime.

In these productions boys had opportunities to display their talents in smaller and less serious works as well as in longer and more challenging pieces. 1956 saw *The Walrus and The Carpenter,* 1960 *The Burglar Alarm* by Ian Hay, and 1957 *The Tide of Life,* written by a member of staff and performed by forms 1, 2, and 3. But more ambitiously, Kevin Reade produced Chekhov's *The Bear* in 1955; Priestley's *Laburnum Grove* was the Shrovetide play in 1954, and Gilbert's *The Old Bull* at Proclamation in the same year.

Pantomime seemed to have returned with a vengeance in the mid-fifties. Fr. Hopkinson produced *Aladdin* in 1955, *Jack and the Beanstalk* in 1956 and *Ali Baba* in 1957 - all given due praise in the Magazine. In the 1957 production J.W. Naughton was said to have acted 'even better than he does in the classroom'. Some Old Xaverians will also have fond memories of the 1960 *Cinderella* produced by Mr Reddy SJ and Mr Nye SJ, which was commended highly in the Magazine review; the singing of the Chorus - particularly Knick-Knack Paddy-Whack - came in for special mention.

For a few years in the seventies the pantomime was very successfully revived under Mr. John Rourke, but then largely disappears. It re-surfaces as a regular offering in the 1990s under the influence of Mr Bailey and Mr. Toal, who to judge from the titles were not traditionalists - *Robin Hood, Sherlock Holmes, Dracula,* and recently *Star Trek.* However *Cinderella* and *Aladdin* restored some historical balance in the last three years. 1967 saw a return to the full-length major item with a successful production of *A Man for All Seasons.* But the early Sixties generally kept to extracts like the trial scene from *A Man for All Seasons* and shorter plays like *Wanted Mr Stuart* by Arthur Watkyn, and *The Billion Dollar Saint* by Natalie White.

*Trial by Jury* and *Pinafore* in the mid-sixties had obviously whetted appetites and the more ambitious *Pirates of Penzance* was put on to great acclaim in 1967. For a few years Gilbert and Sullivan productions - such as *The Mikado* in 1968 - became annual events, as they had been in the 1890s.

*The Mikado*
*D. Burns as Pooh-bah. R. Staunton as Pitti-sing. W. Corbett as Nanki-poo.*
*S. Clarke as Yum-Yum. D. Griffiths as the Mikado. D. Staunton as Peep-bo.*
*L. Murray as Pish-tush. J. Thistlethwaite as Ko-Ko. P.Gallagher as Katisha.*

The School Drama Group revived in 1969, presenting *The Thwarting of Baron Bolligrew* by Robert Bolt. F. Harvey - Dr Moloch, Professor of Wickedness at Oxford - gave 'the most hilarious performance of the evening'.

The Magazine does not report anything of any substance in the 70s, and 80s. In the 1980s two pantomimes were performed - *Snow White* and *Dirk Warrington* as well as a play by Dennis O'Gorman *The Way Out*. None of these were reviewed at any length in the Magazine - still less reviewed in the tart and cutting style to which some of the 1930s and 1940s productions were subjected. Christmas 1983 boys, mainly from the Third Form under the direction of Ms. Wilkie, put on *The Curse of the Mummy's Tomb*, which attracted attention; tombs, archaeologists, princesses, reincarnations and a vase that was supposed to break and wouldn't - all these featured, but the most memorable moment in the play included someone called 'Daphne', dancing the Charleston.

In the 90s things changed again. Three very successful musicals were staged - *Joseph and his Technicolour Dreamcoat, Oliver,* and *Mary Poppins.* These productions were lavishly praised for the very high standards achieved. In 1998 and 2000 the staff showed that there was no end to their imaginative talents with two innovative performances of *The Last Night of the Proms* in the College grounds. The deplorable weather on both occasions soaked performers and instruments, but failed to dampen spirits, enthusiasm or brio.

## St. Francis Xavier's College Choir

This section can be brought to a close on a high note. In the last ten years a College choir has been trained to such a standard that it has carried the name of the College to the furthest corners of England and beyond. The choirmaster, Mr Knowles, has restored SFX to a place in the sun for artistic endeavour, which it has not enjoyed since the performances of Macbeth in 1923. One musical, geographical, logistical and physical achievement must be mentioned - the SFX College Choir has sung in every Anglican cathedral in England, a feat which gained an entry into the Guinness Book of Records.

Although a tradition of choral work can be traced back to the early years of the school, it can safely be claimed that during the years since 1992 the choir has established a reputation for excellence which has never been achieved at any time in the past. Of particular merit have been the numerous tours at home and abroad and the attendant publicity which have done much to enhance the reputation of SFX College.

The first significant public performance was given in 1994 when a chamber choir of twenty-four boys sang Choral Evensong in the Cathedral of Bury St. Edmunds. In the following year 1995 a more ambitious venture was undertaken when the College Choir of thirty-six boys embarked on a tour of Italy. The highlights were the singing of a full choral mass in Florence Cathedral and a vigil mass of Sunday in St Mark's, Venice. A visit to Poland in 1996 included the singing of the mass in the church of Wadowice, the birthplace of Pope John-Paul II. The following year saw the choir visiting France, where, amongst other places, they sang a choral mass in Chartres Cathedral and performed at concerts in Notre Dame, Paris and in Rheims Cathedral. The return visit to Italy in 1999 is considered by many of the choristers to have been their most memorable venture.

This tour culminated in Rome where, on a Sunday, the SFX College Choir sang Pontifical High Mass in St Peter's before a very large congregation. An even wider audience was reached since the service was broadcast world-wide. More recently the College Choir has toured in Germany and performed at Bonn, Koblenz and Cologne Cathedrals.

In 1997 the Choir produced its first compact disc - Heavenly Voices - which was very well received. A further two discs have been produced. At the Queen Elizabeth Hall in January 2000 the SFX College Choir was successful in the National Finals of 'Schoolsong 2000', and was then crowned National School Choir Champions. The highlight of the year came over the Christmas period when the choir sang carols on six evenings leading up to Christmas, performances which were broadcast on Granada Television.

The outstanding quality of choral work at the College was recognized in the OFSTED Report of 2001 where the inspectors noted that 'standards attained by the Boys' Choir are readily comparable with those achieved in most choir schools'. In 1987 Andrew Robinson was awarded an Open Scholarship at Trinity College, Cambridge with the post of College Organist. Trinity wrote to say that this was the first time this post had been held by a Catholic. Fred Devereux reminded them that it was the first time since the Reformation.

*Choir, College Magazine 1934*

*It is many years since notes of this nature appeared in the College Magazine, but the activities of the College Choir should be recorded side by side with other College events if only to prove that the musical tradition, which the school has enjoyed since the days of the operas, is not yet dead. The present Choir has been in existence for more than two years. It has a membership of about 35 boys.....This article is by way of being an appeal for volunteers. It would be a pity if such a highly educative branch of activity should suffer extinction through want of recruits. "College Magazine 1934".*

## Writing, Acting and Entertaining

It only remains to call attention to some Old Xaverians who have distinguished themselves in the world of literature and entertainment. The roll call is very short.

We have very many distinguished teachers, professors, lawyers, administrators, bishops and business-men amongst the ex-pupils of SFX. Could the lack of artistic and literary success amongst Old Xaverians - if such there is - have anything to do with the curriculum at the College or with the way that curriculum was taught? Were boys encouraged to write for themselves at any stage? The author can recall Mr. (later Fr.) Byrne setting 2A the task of writing a murder story in 1942. Peter Ruane, one of the College's Cambridge successes and afterwards Director of Education for Huyton, was judged to have come out best with *Murder at the Blue Boar.*

Fr. Garrold, a teacher, not a pupil at the College, at the beginning of the twentieth century, wrote four novels, one of which is set in a school that is clearly SFX. *The Boys of St Batt's* is unusual in that it is set in a day-school, not a boarding school. It is an early example of a novel that tells its story from the boys' point of view. You can almost smell the stairs, the corridors and assembly hall of Salisbury Street in the writing. It was said of the book that 'it proves how accurately he already understood *from within* the psychology of schoolboys and may in a true sense be called his comment on his first two years of teaching'. Not an Old Xav, but his contribution to the life of the College and the contact he kept up with pupils after they left entitle us to count him as one of ours.

Another of his books - *A Fourth Form Boy* - was also very well reviewed.

> 'Greatly daring the author put the whole narrative directly into the mouth of his 'Fourth Form Boy'. Just as, after reading that amazingly clever book *Stalky and Co.* we obstinately affirm, 'No, that is not how boys talk'. So here we give our most real assent and cry ' Yes, that is it word for word. That is how they think and talk and feel.'

Ted Whitehead, who left the College in 1952, is one of our most successful playwright to date and indeed one of the few OX writers of national and international reputation. He was Writer in Residence at the Royal Court in London in the 70s; his most successful play was *Alpha Beta* which starred Albert Finney and Rachel Roberts and which won him an international reputation. Some readers will remember a play of his which was televised on BBC2 in 1982 because of its subject matter. Called *The Punishment* it is an interview between a sixth form pupil and his Headmaster. This is a verbatim account of an actual encounter between himself and Fr. Neylan in his office in 1953.

On literary encouragement at the College Ted Whitehead writes:

> 'Very little. Most of the teachers seemed to take their cue from Neylan, who scorned any creative work not written in Greek or Latin. Hence his fury with me when I told him that I proposed to switch from Classics to English Literature at Cambridge: he advised me to clear my desk immediately. The one exception was Putty Grace, who encouraged me and others to read major Catholic authors such as Graham Greene, François Mauriac, Georges Bernanos and Proust. He presented me with a thirteen volume edition of "Remembrance of Things Past"; at seventeen I found it just intimidating; in my late twenties it was a revelation. Putty read my adolescent attempts to imitate these writers, and also showed me some of his own adolescent efforts. (He had lived in the Far East for a time before he started to teach at SFX and he had had a short story published in the Malay Times, which he occasionally showed to pupils to illustrate the faults in adolescent writng). He was an inspiration.

> I'd also like to salute the memory of one priest, I think called Father Reynolds, a gentle, patient teacher who illuminated the spiritual significance of Shelley and the Romantic poets (rather than just making us memorise the text!). I wonder if others have mentioned him?

> As for Neylan's attitude to literature, I suspect that the root problem was that his whole emphasis lay on precision and clarity of expression: no sense of the unspoken here. I remember struggling to express my thoughts about a particular Greek text, and when I said I could not yet find the words, he snapped: "You can't have thoughts if they are not already in words!" That may be no more than a semantic argument but I do think he was insensitive to the elusive, indeterminate, perhaps inexpressible area of meaning that makes great literature great.'

Ted has recently completed a new stage play, and a collected edition will be published later this year (2002). He has also written many adaptations and original pieces for TV, including an episode of Cracker. Most recently he has completed an adaptation of Thomas Hardy's "The Mayor of Casterbridge", which will be shown in the autumn.

Terry Feeley, a pupil in the forties, was a scriptwriter and a playwright for nearly fifty years. A steady stream of successful productions of his work appeared on stage, screen and television.

John Gregson (OX 1936), the film star, is best known for his role in the film *Genevieve*, but he had dozens of other parts - mainly in films.

(Item: Gregson was sitting next to Cardinal Heenan at a lunch one day. There was a selection at the main course and he chose the fish. Heenan, sitting next to him chose the meat. Gregson leaned over and murmured: "Have you forgotten it's Friday, Your Eminence?" "No, I haven't. Have you forgotten it's a Holy Day of Obligation?")

David Burke (OX 1953) has played leading roles in the West End and on Broadway, and has appeared in many R.S.C. productions. He was a very successful Dr Watson in the TV series *Sherlock Holmes* and is credited with bringing a new and more serious interpretation to the part. More recently he shared the lead in Michael Frayn's *Copenhagen*, playing the part in both London and New York.

Jimmy McGovern (OX 1966) has an impressive record writing for television and film. He is perhaps best known as the creator of Cracker, the hugely successful television dramas of the nineties. The subject was his idea as was the creation of the character and the milieu. He wrote the first series, most of the second and some of the third. He was highly praised for his work on the docudrama of *The Hillsborough Disaster;* and his play about the Bloody Sunday massacre is currently being praised for the accuracy of its writing and its careful observation; for many people it was a tour de force and an important contribution to the debate. His film *The Priest* tackled the important issue of sexual abuse and ruffled more than a few feathers amongst the clergy. He disliked his time at the College intensely and, like some others interviewed, he could not wait to leave. Unsympathetic teachers, he feels, did not help working-class boys from poor environments to integrate.

During his career as a Foreign Office diplomat Laurence O'Keeffe(OX 1950) wrote two novels - *Simultaneous Equations* and *Abiding City* as well as a book of essays, *Ancient Affections,*a study of the American political scene,

After the War Geoffrey Quinn(1930s) launched himself on the entertainment world as Paul Raymond. He made his name and his fortune as a publisher and a Soho impresario, and he invested wisely in the London property market. In 1993 the Editor of the College Magazine wrote : "Some of our readers will be aware that an Old Boy has been listed as the richest man in England. Although his route to the top demonstrates the versatility of Old Xaverians, his success has not been closely followed in these pages."

In 1880 and 1881 Gerard Manley Hopkins SJ was on the church staff at St. Francis Xavier's. According to the College Magazine (1995) he found Liverpool squalid and its inhabitants repulsive. Slight though his connection must have been with the College, it is too tempting not to mention him here. But better he speaks for himself with one of the poems written in Salisbury Street.

*Ted Whitehead (OX 1952)*

108

FELIX RANDAL by Gerard Manley Hopkins SJ

FELIX RANDAL the farrier, 0 he is dead then? my duty all ended,
Who have watched his mould of man, big-boned and hardy-handsome
Pining, pining, till time when reason rambled in it and some
Fatal four disorders, fleshed there, all contended?
Sickness broke him. Impatient he cursed at first, but mended
Being anointed and all; though a heavenlier heart began some
Months earlier, since I had Our sweet reprieve and ransom
Tendered to him. Ah, well, God rest him all road ever he offended!
This seeing the sick endears them to us, us too it endears.
My tongue had taught thee comfort, touch had quenched thy tears,
Thy tears that touched my heart, child, Felix, poor Felix Randal;
How far from then forethought of all thy more boisterous years,
When thou at the random grim forge, powerful amidst peers,
Didst fettle for the great grey drayhorse his bright and battering sandal!

Fr. Hopkins left St. Francis Xavier's in September, 1881, and we may assume that he had few regrets about his going. His ultimate verdict can he found in a letter where he even compared Liverpool unfavourably with Glasgow: 'Things are pleasanter here than at Liverpool. Wretched place too Glasgow is, like all our great towns; still I get on better here –.' Beyond doubt Hopkins was happy to have seen the back of Liverpool.

The Xaverian and the College Magazine alone have been consulted for this list. Apologies must be offered for any omissions, errors and oversights, which will be corrected in the second edition.

"Jimmy Tarbuck, the well-known comedian and television personality, has few happy memories of his time in the `50s at SFX Prep School. He remembers 'cruel and vindictive teachers like Fr. McCann and Fr. Burns', and the atmosphere of fear generated by the ferula in such small boys. At the age of 10 he started to play truant and was caught when he chose to go to Woolton Baths on the same afternoon Fr. McCann took his class there. He refused to be beaten, was chased around the room by Fr. McCann and escaped through the window. He never went back.

Glimmers of light were playing football at Melwood, (which included at least one hat-trick), turning out for the Old Xavs Football team in the `60s, and some of the good friends he made - like Pearson, of the undertaking family on Allerton Road."

*Fr. Gerard Manley Hopkins SJ*

**Addendum.**

Fr. Garrold devised for his classes a banking method of fictitious money. Good homework themes were rewarded according to the tariff printed below, and fines inflicted for poor behaviour. Each boy had his bank-book and cheque-book, and accounts were balanced each week. Privileges could be bought by pupils in credit.

---

### RICHARD PHILIP GARROLD

I append the original Fine-Lists and Theme tariff.   (d. = a penny.   /- = a shilling)

#### FINES.

Rowdiness - 5/- to 30/-

| | | | | | |
|---|---|---|---|---|---|
| Semi-rowdiness | 2/6 | | Demi-semi do. | 1/- | |
| Talking - first time | 2/- | | 2nd time | 3/- | 3rd time 10/- |
| Leaning back | | | | | |
| Ist time | 1d. | | 2nd time | 2d. | 3rd time 6d. |
| | | | | | |
| Banging desk | I/- | | do (special) | 2/6 | |
| | | | | | |
| No capital . | 6d. | | No book given in | 3/- | |
| Chewing | 2/- | | Standing up | 6d. | |
| Grimaces | I/- | | Wrong account | I/- | |
| ' Start ' for ' begin' | 6d. | | Wrong subject | I/- | |
| Dropping things | 6d. | | Needless question | 2/- | |
| Clicking fingers | 1d. | | Unsolicited comment | 1/- | |
| | | | | | |
| Mad answer . | 6d | | Leaving place | 1/- | |
| Inattention | 5/- . | | 'Please Father ' tax | 1d | |
| Leaving room | 2/- | | Yawn . | 2d | |
| Undisguised yawn | 6d | | | | |

#### THEMES. (HOMEWORK)

| | | | | |
|---|---|---|---|---|
| A + | 3/- | B | 6d. | |
| A | 2/6 | B - | 3d. | |
| A - | 2/- | C | - | |
| AB | 1 /6 | D | 1/- fine. | |
| B + | 1/- | D - | 2/- fine. | |

## Chapter 6

# Curriculum : Other Areas

### Science at SFX

As early as 1877 the Superior General of the Jesuit Order, Fr. Beckx, had written to the English Provincial, Fr. Gallwey, urging him to ensure that more time was given in the English schools to modern languages, arithmetic and chemistry. It would seem that the General was aware of the need for a re-examination of the curriculum in the Order's colleges, as well as being aware of the wishes of parents for a curriculum more suited to the times. The teachers at SFX responded to this invitation with a will, and the College can be considered a leader in the promotion of science teaching both in the city and nationally towards the end of the nineteenth century.

Professor Maurice Whitehead of the University of Wales at Swansea has drawn attention to the contribution the Jesuits made to the development of science education in Liverpool in the nineteenth century in an article for Annals of Science No 43 (1986 pp.353-368) and most of what follows is taken from that source.

At SFX a new 'Science Class' had been introduced in 1875 by a Jesuit scientist, Fr. Gerard, a Fellow of the Linnaean Society and a prolific writer on scientific topics. He was firmly in the tradition of international Jesuit academics, who for centuries had made their marks in astronomy, geography, physics, chemistry and biology as well as in the arts subjects.

Fr. Gerard, appointed Prefect of Studies in 1876, saw to it that a teaching area for science was included in the plans for the new College opened in 1877. Fr. Vaughan, a teacher on the staff, was asked by the Provincial to begin formal training in chemistry at the age of 50, and he proceeded to teach the subject from 1877 onwards. He spent term time teaching at the College and vacation studying the subject in London.

It is salutary to read that at the specific request of the General it was the intention as early as 1877 that every boy in the College should study science - not just an able class of older boys as happened elsewhere.

Fr. Vaughan and Fr. Gerard both taught science classes from 1877 onwards - together with Fr. Sergeant, who had arrived in 1876. From 1877 Fr. Vaughan also taught 'a night chemistry class for young men who had not had the opportunity of studying the subject at school.' Fr. Gerard also did his share. He gave a series of lectures on scientific subjects for the general public between 1878 and 1879 : On Beer; The History of the Apple; and African Geography.

The work of these men put SFX in the forefront of science teaching not only in Liverpool, but also nationally. Fr. Vaughan taught the subject for 15 years until he retired in 1892 - a continuity that did much to enhance the status of the subject and that of the College. When Fr. Gerard departed for Stonyhurst in 1879, matters at SFX faltered - generally and scientifically. There were three Prefects of Studies and numerous staff changes between 1879 and 1888. There were Prefects of Studies like Fr. Tarleton, who in 1888 wrote to the Provincial to ask: 'Is it worthwhile to continue the teaching of chemistry?'

From September 1889, SFX settled down to a new period of growth and development - not least in the area of science and technical education, when Fr. Donnelly, another scientist, was appointed Prefect of Studies. He came to SFX from Glasgow where he was one of the people responsible for the establishment of an athletics club that became Glasgow Celtic. He made an equally impressive impact on Liverpool. In

1896 he opened a new science course in the Commercial School. The same year two large classes in practical chemistry were timetabled. Scholarships in science were awarded to SFX pupils. Laboratory assistants were appointed. Proper laboratories were fitted out.

The introduction of science into the College curriculum, combined with the policy of entering pupils for London Matriculation, the Oxford Local Examinations, and, from 1890, the South Kensington Arts and Science Exams, made a considerable impact on the work done in Salisbury Street. These developments also helped to build up the reputation of the College. They also make it all the more difficult to explain why - as pointed out in Chapter 3 - the roll fell so dramatically in the nineties.

Though Fr. Donnelly was to remain as Prefect of Studies until the summer of 1898, it is clear that by the end of 1896 he felt he had successfully accomplished the task he had set himself on taking up office eight years earlier. Speaking to the boys' parents at Christmas 1896, he gave an address which serves as a fitting testimony to his work at St Francis Xavier's College:

> 'The studies have been placed on such a footing that no one need now complain that he has not got a chance. In proof, I may refer ... to the case of the three Scholarships won during the last two years at University College, Liverpool, and open to competition in the whole of Liverpool. Our students were pitted against those of Liverpool College, Shaw Street, the Liverpool Institute, Mount Street, and other non-Catholic institutions, and acquitted themselves most honourably.
>
> We have added a Fifth Form to the Commercial Course by means of which such boys as wish may obtain a thoroughly good scientific training. The study of Practical Chemistry has been begun in the lowest forms of the Commercial Course, and I know no study to which our boys turn more eagerly. It has been a problem with me for years to see whether we cannot start the study of Mechanics and Chemistry lower down in the Classical Course, and I hope to see something done in that direction after Christmas. There is no doubt that it tends to rouse and develop a boy's powers of observation in a marvellous way, and that some minds that cannot be excited or stirred by the study of literature are roused from a prolonged state of torpidity by the wonders of the world of science.
>
> It is now eight years ago, almost to a day, that you were told that the authorities of the College were fully alive to the requirements of a great commercial city like this, and were fully determined to respond to your desires, as far as possible, of giving your children such an education as would fit them to go forth on terms of equality with their non-Catholic fellow countrymen. This I claim that we have done.'

| *Fr.Gerard* | *Fr. Vaughan* | *Fr. Tarleton* | *Fr. Donnelly* |

In 1898 the next Prefect of Studies, Fr. McHale, responded with alacrity to a suggestion from the Provincial that he should apply for the status of School of Science on the grounds of 'examination successes and a first-rate science laboratory'. A physics laboratory was equipped to complement the chemistry laboratory and a newly equipped woodwork department was opened. Approval was given and the School of Science was opened in autumn 1899. It was noted in reports that 'more emphasis was being placed on practical experiments by pupils'.

Professor Whitehead concludes his article with these remarks:

> 'The emphasis laid on the provision of scientific and technical education at SFX between 1875 - 1900 marked an important new departure in the educational work of the English Jesuits. It introduced the world of science to a wide range of pupils who would otherwise have been deprived of such an education and it established science as an integral part of the curriculum at the College.'

The work begun by Fr. Vaughan, Fr. Gerard, Fr. Sergeant and Fr. Donnelly in the nineteenth century laid the foundations on which science teaching could build in the twentieth century. Mr Mollard, Mr Bradshaw, and Mr Birmingham - names familiar to many readers - toiled profitably in this particular vineyard in the first half of the twentieth century. The last of these - Mr Birmingham - who had joined the staff in 1922, established the Mollard Prize for Chemistry in honour of his former teacher and colleague. It goes to the candidate with the best chemistry results at Advanced level.

It is convenient to register here the names of some of the stalwarts of the Maths Department. At Salisbury Street Mr Dunn, Mr Crook and Mr Beaky Jones taught both before and after the war. At Woolton Mr. Mike Benton, Brother Edmund and Mr. Paul Bright, amongst others, will long be remembered for their contributions to the work of the department.

Since 1961 a new cohort of science teachers has made its mark at Woolton. The new science facilities at High Lee were 'state of the art' and a considerable improvement on what was provided at Salisbury Street. The laboratories and equipment were constantly up-dated, drawing favourable comments from Inspectors. In recent years the introduction of the latest technological support has the enthusiastic backing of Brother Francis, and at SFX provision in this area has been second to none.

The "giants" of the science staff between 1961 and 2001 have been John Sherrard, John O'Malley, Brother Augustine, Mike Emmott, Paul Prescott and Ian Blackhurst. A steady stream of their science students have gone on to higher education to study medicine, dentistry and the various branches of engineering. Mr O'Malley, a pillar of strength in the department and the longest-serving member of staff, introduced electronics as an O Level subject in the Lower Sixth with outstanding success.

The move to Woolton was of special importance for biology. The subject was taught for public exams in the last years at Salisbury Street, but the laboratories at Woolton enabled the subject to achieve parity with physics and chemistry. Between 1961 and 1969 biology prospered - especially under Tony Matthews. In the next thirty years under Ian Blackhurst it has become one of the most successful subjects on the curriculum.

## Concertatio

From the early days the Jesuits looked for different ways to stimulate the involvement and interest of pupils in their learning. St Ignatius had drawn attention to the usefulness of oral work and recitation, and in the early days, as the Ratio was being put into practice, there seems to have been a certain amount of experimentation in teaching approaches.

One such technique found its way to Stonyhurst from the continent in the eighteenth century and thence to SFX in the nineteenth. It was still being used in the 1920s. This was called the Concertatio.

The Concertatio was a contest in subject matter between two different classes or two sides from the same class. A subject or topic was chosen and questions were fired across the room alternatively. A mistake meant a 'victory' for the other side and the side with most victories was the winner, and extra play was awarded. To render the rivalry more acute, sides were named Romani and Carthaginienses at a special ceremonial match - called, it is thought, Concertatio Pro Patria' - at the beginning of the year. The three best pairs of boys in each side were called Imperatores, Praetores and Tribuni, and they wore special insignia with badges and medals. At SFX the contest would take place in class, or publicly in the Exhibition Room after the 1855 College was built, or often during dinner in the Priests' Refectory.

For many reading this, the fortnightly Latin Grammar Test Papers of the 'fifties will seem a poor replacement.

A variation on this in the nineteenth century only were the Compositions. They were held at the end of each of the four (sic) terms. Boys had to compose and recite in English, French, Latin or Greek. Much-valued privileges were granted to those judged to be the best performers. Perhaps these sort of public performances survived in shadowy form well into the 1950s. Many Old Xaverians will remember being chosen to read at lunchtime to the Fathers and Scholastics, or to stay behind after school to read, as they ate their meal in complete silence. It could be a nerve-wracking experience - particularly if an extract from the Lives of the Saints struck the reader as funny enough to make him want to laugh out loud.

## The Intercollegiate Examinations

From the 1880s onwards Fr. Provincial had awarded sizeable monetary prizes to the boys from a Jesuit College who scored the highest and next highest marks in Latin and Mathematics in the Senior Oxford Local Exams and in the Junior Oxford Local Exams - the day's equivalents of A Level and GCSE.

In 1920 the Provincial revised the system, since different colleges now sat the exams of different Boards. He decided to award the prizes on the results of a special examination, common to the nine colleges of the Province. In the first four years of the new Intercollegiate Exam SFX carried off five of the sixteen first prizes. In 1949 we won all four first prizes in one year - a unique achievement. The Intercollegiates became highly competitive, although various minutes of meetings show that the rivalry was largely between Headmasters. The vast majority of pupils  - even those sitting the papers - were little aware of their significance and even of their existence. In retrospect it seems like another example of the twentieth century inclination for the tail to wag the dog - at least at SFX. Fr. Neylan in particular regarded with special malevolence any boy who did not win an expected prize, the boy being left in no doubt that he had failed.

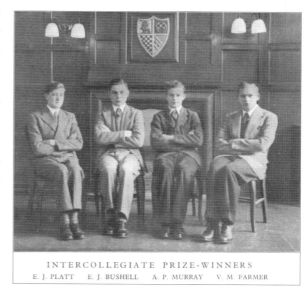

INTERCOLLEGIATE PRIZE-WINNERS
E. J. PLATT    E. J. BUSHELL    A. P. MURRAY    V. M. FARMER

## Religious Education

From 1970 onwards the more open and less didactic approach to religious education in schools brought changes in the way the subject was tackled at the College. In the recent OFSTED Report on SFX the work of the RE department was highly praised and this public document can be consulted by those interested.

Before 1970, the teaching of religion was much more stereotyped than it is today and an attempt is made here to draw some sort of picture. The opinions of only a very limited sample - some half-a-dozen 80-year-olds from the 'thirties and about twenty pupils post-war - have been canvassed, and therefore the results may well be skewed, but a clear enough picture emerges. Religious Doctrine, as it was called, always seems to have permeated the life of the College, as one would expect. Whether the account is about the 'twenties and 'thirties or the 'fifties and 'sixties, the pattern is the same.

The lower forms largely had lessons based on the Catechism, which they were expected to know by heart, along with some study of the Gospels. In years four and five the Gospels were studied in some detail and the pupils sometimes, but not always, were entered for external examinations. In the sixth form the serious business of explanation and argument was undertaken, and the principles of the Catholic faith subjected to scrutiny, often in a very liberal atmosphere. There were exceptions to all this, when a particular priest took it into his head to be more challenging lower down the school.

Ritual was never neglected. Weekly Mass, the Angelus at mid-day, fortnightly Confession, strict observance of High Days and Holy Days, the Forty Hours, Tuesday or Wednesday Benediction, and Hail Marys said - often perfunctorily - at the beginning of each lesson. Natty Lucas (history teacher) would start the Hail Mary as he crossed the door and the prayer would be finished by the time he reached his desk. Before the war to be late for Mass meant an automatic 6 ferulas.

Prayer and good works were cultivated in the pupils with some energy. The Society of the Sacred Heart of Jesus, instituted as long ago as 1868 by Fr. Harris, and later in 1874 the Sodality of Our Lady sought to develop in the boys an attitude to prayer and to its value and practice which one would find in any Catholic school of the day. The St. Vincent de Paul Society, which similarly had a long history in Salisbury Street, sought to bring out in those who joined a sympathy and a practical help for the poor, which after all had been one of St. Ignatius' original purposes.

The R.D. classes in the Lower School are usually recalled as extensions of the Catechism. There had always been a class prize for R.D.; it did not became R.E. till 1976. For many fifth formers the School Certificate Course in Scriptural Studies was a mixture of the historical and the religious. In 1991 the Proclamation lists students passing examinations in Religious Education, in 1992 in Religious Studies and, in 1993, in Christian Theology.

Any criticism of the religious teaching will inevitably be linked with one's response to the whole educational methodology and practice at SFX at any given time. At times it opened itself to the charge of elitism. To put it crudely, cannon-fodder up to the fifth form, officer material in the sixth. The opinions of those - the vast majority - who left before or after form five reflect a different experience from that recalled by sixth formers. Rote-learning, ferulas, and exclusion seem to characterize the whole curriculum for some who have spoken of their eagerness to be shot of the place as soon as possible. One fifth-form leaver, when asked about drama, simply said 'there wasn't any'. Yet he attended the College when dramatic productions were staged regularly. Was the case the same with RE as with drama - when it came down to the real thing 'only sixth formers need apply'? Maybe not, but were there shades of this approach?

A positive, if rather patchwork, scene is eventually sketched. It came, therefore, as a surprise to read a report written by a priest on the staff for the Provincial in 1936.

## Observations on the Religious Doctrine at St. Francis Xavier's
## July 1936

In July 1936 a Jesuit on the staff at SFX wrote a report for the Provincial on the state of religious education at the College. The report is seven pages long. If his remarks were true, it would represent a damning indictment. It can probably be dismissed as the biased and unreasonable ramblings of one dissatisfied teacher. No record of receipt or reaction by the Provincial of the day can be found in the Farm Street Archives. Ex-pupils, to whom it has been shown, have responded almost unanimously. 'An unfair - not to say completely untrue - description of the state of affairs in the subject in the 1930s, and not at all representative of the teaching of religious education in the 1940s and the 1950s.'

The quotations in the report of the complaining priest speak for themselves.

> The state of religious doctrine in the school is haphazard and unorganized and much below the standard that should exist.

> In 2nd, 3rd and 4th forms the syllabus is simply the Catechism. No official interest is taken in what classes do...it is easy for a master to scamp RD unscrupulously. I know of at least one case where this used to be done. Catechism is mere by-heart work.

> The fifth and sixth formers do not learn at any time the basis on which their faith is supposed to rest.... and leave College completely unequipped to meet any criticism of the Catholic Church. On the relative importance of academic subjects and religious education boys know that they can plead 'scholarship work' in an excuse for not taking RD exams ...and that the plea will be successful.

> The boys know perfectly well that RD is considered a very subsidiary subject. At morning prayers the small boys are kept in order. The bigger boys do what they like.

He goes on to make two very startling - and very disputed - claims:

> It is held by a number of people in Liverpool that, if a Catholic parent wants his boy to receive a good Catholic education and if he wants to be certain that the boy will retain his faith after leaving school, he should send the boy to St Edward's. If on the other hand he is anxious that the boy should pass examinations well and get a job, he should send him to SFX.
> Secondly it is held by a number of people that an unduly large proportion of SFX boys cease to practise their religion after school.
> These claims do not surprise me, since what is wanted in the College is a genuine tradition of spirituality. This is a fairly serious indictment, but not exaggerated at all.

The paper is unsigned and, on that ground alone perhaps, it should be dismissed as irrelevant. There is reason to believe that the paper was written but never submitted. Furthermore the sources it claims are vague in the extreme. It is impossible to say at this distance whether there is any accuracy at all in its descriptions.

But the paper has had it uses, since this writer felt bound to lobby past pupils for responses. Not only do those responses contradict the report, root and branch, but they also register an informative and interesting account of religious doctrine classes.

My own reflection has been that we were treated religiously in an enlightened way. I think we were allowed to grow up - particularly by Joey Woodlock. I would call him a Christian humanist; a bit like Newman.                                                                 1936

We used Sheehan's Manual of Apologetics and enjoyed many lively debates with - I think - Father Freeman.                                                                                          1937

I was taught the Catechism by rote in the early years. It formed a good sold foundation for later. We also studied the New Testament, but little or none of the Old Testament. In the sixth form Fr. Freeman (one of the best teachers we ever had) took us right through both volumes of Sheehan's Apologetics. It was a wonderful and challenging experience. He encouraged interruptions and questions. At annual retreats quite a stress on sins of the flesh.      1938

School mass once a week. Confession in the parish church fortnightly. Our Lady's Sodality with quite a large membership. St Vincent de Paul Conference which involved visiting the poor of the parish.                                                                                 1935

I consider that the understanding of my faith as taught, inculcated, directed, or whatever at SFX was second to none. Fr. Adamson ran what today would be called inter-active RI classes - in the fourth form, I think. Boys were selected to present a topic, which may or may not be in agreement with the Church's teaching, whilst the rest of the class could take other views.
                                                                                                       1948

Fr. Somerville's classes in the sixth form were an excellent grounding for life. His thoughts on Social Justice were way ahead of their time. If you paid attention to him, he prompted you to think about your faith. There was a sound teaching of RD, but in many cases this might have been pearls cast before swine.                                                               1952

Fr. Somerville introduced us to the idea of the minimum wage, earnings for everyone enough to save and go on holiday - according to one's station.                                         1950

My main recollections of RE were of being taught by the priests, who were very serious in their commitment to their RE teaching. I recall Fr.Tomlinson in Form 3; Fr. Doyle in Form 4; Fr. Somerville in the sixth form, who gave me twelve for not paying attention in his RE class - that's how serious he was. Somerville had written a book on Catholic apologetics and it was our text book for the first (and second year?) year sixth. We also had a Fr. Reynolds who wasn't our teacher of RE, but I recall him as very often adverting to religious matters in Greek and Latin lessons.                                                                                  1952

Perhaps the whole community had responded to the criticisms of the unsigned letter by the late forties. Funny though that while my recollections of these priests are so vivid, I have no memories whatever of being taught RE by laymen or scholastics.                           1953

Perhaps you caught the end of the scandalous teaching of the 1930s and I got the benefit of the reforms - which must have been implemented by Neylan if this analysis is correct.
                                                                                                       1951

Fr. 'Baldy' Burton stressed the debt the Church owed to Judaism. Fr. Hand allowed a surprising amount of polemical argument in RE. I recall that the understanding of my faith as taught at SFX was thorough, careful and intellectually stimulating.                                 1949

Fr. Wilkin and Fr. Dooley are fine examples in the 'Forties of priests who took the subject seriously. In the sixth form Fr. Wilkin gave the impression that there was no more important subject on the curriculum.

1947

Looking back, I think the process was one of osmosis. For many of us, who became embedded in the school's life, there was 'a family atmosphere' at the school. What the inward response was of people less caught up is hard to divine.

1938

Religious instruction more like religious indoctrination. You were thrashed into belief, the prime example being the use of the Catechism as an instrument of terror. I mentioned to you the panic I felt in the examination conducted by Jock, when he asked me "What will God say to the wicked," and I (mixing up my catechism answers, but not deliberately like Putty) replied, "God will say to the wicked, Come ye blessed of my Father." Obviously I was one of the damned. The irony was that I was actually an extremely devout adolescent. But there was little sense of the spiritual in the religious education at the college. There was also little attempt to prepare you for the challenges, both historical and theological, which you would encounter later, as I did at Cambridge, and which undermined my own belief.

1953

It is perhaps appropriate at this point to return to the deliberations of the conference on Jesuit education referred to earlier in Chapter 4.

Fr. Arrupe, The Superior General in 1980, spoke at the Conference. Is he putting his finger here on criticism that can be levelled justly at Jesuit schools when they fall short of the Ignatian ideal? In describing the 'Ignacianidad' of a Jesuit school and the Jesuit charism that informs it, he said ' I am not talking about arrogance or snobbery, still less about a superiority complex'. Nor was it 'the training of a socio-economic elite' for future leadership. Elsewhere, he refers to 'convictions of Ours that are too firmly entrenched'. (1965 Magazine p.12.)

Is there not an implication here that some Jesuits had conducted their schools against such a backcloth? The elitism which it is possible to recognize in these remarks will strike many a familiar chord amongst pupils who attended SFX during the terms of Fr. Neylan (1939-1953) and Fr. Doyle (1962-1974), and probably of Fr. McHale (1889-1910). Would it be unfair to claim that for these Heads only Open Scholarships, Intercollegiate Prizes and the highest grades at A Level, O Level and GCSE counted? In the 1960s The Archbishop of Liverpool complained that 'Catholic grammar schools in Liverpool are obsessed with Oxbridge scholarships. And the worst culprit is SFX.'
This approach to secondary schooling might be called 'Jesuitic' as opposed to 'Ignatian'. But more than one correspondent feels there is no such distinction; that perhaps some Jesuit schools might have interpreted their brief in narrow, rigorist, legalistic, mechanical, external, formulaic terms; and others in more humane, integrated, well-rounded, spiritual, reflective, affective terms. Those who think along these lines unsurprisingly are unhappy with the epithet 'Jesuitic' and prefer to talk about a 'continuum' or a 'spectrum'.

The 'Ignatian' education aimed at in Jesuit schools, Fr. Arrupe and the Conference go on to suggest, 'lives and operates out of our own charism'. The marks of such Ignacianidad, it is claimed here, are those that marked the terms of Fr. Warner (1953-1961) and Fr. Woodlock (1919-1937). They are also the marks of any good modern Catholic school and will be those which Brother Francis and his staff would want pursued in the College today:

      total formation of each individual based on individual capacities
      individual care and concern for the person

emphasis on activity

reasoning reflectively, logically and critically

adequate pastoral care and concern for the poor

pursuit of excellence, but without comparison with others

competition between groups rather than individuals

collaboration and spirit of community

a general co-operative and communitarian approach

And lastly - non multa, sed multum - depth rather than breadth.

Is this distinction between 'Jesuitic' and 'Ignatian' education fanciful and artificial? There is a wealth of anecdotal evidence that could be said to support it. Or is it just that those referred to here as 'Jesuitic' were simply those who failed to measure up to 'Ignacianidad'? Certainly St Ignatius' view was a world-view. Its inspiration, its values, its attitudes and its styles propose Christ as the model for all human life. For some Old Boys this was their experience at SFX. For others, unfortunately, it is not a picture that they recognize.

Opinions have been canvassed from individuals who might be said to have had a professional interest in this aspect of the curriculum. Some have pointed out that the accounts given by pupils above, represent religious instruction at any Catholic grammar school in that period (1930-1960); but there will have been teachers of religion of outstanding quality to counterbalance, just as there were at SFX. Fr. Somerville comes to mind as well as Canon Drinkwater in Birmingham, who strongly opposed what he saw as a travesty of religious education.

Fr. J. Gillick, SJ, who was Captain of the College in 1933-4, seems to strike home in a number of ways and with his permission his letter is reproduced here. It restores overall balance to the debate, and sets some of the earlier comments in a much-needed context.

> 'My heart goes out to anyone trying to make a fair judgement on Religious Education in any institution. The first difficulty comes in deciding what exactly we are assessing. I can feel some sympathy with the writer of the 1936 letter and those whose experience it mirrors. But it is presuming that the task is to TEACH the faith, whereas this is only one element in our task of rousing and handing on FAITH to the next generation. Faith is caught, not taught. {An analogy might be drawn here with science. We teach pupils 'how to do science', not 'what science to do'. P.H.} Instruction in the doctrines of the faith is only one part of it, and far from the most crucial. Having tried to teach it to boys for many years, I know how difficult it is and how few there are with a flair for it. In my time at S.F.X. ('24 - '34) the teaching wasn't perfect, but, on the whole, I would agree with the favourable assessments of past pupils printed above. It might be good to remember that this is how religious doctrine was taught generally before the catechetical reforms of the '60s - and that Fr. Sommerville was one of the leading figures in that movement. On the negative side, perhaps some of the positive elements have been blotted out by the memory of ferulas and the rather medieval disciplinary system of teaching - which was shared by most schools at the time.
>
> But I think it is misleading to concentrate on the TEACHING OF DOCTRINE in the effort to rouse faith. This is a task shared by the parents and family, the school, the peer group and the zeitgeist. The school is only one element, and not the most important. Personally I look back with gratitude for all that was done to help us to grow in the faith and I would disagree with the assertion that "what is wanted in the College is a genuine tradition of spirituality." Looking back, my memories tally with the other accounts you report. The major task of the College was to provide us with a Catholic atmosphere and culture and stimulate the seeds

of faith and practice in us. I can still remember the impact of the Tuesday benediction, Brother Shaw's Forty Hours, the habits formed of fortnightly confession, the annual retreat and the quality of the retreat fathers, the Knights of the Blessed Sacrament and the Sodality, the influence on a growing boy of men like Fr. Woodlock and Fr.McCann and some of the scholastics and the hours they spent with us in the playground and at Melwood, lay masters like Les Bailey, Frank Grace and Frank Checkland. I think that those in charge worked hard to provide us with the ground in which the seed of faith could grow.

I'm not sure that I grasp what is being said about the distinction between Ignatian and Jesuitic teaching. I would suggest, rather, that there is only one Ignatian ideal and that in the history of all our institutions there are periods when this ideal predominates and others when we fall short. I think it would be fair to say that in the times of Fr. Woodlock and Fr. Warner the Ignatian ideal was the main thrust, with less emphasis on the struggle for academic excellence. Unfortunately there were others, when incompetence or obsession with the classics and Oxbridge scholarships tarnished this reputation.'

Fr. Jack Gillick SJ

Others have remarked that competition, academic excellence and Oxbridge scholarships have their place. Most Catholic grammar schools up until 1960 operated in a cultural context in which they saw their prime function as lifting the status of the largely working class or lower middle class pupils as a means of lifting the status of the whole Catholic community. Oxbridge was one of the tools to this end. It never seemed to be an issue with most teachers that this approach short-changed the mass of pupils who never had such high academic prospects.

*The College Shrine to Our Lady of Lourdes*
*(first floor Salisbury Street)*

*The Shrine of Our Lady at Woolton*

*SFX Pilgrimage Group at the Chapel of St. Bernadette 1957*

## Sport

There has been so much sporting activity at the College over the last 160 years that any attempt to record it fully will probably fail and certainly bore. It is hoped that the selective approach adopted will not offend - an overview only - with some sports, events and occasions presented in more detail.

Until fairly recently football in winter and cricket in summer were the only consistent items on the sporting agenda at the College. In the early days the games were internal between different forms, and then against other schools. The Xaverian reported these matches - often in great detail. The annual match with Stonyhurst in the nineteenth century was something of an event with the home game being played at Goodison Park - thanks to Mr. Baxter, who was an Old Xaverian and a Director of Everton. The fixture was only abandoned in 1918 when Stonyhurst changed over to rugby.

The difficulty of renting decent playing fields was a regular problem for those trying to promote a programme of games. Melwood was bought in 1921, but before that for over thirty years pitches were rented all around the City. Kensington Fields, rented by Fr. Porter in the 1860s, Wavertree Playground, Black Horse Lane, Childwall, Green Lane, Clubmoor, Fairfield - a testament to the open spaces still inside the city boundaries at the time.

Between 1913 and 1920 the College rented five pitches at Clubmoor. But one night in 1920 the wooden pavilion, which we owned, was totally removed right down to the foundations. It was reliably and, given the poverty of the day, sympathetically reported that the locals had taken it for firewood. Grounds in West Derby Road were used for the rest of year, but the whole episode prompted Fr. Woodlock, Prefect of Studies, and Fr. Melling, the Vice-President (deputy head), to look for our own premises.

In 1921 fourteen acres were bought near West Derby village, the terminus of the Number 12 tram, for £6,000. A competition was held to decide a name for the new ground, which was won by a junior boy: Melwood Bridge Estate - named after Fr. Melling, the Vice-President, Fr. Woodlock, the Prefect of Studies, and Fr. Bridge, the Rector. It can be assumed that that young boy made his mark later on in life.

*The original pavilion at Melwood built 1921*

*The Pavilion Extended 1932*

## Intercollegiate Athletics Competition

The Liverpool secondary schools competed annually in an Intercollegiate Competition, which was first held in 1913. The College made no impact for ten years and then won the trophy three times between 1924 and 1927. If the records in the College Magazine are any indicator, this competition does not seem to have survived the war. More recently inter-school athletics competitions have been revived and we have sent successful teams to Liverpool and Lancashire meetings.

LIVERPOOL AND DISTRICT SECONDARY SCHOOLS

ANNUAL ATHLETIC SPORTS

WINNERS OF OPEN CHAMPIONSHIP

1913. Liverpool Institute.
1914      do.
1915.      do.
1916-7-8.    No competition owing to war
1919. Liverpool Institute.
1920. Liverpool Collegiate School.
1921.      do.
1922. Liverpool Institute.
1923. Liverpool Collegiate School.
1924. St. Francis Xavier's College.
1925.      do.
1926. St. Edward's College.
1927. St. Francis Xavier's College.
1928/29. Liverpool Collegiate School
1930.    L'pool Inst/Quarry Bank HS.
1931.    Quarry Bank High School.
1932/33/34 Liverpool Collegiate Sch.

*The Fr. Parry Shield*

*This shield was paid for by the friends of Fr. Parry in 1921 in recognition of his 23 years devoted service to St. Francis Xavier's College. The College Crest in the centre is in beaten silver, inscribed 'The Father Parry Shield : Victor Ludorum'. The mid-circle consists of the national emblems - the rose, the thistle, the shamrock and theleek. There is a narrow border of bay leaves around the outside.*

From 1920 onwards a College Sports Day was organized at Melwood, and athletics has remained a strong contender for sporting interest since. Between the wars the Victor Ludorum at each meeting was awarded the Fr. Parry Shield, a magnificent piece of silverware, which the College may still possess. If it can be found, it could well be competed for again. The summer athletics meeting became a regular fixture and it gained in strength after the move to Woolton.

Extract from College Magazine 2000.

'The athletics season at the College usually begins at the start of the Summer term, occupying games sessions for five or six weeks. At times, however, the weather can stop this progressing as we would hope. You really need the track at High Lee to be fairly firm for the runners and there are obvious dangers for the field events in poor conditions.

Over the past few seasons, we have always done well in the hurdles (at the G.M. Meeting in Blackburn, our hurdlers won in all year groups),

*Standing* :—M. Raftery ; A. Walton ; G. Woods ; J. A. O'Brien ; J. McDermott ; H. Garnett ; R. Burke.
*Seated* :—E. Tryers ; J. Lennon ; J. Bass ; G. Doran ; B. Wallace.
*On Ground* :—B. Simpson ; C. Mathews ; G. Wilson ; R. Paden.

*Athletic Sports, 1931, First Prize Winners*

*Top Row (left to right)* :—440 Yards, Open ;  Senior Boxing Championship ;  The ' Fr. Parry ' Shield—Victor Ludorum ;
    Cross Country ;  High Jump, Open.
*Middle Row* :—Junior Football, Class Cup ; Senior Sports, Class Cup ; Mile, Open ;  Under 15 Championship ; Junior
    Boxing Championship ;  Senior Tug-of-War, Class Cup.
*Lower Row* :—100 Yards, Open ;  Under 13 Championship ;  Under 11 Championship ;  Art Essay Cup ; Junior Cricket,
    Class Cup ;  Senior Football, Class Cup ;  Junior Sports, Class Cup.

*Challenge Cups competed for in the 1930s*

and this really corresponds to the number of times pupils can practise the event, given sunny weather. The throwing events, being more technical than the track, require constant repetition if real progress is to be made. A great many pupils show a talent in a sport they had not previously known, and it is a discipline that allows boys of all shapes and sizes to take part. Many enjoy trying to take 2 seconds off their best 800 metre time or throwing the javelin 5 metres further than last year.' Since 1997 it has been possible to take a GCSE in Physical Education in Years 10 and 11 - a very popular option.'

## The Senior and Junior Shields

The Senior and Junior Football Challenge Shields, competed for annually by Liverpool and District Secondary schools, have been the central attraction in the football programme nearly every year since 1895. The records for the Senior Shield are sometimes contradictory and the records of the winners of the Junior Shield are incomplete. No doubt corrections will be received.

The Senior Shield was presented by Everton Football Club in 1894 and was won in its first year by Liverpool Collegiate in 1895. SFX did not register its first success till 1919-1920 when the Catholic Institute was beaten in the Final 3-2.

The First XI has won the Senior Shield eleven times. In the 'twenties we won it in 1920, 1925 and 1926. The 'thirties were completely barren years . Our best spell came in the 'forties, when we appeared in the Final in seven out of ten years; victories in 1942, 1943, 1947 and 1950; and defeats in 1941, 1948, and 1949. In the 'fifties and 'sixties we went empty-handed, although we did make the Final in 1956 and 1960. Success came our way in the 'seventies - in 1971, 1975 and 1976. We won the Shield again in 1987, but had no success in the 'nineties. We are the current holders, winning it last year 2001.

The Junior Shield has been won by SFX 12 times according to partial records. The SFX successes came in 1922, 1924, 1925, 1927, and 1937. Since then the Juniors have won in 1944, 1951, 1959, 1982, 1984, 1997, and 2000. The Junior Shield was presented by Liverpool Football Club and was won for the first time in 1916, when Birkenhead Institute were the winners. SFX's first victory came in 1921-1922.

*Senior Shield Winners 1947.*

*Junior Shield Winners 1959*

## SECONDARY SCHOOLS ASSOCIATION FOOTBALL CHALLENGE SHIELD.

Won by the Everton A.F.C. and presented for competition between Liverpool and District Secondary Schools.

1895. Liverpool Collegiate
1896. Liverpool Institute
1897. Liverpool Collegiate School.
1898.        do.
1899. Liverpool Institute.
1900. Liverpool Collegiate School.
1901.        do.
1902.        do.
1903.        do.
1904. Liverpool Institute.
1905.        do.
1906. Wallasey Grammar School.
1907. Liverpool Institute.
1908. Liverpool Collegiate School.
1909. Birkenhead Institute.
1910. Liverpool Institute.
1911.        do.
1912.        do.
1913. Liverpool Collegiate School.
1914.        do.
1915. Liverpool Institute.
1916. Liverpool Collegiate School.
1917. Liverpool Institute.
1918. Liverpool Catholic Institute.
1919.        do.
1920. St. Francis Xavier's.
1921. Liverpool Collegiate School.
1922.        do.
1923. St. Edward's College.
1924. Liverpool Collegiate School.
1925. St. Francis Xavier's.
1926.        do.
1927. Liverpool Institute.
1928. Wallasey Grammar School.
1929. St. Edward's College.
1930. Bootle Secondary School.
1931. Alsop High School.
1932. do.
1933. Oulton Secondary School.
1934. Quarry Bank High School.
1935. Alsop High School.
1936. King's School Chester
1937.        do
1938. The Collegiate
1939. ——
1940. The Institute (beat SFX 2-0)

WINNERS OF THE SENIOR SHIELD, 1942, LIVERPOOL AND DISTRICT SECONDARY SCHOOLS.

*Standing:*—D. MOLONEY, T. LEDDY, J. FITZPATRICK, A. HORAN.
*Sitting:*—P. GILL, E. O'CONNOR, F. J. DUNN, R. STRAUCH, B. WAH.
*On Ground:*—R. LAPPIN, J. KANE.

*Winners 1942*

*Shield winners in the 1920s.*
*Les Bailey standing on extreme left.*

THE WINNERS OF THE SENIOR SHIELD
MARCH, 1950

*Winners 1950*

1942. St. Francis Xavier's (beat Quarry B. 4-0)

1943. St. Francis Xavier's (beat Institute 3-1)

1944. Prescot

1945. Quarry Bank

1946. Alsop

1947. St. Francis Xavier's (beat Alsop 2-0)

1948. The Institute (beat SFX 1-0)

1949. Bootle Grammar

1950. St. Fr. Xavier's ( beat Collegiate 4-3)

1951. Bootle GS

1952.  do

1953. The Institute

1954. Quarry Bank

1955. Liverpool Institute

1956. Quarry Bank (beat SFX 5-1)

1957. Collegiate

1958. Holt & Prescot

1959/60/61 Prescot (beat SFX 4-2 1960)

1962 /63 De La Salle

1964. Prescot

1965. Holt

1966. Prescot

1967. Prescot

1968. The Collegiate

1969. Ruffwood

1970. Holt

1971. St. Francis Xavier's (beat West Derby 6-1)

1972. Prescot

1973/74 De La Salle

1975. St. Francis Xavier's & St Kevin's

1976. St. Francis Xavier's

1977. Ruffwood & Prescot

1978. St. Margaret's & De La Salle

1979  Bluecoat

1980. Cardinal Allen & De La Salle

1981/82. De La Salle

1983 De La Salle/Bluecoat

1984/85/86  De La Salle

1987 St. Francis Xavier's (beat St. Margaret's 3-1)

1988 /89 De La Salle

1990-92 Records blank

1993 Bluecoat

1994 Birkenhead 6th Form College

1995 All Saints

1996 Blank

1997 Knowsley Community College

1998 Carmel college

1999 Bluecoat/ Hugh Baird College

2000 Bluecoat

2001 St. Francis Xavier's        (see Mag. May 1924 p. 97 and engravings on the trophy  for partial lists.)

FIRST ELEVEN 1970-71
*Back Row (l.-r.):* P. Jones, P. Roach, A. O'Leary, W. Quirk, D. Moore, J. Cotter, J. Burke, J. Weston, S. King
*Front Row (l.-r.):* K. Stoddart, K. Vaughan, T. Starkey, A. Fernandez (*Capt.*), P. Gibney, C. Corkhill

*Senior Shield Winners 1971*

*Senior Shield Winners 1976*

FIRST ELEVEN SENIOR SHIELD WINNERS 1987
Standing (L to R) N. O'Hare, F. Ryan, A. Tabberner, J. Williams, A. O'Hare, I. Falshaw
S. Fallon, S. Burke, P. Quigley, J. Graham, P. Bedson, Mr. T. Brophy

*Senior Shield Winners 1987*

**Winners of the Junior Shield**   Presented by Liverpool F.C., 1916,

| | |
|---|---|
| 1916 | Birkenhead Institute |
| 1916-17 | Catholic Institute |
| 1917/18/19 | Cath. Inst. & L'pool Inst. |
| 1920 | Bootle Secondary School. |
| 1921 | St. Edward's. |
| 1922 | St. Francis Xavier's |
| 1923 | Birkenhead Institute |
| 1924 | St. Francis Xavier's. |

1925, 1927, 1937  St. Francis Xavier's
1944, 1951, 1959      do

1925- 74 Full records not available

1975 De la Salle
1976 Woodchurch
1977 Savio.
1978 Collegiate.
1979 Cardinal Godfrey
1980 Brookfield
1981 St. Mary's( Wallasey) Bluecoat.
1982  St. Francis Xavier's
1983  Savio.
1984  St. Francis Xavier's
1985/86  Savio.
1987 De la Salle.
1988 Our Lady of Fatima
1989 Savio / De la Salle
1990 De la Salle
1991 St. Wilfrid's
1992 Savio
1993 Campion
1994 Gateacre
1995 Bluecoat
1996 Cardinal Heenan
1997 St. Francis  Xavier's
1998/99 Bluecoat
2000 St. Francis Xavier's
2001 Bluecoat

*Ruane, Iliff, Murphy, Worrall, Fitzgibbon,
Scott, Atherton, Grisewood, Hassett, O'Connor, Heery, Blundell*

*Second XI 1947-48*

THE WINNERS OF THE JUNIOR SHIELD
MARCH, 1951

*Junior Shield Winners 1951*

**Cricket and Tennis**

THE FIRST ELEVEN, 1962
*Standing :* J. Thornhill (*scorer*), M. Best, C. Dunn, E. McNerney, D. Kirwan, A. Stanfield, P. Langton
*Sitting :* J. Harrison, M. F. Cogley, M. Redmond (*Captain*), D. Reynolds, J. Halsall, (*Absent* P. Bailey)

THE TENNIS TEAM
*Standing :* M. G. Forth 4B, J. B. Atherton S2, T. M. Powell M1, J. M. Fernandez S2, G. J. Wilson M1
*Sitting :* M. J. Hardman S2, E. D. O'Neill M2 (*Captain*), M. F. Cogley C3

*1962*

FIRST ELEVEN, 1960
A. Boyle, T. Rotherham, J. Harrison, B. McGuinness, F. McNerney, P. Halsall, C. Byron
J. Giles, A. Dunn (*Captain*), M. Redmond, S. Grue

*1960*

*Three of the best Magazine photos of the First XI Cricket Team/Tennis*

**The Scratch Eights**

In May 1917, since the weather made cricket impossible, a competition called The Scratch Eights was inaugurated. The names of those boys wishing to take part were put in a hat, and teams of eight were drawn. Games were played in the playground, fifteen minutes each way, at lunchtime. At the end of each round the names went into a hat and new teams were drawn, till two teams contested the Final.

The Scratch Eights Competition, revived in 1956, was won by the Middlehurst Eight. Played again in 1957, the winner was the P. Duffy Eight. But there is no magazine entry subsequently. This report is from the 1956 Magazine, p.47. The Eights continued to be played till the College moved to Woolton in 1961.

**Scratch Eights Competition**

For one reason or another traditions die out and often it is the good ones that do the dying. Occasionally, like the Phoenix from the ashes, they rise again, and this year it was the Scratch Eights bird that emulated its more illustrious predecessor, bringing improvised goal-posts, the sound of the whistle, the cries of spectators and the watchful eyes of the staff to the playground, at the unwonted hour of 1.35.

Teams of eight, made up of a mixed bag from Second to Sixth Form boys and captained by a member of lst or 2nd XI, took part in a knockout competition played ten minutes each way, while prefects sought to control the human touchline on each side.

Few will deny that many of the games were exciting, with the younger element by no means overawed by the unusual presence of their elders in association and opposition. Accidents were very few and all were slight, football was varied in standard but invariably exciting, with many an entertaining and amusing struggle between even sides. Few, we suspect, supported the eventual winners, Middlehurst's VIII, for loyalties were fairly evenly divided and support seemed centred on class representatives rather than the team for which they played.

Was the competition a success? We think so, if for one reason only - it was enjoyed by all who took part and by many who did not (we suspect quite a few of these will be taking part next year!) but by none more than the members of the winning team who found themselves possessors of very welcome prizes.

Lest it be thought the First Forms were left out of all the fun, suffice it to say that their Sittingdown Football contest in the warmth indoors brought medals (!) to the winners.

On the surface, the Scratch Eights Competition might seem to be but a moderately pleasant way of shortening a long dinner-break: but it may well do more than that, for it links the School in friendly competition as few other enterprises do and, as such, is a force for unity and a fosterer of the good spirit we are so happy to notice throughout the College. May its revival be sustained, may it become still more popular with those for whom it is intended - the boys from 12 to 18.

## Other Sports

The list of sports played is, of course, much longer than this. The Boxing Club was started - or revived - in 1920 by Fr. Woodlock, an enthusiast for the sport. It flourished until he retired in 1937, and was revived again by Fr. Pearson and Fr. Earle in 1947. Swimming suffered until 1961 from want of a pool of its own. It became an important part of the College sports programme when it moved to Woolton with its own swimming-bath.

Athletics, largely a summer and a minority interest for many years, nonetheless attracted enthusiastic participants and in recent years has engaged more and more pupils in an increasing number of meetings.

Pupils can also choose from water polo, cross country, golf, squash, tennis, basketball, volleyball, and gymnastics. School clubs, school trips, and outside links with primary schools add to the variety of the Department's activities, which is all complemented by regular representative honours.

*Trophies won by the College teams 2000-2001, including the Senior Shield*

The College boasts a number of successful footballers. J. Healy (OX) played as an amateur for England in 1908. Frank Checkland, a teacher here for 40 years, played as full-back for Liverpool in 1921, the season the team won the Championship; afterwards he played for Tranmere. Sammy Lee, a Liverpool and England player, needs no introduction here; and John Harding (OX 1955) captained Oxford, Pegasus, and Army teams and played for England as an amateur international between 1959 and 1965. His brother, David (1961), played professional football for Wrexham and Preston; he then emigrated and played for Australia in two World Cups in 1974 and 1978. Ian Falshaw (OX 1987) captained Oxford at football. Joe Parker (OX 1994) played for Oxford at both football and cricket in the 1990s. Peter Sweeney and John Harding (Oxford), Mike Bushell (Cambridge) played regularly in the University First Eleven. Inevitably questions will be asked about the failure to deal with other subjects such as History, English, Geography, Classics, Modern Languages, Business Studies, Technology and Art. To list them is to answer the complaint. The successes pupils have achieved in these subjects and the teachers responsible are regularly celebrated in the College Magazine. That will have to do, Putty Grace notwithstanding.

**FOOTBALL REPRESENTATIVE HONOURS 1994-95**

*Football 1994-95 Representative Honours: Left to Right: David Barnicle, Liverpool U14; Simon Clarke, Merseyside U19, Liverpool U19; Lee Lunt, Merseyside U19, Liverpool U19; Paul Jackson, Merseyside U19, Liverpool U19; Steven Duggan, Liverpool U15; Martin Battle, Liverpool U15; Lee Andrews, Liverpool U15; Michael Ness, Liverpool U15. Front: Michael O'Brien, England U15, Liverpool U15.*

*Chapter 7*

# **S**couse

It is alleged that George Ridge (teacher 1948-1983) arranged for a boy with a pronounced stutter to attend a Speech Therapy Class during the summer holidays. On the first day of the Autumn term, George asked the lad how it had gone. He replied: "Well, Sir, I can say 'Peter Piper picked a peck of pickled pepper.' b-b-b-but it's t-t-t-t-t-terribly d-d-difficult to work it into a c-c-c-conversation."

In researching this book many such nuggets have turned up, which are difficult to weave into an impersonal history. Some of them are gems: it would be a shame to leave them languishing, unshared, in the notes. Others are items of interest or anecdotes which do not easily fit into the main body of the book. I include them in this chapter under the heading of Scouse - as an infinitely variable stew flavoured with a salt that is peculiarly Liverpudlian.

The last chapter has undoubtedly been the most difficult to write. Up till now the book has been dealing largely with matters of record. I do not claim that everything so far written can be supported by chapter and verse, but available sources - letters, files, newspaper reports, articles, books, chronicles, archive material and interviews - have all been used at least as a starting point. The first six chapters could not have been written without them. I can only hope that my extrapolations and assumptions - my leaps in the gloaming - do not strike too many people as totally arbitrary and without foundation.

Chapter 7 moves me on to new ground: the ingredients thrown into this pot are personal and impressionistic. A juxtaposition of suggestions, opinions, and surmises from many sources - recollections of events which, in most cases, happened - or did not happen - many years ago; some now distorted by time, but, it is hoped, kept honest by a judicious admixture of supporting evidence from the College Magazine. Things here, as generally throughout the book, are biased in the direction of Salisbury Street, because I was educated there and because most of the people who have responded to my request for copy were pupils there, too.

Inevitably viewpoints differ. The people I am talking abut here are mostly Salisbury-Street-educated boys.Their recollections have fallen into two obvious groups. One group - much the larger - consists of academically successful OXs who look back on their time at College with some affection. They are prepared to make allowances for some of the more negative, even brutal, aspects of their time at school, which they admit were very real.

Contributors to the second group, whom I have contacted, or who have rung or written to me, have no such rosy account to give of their experiences. They complain of ill-treatment, of beatings, petty restrictions, and worse. They demand that there be no whitewash of persons or events. It is ominous that one particular member of the staff regularly occurs as the target of this group: more than once it has been suggested that he should not be granted the protection of 'Nil nisi bonum de mortuis'. From first form to fifth form they detected - mostly in retrospect - an elitism in the classroom, in sport, in school activities, in the prefect system, in any and every sort of pupil engagement and even in the character of teacher-pupil relationship offered to some boys, but not to others.

Whilst I hope that in what follows I have given due consideration to the full range of these experiences, it is not my intention to blacken reputations further on the basis of hearsay and uncorroborated accounts; nor to protect anyone by whitewashing the past. Not too much purpose would be served, if I went into detail. I can only hope that only a few will consider that truth has suffered thereby.

There were undoubtedly pockets of petty crime and minor vice in the school in Salisbury Street. Items would occasionally go missing from the basement cloakroom, which doubled up as lavatory and meeting place: the scent of cigarettes often hung in the air at the cubicle end. (Mr Crook, maths teacher, once threw a large jug of water over the door of one cubicle, soaking the occupant. He claimed he saw smoke and thought there must be a fire.) Tattered copies of Hank Jansen novels - the porn of its time, but which these days would unhesitatingly be accepted by Mills and Boon - were furtively passed around the yard. Nevertheless, I do not recall any obvious atmosphere of deep-seated badness. It is hard to believe that bullying was totally non-existent amongst the boys - particularly with the official and legalized bullying of the ferula as an example. But no one seems to recollect pupil-on-pupil bullying as looming large, or at least no one who has been in contact with me. Several consider it to have been absent entirely. I am prepared to be disabused of the idea that this is in fact an accurate description.

The College throughout its existence has been less than perfect; more so for some than for others. For some, any perfections there might have been were buried deep enough to be undetectable. Presumably one group is not entirely right and the other group entirely wrong. I hope that this chapter, like a pan of good scouse, has sufficient to cater for all appetites. Some readers will cry 'Not so much scouse as blind scouse'. Well, if anyone finds parts indigestible, he should leave it on the side of the plate and savour such bits as he finds tasty. If this proves beyond him, he is probably looking for a different book, based on a very different research approach, and with very different intentions.

Before I started writing, I extended an open invitation to Old Xaverians to submit accounts of their memories of SFX, good, bad, funny or sad. Many of these submissions acted as catalysts or leavening in writing the main body of the text, without necessarily being accorded a direct accreditation. Other submissions defied categorization. They were all gratefully received and there is no doubt that they convey much of the attitudes, wit, and character of a wide spectrum of past pupils and teachers. It would be unfortunate if they were to be lost to history.

This representative selection makes up the farrago, the hodge-podge, the charivari that is Chapter 7. I have made no attempt to organize, categorize, or sterilize them. I have adopted a pick-and-mix strategy: relish what you like, disregard what you find unpalatable. Accounts, photographs, anecdotes, obituaries and records of one kind or another, are presented with the minimum of editorial comment. The footnotes I call Trivia at the end of several sections I have been advised to cut out as being too trivial. Rightly or wrongly I am ignoring this advice.

I also received a great number of photographs and I have interspersed these with the stories to complete a picture of life in the College. Like the anecdotes, the pictures vary: some are included on their own merits, some because it is all I have of that period, whereas others have earned their place as historical records of the people, the events and the achievements of 160 years of St Francis Xavier's College.

It cannot be denied that, love it or hate it, the College has left its mark or scars on most of its alumni.

## a. The Ferula

No excuse need be given for starting with the ferula. It may be going too far to describe the ferula as a surrogate headmaster, but it personified Authority for a good part of the College's history as nothing else did and it is an abiding memory for too many Old Xaverians not to be given pride of place here.

The ferula is defined in the dictionary as 'an instrument of punishment, esp a flat ruler'. The ferula used at SFX and in all Jesuit schools was reputed to be a piece of whalebone wrapped in rubber. In point of fact it was some sort of composition, pliant and flexible, about a foot long or slightly less. As can be seen from the pictures, some were moulded or shaped. Some pupils recall a  narrowing at one end, the better to fit into the hand. And let's be clear from the outset - it hurt.  It could be very painful indeed, depending on who was administering the punishment.

*A ferula in the archives at Stonyhurst*

If the teacher judged that an offence had been committed, he wrote out a bill. He gave the offender a small piece of paper - name, date, number of ferulas, the offence and teacher's signature. Ferulas usually came in 3s, 6s, 9s, or 12s. Twice 9 and even twice 12 were not unheard of. (A pupil in 5S in 1953, Bill Bewley, received twice 12 for knocking Fr. Neylan to the ground; he had hurled a gym bag at some speed through the classroom door, as the good father was entering. Six on the right hand, six on the left, six on the right, six on the left. Boys other than Bill judged these ferulas to have been well worth it. It should be noted that Fr. Neylan was exempt from the system. He ordered ferulas, administered them, and never wrote a bill). It was an essential part of the system that the pupil took the bill to be counter-signed by the Prefect of Discipline or the appropriate Head of Upper, Middle or Lower School before the visit to the book office - 'a crude Appellate Tribunal,' as one OX describes it. Then at Salisbury Street the offender would go for

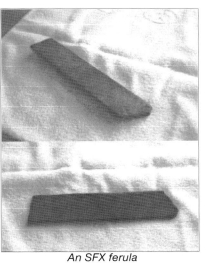
*An SFX ferula*
*(kept by George Ridge)*

punishment to the place of execution: 5A classroom upstairs, then the Book Office on the first floor and in later years to the Gym Office. Punishment was not only approved but sometimes inflicted by the Prefect of Discipline, although at SFX under Fr. Woodlock and Fr. Neylan the Scholastics were usually assigned this particular task.

More than one ex-teacher has pointed out the dangers of judging the past by the standards of later times, and there are places where these notes have carelessly veered in that direction. The importance of putting any system into the context of its times must be acknowledged. Attitudes to corporal punishment changed. One teacher wrote that the system under Fr. Harris would have been regarded as intolerable in the College of Fr. Neylan. Just as the punishment regime of Fr. Neylan compares unfavourably with that at Woolton in the 1970s. In 1942 Putty Grace could write in the magazine that 'Nowadays a boy may pass his eight years or so at the College without being incommoded in this way (ferulas) even once.'

For particularly meritorious work or behaviour a red bill was issued. Technically this could be used to cancel out an ordinary bill, but only for an offence in the same category. The two categories were work or behaviour. This meant that, since most red bills were given for good work, the opportunities for redemptions were few and far between. In any case red bills were a pretty rare phenomenon.

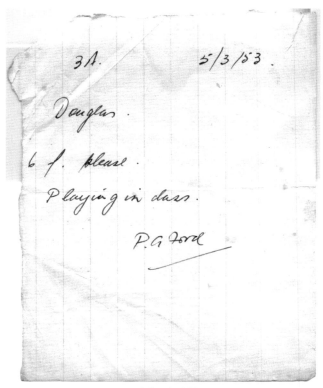

*A ferula bill.*

The Ratio Studiorum and then the commentaries on it written in the eighteenth century talk about the basis for authority in the classroom. The teacher should have esteem and affection for the pupil. The pupil should have a fear for the teacher - but this was to be a timor reverentialis , not timor servilis. That is the respect of a child not the fear of a slave. Moderation was enjoined in all cases. The whole issue of punishment was debated and laid out in clear terms. The restricted use of corporal punishment and its 'last resort' nature seem to have been the order of the day in the seventeenth and eighteenth centuries. (Schwickerath 1904 p. 614). But things changed in the very different climate of the nineteenth century.

Any attempt to discuss corporal punishment and its use at SFX is fraught with difficulties. No punishment books seem to have survived, which might have provided some objective evidence. But there is sufficient comment - mainly in the Xaverian - to justify a few harsh words about Fr. Harris and Fr. McHale. A more severe regime of physical punishment - often in public - would appear to date from the arrival of Fr. Harris in 1866. His successors seem to have been less addicted to the ferula, but the appointment of Fr. McHale in 1898 heralded a return to boy-beating on a scale

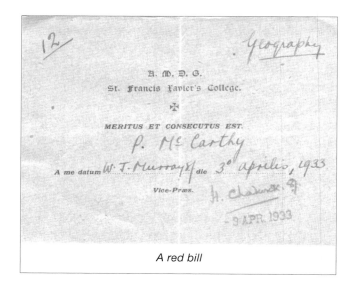

*A red bill*

that was excessive even for the day. The boys cheered uncharitably when it was announced that Fr. McHale had died. But he, they will have thought, never dispensed much charity to them. Such judgements, it is emphasized, rely on second and third hand recollections.

During Fr. Woodlock's time Old Xaverians recall a fair amount of corporal punishment, but it does not seem to have been inordinate. Whilst we now have first-hand recollections, it should be noted that such recollections are those of a very small handful of people. Nonetheless, Fr. Woodlock's reputation as a humane and kindly man lends credence to the reports. No school of which he was the Head was ever likely to be labelled cruel and sadistic.

The same could not be said of the College under Fr. Neylan. There is no shortage of Old Xaverians of the 'forties and 'fifties who claim that under Fr. Neylan there was a return to a more illiberal approach. He was ably supported by Fr. Brennan, who joined the staff in 1948 and who was a strong believer in the motivation of fear.

The injustice of being beaten for failing to understand work still rankles with some. After all whose job was it to see that the pupils did understand? Misbehave and get caught - one could see the justice in what happened next. But ferulas for wrong or poor work - boys too often saw that as unfair. Old Xaverians still vividly remember the Maths teacher, Beaky Jones, distributing homework books. The book was held up and shaken to see if a bill dropped out. Not for untidy work or incorrectly laid out work, but for getting fewer than 7 sums right out of 10. Lay staff like "Beaky" Jones and Putty Grace as well as the Jesuits had recourse to The Man, as one teacher customarily referred to the allocation of ferulas.

> 'A brutal and sadistic regime of teachers and Jesuits whose only answer to any problem concerning a boy was THE FERULA'                                                                    1945.

> 'I recall some boys crying even before they had been thrashed.'                                1951

> 'The pain was excruciating.. palms of the hands bright red and swollen.' 'Severe and repressive discipline.'                                                                                        1943

> 'I was given 6 ferulas three days running for making mistakes in the use of the Greek Middle Voice - without any attempt to explain what I was doing wrong.'                       1944

> 'Have a memory of a senior boy going into the Book Office as I came out. He shuffled a pile of ferula bills, held them out to the Scholastic on duty with the memorable words "Pick a card!"
>                                                                                          1941

> 'In the past many people regarded corporal punishment as a teaching aid. At the time when child-centred education was fashionable, one Jesuit said " Our job is to flog it in, not to draw it out.' Nor was he thought to have been speaking figuratively.

One Old Xav has written to claim the record for the number ferulas in one term - 106. Any challengers? Another got nine bills in a week. Yet another received two bills from different masters inside ten minutes. He protested to the second master that he already had one bill that morning 'and it was only ten past nine.' The teacher relented and said ' All right, I'll put tomorrow's date on mine'!

This system of postponed punishment is often contrasted favourably with the casual, instant and often arbitrary use of corporal punishment in schools such as St. Edward's. 'The Jesuit disciplinary system was more civilized than the cane-beating one got at the Christian Brothers' schools' (1941) - by a pupil who attended both. But amongst those pupils who attended College in Fr. Neylan's time there is a feeling of an unnecessarily cruel system - used probably by only a small number of staff, but with an impact way beyond their numbers. After all there were staff who never gave ferulas, and others who only gave it for serious misbehaviour. They unfortunately get tarred with the same brush. The final - hypocritical ? - words of the Inspectors' Report for 1953 read 'there was some discussion on the extent to which corporal punishment was used in the School. Fr. Neylan agreed with the Inspector that it might be more effective if used less often.' It must be left to people in a better position to comment on the disciplinary system at the College in the years that followed. Fr. Warner's period as Headmaster seems to have ushered in a more gentle regime, where corporal punishment was concerned. There was a return to much stricter punishment practices under Fr. Doyle, although that may more rightly be put down to Fr. McMorrow's influence. Fr. McMorrow, the teacher in charge of discipline, was thought to be very severe when it came to corporal punishment. At Benediction, if the hymn was the familiar one, the boys would sing :-

Lord, for McMorrow and his needs
we do not pray.
Keep me, my God, from meeting him,
Just for today.

But he was probably compassion itself, compared with Fr. Harris and Fr. McHale and the systems they operated a hundred years before him.

At Woolton up to 1974 the College remained under the Jesuits. Fr. Doyle and Fr. McMorrow maintained the system, but there was considerable scaling down in the use of corporal punishment. After the Jesuits left, although the system was retained, many members of staff never used it. Then in 1983 corporal punishment was abandoned altogether, and shortly after that it was prohibited by law.

# Prefects of Studies : 1842 - 1919

Aut disce aut discede
  (written over classroom door after a year of poor results in the 1860s)

Only those Prefects of Studies who held the post for more than two years are listed here. The information is taken from The Xaverian May 1890.

| | |
|---|---|
| 1844 - 1852 | Fr. J. Johnson (absent in 1848) |
| 1853 - 1856 | Fr. Collyns |
| 1857 - 1858 | Mr. R. Payne (and 1864 -1865) |
| 1866 - 1874 | Fr. Harris |
| 1876 - 1879 | Fr. Gerard |
| 1882 - 1885 | Fr. R. Cardwell |
| 1886 - 1888 | Fr. Tarleton |
| 1889 - 1897 | Fr. Donnelly |
| 1898 - 1910 | Fr. McHale |
| 1910 - 1915 | Fr. J. Bridge |
| 1915 - 1919 | Fr. H. Irwin |

Between 1842 and 1865 there were seven Prefects of Studies. Three served for one year only. Four others, Fr. Johnson, Fr. Collyns, and Fr. Payne all held the office for at least four years. From such evidence as there is, they seem to have been humane, popular and well-liked - sound teachers, if in some cases recollected as demanding - although kindly recollected. The Xaverian records that for one whole year in the 1860s the ferula was hardly used and that a report card system successfully took its place. 'A well got-up card works admirably. The cards have almost done away with ferulas and penances. During the whole year we have had not one case of disobedience nor one case of serious quarrelling.' (NB. this followed an intervention in 1867 by Fr. Porter, who ordered that the use of the ferula was to be reduced. He suppressed it all together for one month).

(Letters and Notices 1867 p. 36).

*Fr. Harris*

Fr. Harris came in 1865 and is usually credited with turning a faltering College round, increasing the numbers and setting it on the road to permanent success. But he is also credited with a different sort of innovation - the use of fear to obtain the pupils' co-operation. Fr. Harris, it was said, had come to the conclusion early that no useful purpose was served by postponing all punishment until the next world. Discipline became spartan. His notices included ' Any boy found standing still or loitering on the penance walk will be liable for 12 ferulas.'

After a snowball fight with the Collegiate in 1871, Fr. Harris judged that the College had been disgraced. He proposed to punish the whole school. But he was prepared to exempt any boy as follows:

> 'If any scholar can in the sight of God and his own conscience truly and sincerely and honestly declare that during the last six months he has not broken the College regulations in the street - viz that he has not been guilty of violent running, knocking on doors, ringing at bells and then running away, playing with and talking to, fighting with and quarrelling with street boys, keeping low company, throwing stones, mud, snow-balls, tossing other boys' caps about the street, running against persons, hustling them, romping with his school companions, running into shops - then he should hand in his name to Fr. Harris.'

It is possible that accounts of him as a strong disciplinarian have clouded his virtues as a teacher and a priest. The Xaverian of January 1893, lending some balance, describes Fr. Harris in glowing terms. '..a remarkable man... a powerful preacher...he found the College somewhat of a weakling; he left it crowned with the strength of a vigourous and lusty prime. Whole-souled devotion to his work...truly a labour of love.. a real and original educator, and a good and worthy priest and religious.' And there are certainly plenty of references to his popularity with the boys - even if they also feared him. It should be added that he was a publicist extraordinary who kept the name of the College in the Liverpool public eye. In 1869 he advertised 30 times in the Daily Post, 10 times in the Liverpool Mercury, 14 times in the Daily Courier, and 4 times in the Catholic Northern Press. In 1870 the Proclamation was held in St George's Hall with over 1000 people in the audience. He admitted non-Catholics to the College, charged parents according to means (with the Jesuits paying the fees of the poorest) and introduced a programme of home visits.

Fr. Gerard and Fr. Donnelly followed Harris. They seem to have been more in the mould of the earlier Prefects of Studies. Perhaps they were stricter in the demands they made on their pupils, since numbers now were much larger and the curriculum more extensive. Their contribution to the establishment of a strong science department has been detailed earlier.

The College now had such support from the Old Boys and the parents that at the Proclamation of 1888 there were 3000 people crammed into the College Hall. The Association of Old Xaverians was founded in the autumn of 1884, and it soon had debating, football, cricket, dramatic and cycling clubs. It took an active part in promoting the College and it wielded an influence that it has perhaps not had since.

*SFX 1887 Joseph Unsworth 4th from left.*
*Alexander Keogh 2nd from right*

*SFX class of 1883-84 c.*

*Masters at SFX 1896*
*Standing : C. Bert, C. Cooksey, A. Kopp, Ph. George*
*Seated   : T. White, L. Mooney, F. Parry, R. Quick*

In Fr. McHale (1898 - 1910) there was a return to the stern discipline of Fr. Harris. When he died, one obituary had it that 'he treated no one with more severity than himself'. His reputation was such that some of his pupils would have doubted how that could be.

At the General Inspection of 1904 Fr. McHale objected to one of the criticisms of a member of staff. The inspector had written 'The class is somewhat cowed by the master who rated and set impositions with an excessive vigour'. Fr. McHale persuaded him to change it to 'The class is somewhat disheartened by reproofs and impositions to which the master freely resorted'. Another inspector objected to a master who let pass without correction or even observation a pupil who had written "Poverty in this world is a safe and sure guide to Heaven", and "Laughter is a kind of an imperfection in the nature of man".

His period of office was noted for improved academic results and for the fact that he encouraged the College to play football games against other schools. For the record, the College's first 'out' match was in 1898 against HMS Conway Training Ship moored in the Mersey. We lost 7-1. But between 1908 and 1910 the College First Eleven played 54 games and won 51 of them.

Fr. McHale was very highly regarded all over the city and he generated such a spirit of work and enterprise that his obituary felt justified in claiming that 'after three years of his control SFX was looked upon as the most successful school not merely in Liverpool, but also in England.' !

*' V Classical 1910-11 Football Team'*

Some statistics from the HMI Inspection of 1915 will be of interest.

---

**Public Record Office KEW . Ed 109/3009.    1915 Inspection**

**Statistics of Pupils.**

---

9. Actual  FIGURES  at date of inspection :
(a) Total number of boys (including 5 Bursars), 367 (all Day Scholars).

(b) Distribution of boys according to their age on 31 July 1914

| Age | Number | Age | Number | |
|---|---|---|---|---|
| Under 9 | 17 | 14 | 55 | |
| 9 | 17 | 15 | 41 | |
| 10 | 32 | 16 | 16 | |
| 11 | 36 | 17 | 7 | |
| 12 | 65 | 18 | 3 | total 367 |
| 13 | 78 | | | |

11. PERCENTAGES based on Returns for School-Year 1913-14

| (a) Class in life from which boys are drawn:- | | b) Areas from which boys are drawn: | |
|---|---|---|---|
| Professional | 14 | Liverpool | 68 |
| Farmers | 2 | Rest of Lancashire | 14 |
| Wholesale Traders | 7 | Rest of England | 17 |
| Retail Traders and Contractors | 29 | Outside England | 1 |
| Clerks and Commercial Agents | 16 | | |
| Public Service | 7 | | |
| Domestic Service, postmen etc. | 4 | | |
| Artisans | 13 | | |
| Labourers | 7 | | |
| Occupation none or unknown - | I | | |

*Form 1B 1918 (Joe Lane end of second row left, Jack Lane second row end right)*

# The Woodlock Years : 1919 - 1937

The history of the College between the wars and the life of Fr. Woodlock are inextricably entwined.

*Fr. Woodlock*

*Fr. Woodlock and Fr. McCann*

From all accounts Fr. Woodlock was an extraordinary Headmaster, an extraordinary teacher, and an individual with a unique combination of qualities. Old Xavs, now in their eighties, still consider themselves fortunate to have been his pupils. Appreciations, notices and obituaries all speak of a gifted, devoted and approachable priest, yet with it all modest and unassuming. Fr. Woodlock left abiding witnesses to his personality and strength of character  - even more so than Fr. Harris.

The records show that he not only stood physically taller than all the other Prefects of Studies - he was well over six foot - but intellectually he seems to have had no match. Before coming to the College he had taken firsts in Mods and Greats at Oxford, and throughout his life he applied himself to a wide range of academic pursuits.

His colleagues recall that Fr. Woodlock brought a spirit of youthfulness, spontaneity and simplicity to all the pursuits he engaged in - and they were many. Astronomy - the astronomical telescope in his room became a communal possession; he worked with Fr. Rowland in the observatory at Stonyhurst. A keen photographer - his action photos of College activities were very impressive. He was a consummate fisherman, an expert in manufacturing as well as casting a trout fly. He was active and proficient in any number of sports; his skating was said to be of international standard. All  his life he coached football and cricket teams with the zest of a young man. He counted differential calculus (cultivated while at the Front), crossword puzzles, and philosophy amongst his spare time interests. The great classical authors were his guides, philosophers and friends. He engaged in X-ray work. He was a bird-watcher. Boxing, butterflies and snakes - in these fields he was more than just an amateur; he bred snakes; he had articles published in the Journal of Genetics; and he had a standing invitation to the boxing matches at Liverpool Stadium.

He took up the game of bridge late in life and became an expert on the rules. He had served as a chaplain in the First World War, going missing behind German lines at one point, but managing to escape. In the 1930s - prescient as ever - he had a letter in the Times about fox hunting in which he made some moral and theological observations about the sanctity of life; he received letters of commendation in reply from people on both sides of the argument.

But, for all Fr. Woodlock's accomplishments, pride and arrogance, which in him of all people might have been completely lacking.  'For gladly would he learn and gladly teach', as someone said of him. He knew every boy in the school by name and all the details of his failures and achievements. 'He was utterly devoted to his boys.....noted for his personal interest in the boys for whose schooling he was responsible.' He taught Latin in particular with 'phenomenal success' year after year. As Head 'his yoke was sweet and his burden light'; he gave a master a freehand to teach as he liked. He had an immense vitality and enthusiasm and the great gift of communicating this enthusiasm to others.

What a blessing it must have been to have had him as a teacher and a headmaster!

*Frank Hart (later school captain 1937-1938) talks to himself ( one of Fr. Woodlock's trick photographs)*

*A. M. D. G.*

# St. Francis Xavier's College,

## LIVERPOOL.

# Solemn Requiem Mass

### AND

# Unveiling of the War Memorial

### IN THE COLLEGE HALL

### BY

## VERY REV. FATHER RECTOR

### (Rev. James Bridge, S.J.)

**Saturday, December 11th, 1920, at 10 a.m.**

*Unveiling of the War Memorial December 1920*

About one thousand Old Xaverians fought in the War, and over 150 were killed.

Names of dead listed at the unveiling

Privates.

| | | | | | |
|---|---|---|---|---|---|
| A. Birchall | J. Blundell | A. Booth | B. Bradley | A. Breen | F. X Brierton |
| C. V, Brown | P. B. Burd | P, J. Byrne | F. Carew | J. Carroll | J. Caulfield |
| F. Chew | J. E. Clague | L. Conroy | A. Costello | J. Cummings | F. W. Dobson |
| J. Doyle | W. Duffy | F. Dunn | C. W. Fitzgerald | J. Fitzgerald | H. Garnett |
| T. Gilgan | T. Green | A. Harris | A. Hudson | H. Keegan | P.J. Kennedy |
| W. Kenny | R. Kiernan | G. Killikelly | A. Lea | W. J. Lee | A. Lynch |
| H. Lovett | B Lowe | G. Marley | F. McCann | E. McCormick | J.J. McGrath |
| G. McGuinness | W. McMahon | J. Morley | C. Murphy | E. Musgrave | M. O'Connor |
| A. O'Halloran | J. Partridge | A. de la Planque | P. G. Powell | W. Powell | E Roberts |
| L. Roche | P. Robinson | H. Segar | J. Schwenter | A. J. Sheridan | W. Shorthall |
| A. F. Smith | H. Sparrow | T Suarez | J. Swift | J.B. Thomas | F Toolan |
| F. Trist | J. Turner | R. G. Wall | Paul White | C Wilcock | A.Winfield |
| W. Wrigley | | | | | |

Engineer J. Connolly    M. O'Brien R.N.   Bonner R.N.V.R.
J. Kelly, R.N.V.R        Cadet F. Talbot   Lieut. R. Morgan, R. N.R.
Lieut. J. Quinn R.N.A.S. C. Boyland R.N.A.S.

**R. I. P.**

The Xaverian 1919 February reports : 'One of our College boys joined up to fight the Hun before his 16th birthday. He is back again at the College in the 5th Form - is still in khaki, as his demobilization leave is not yet up - and he has two blue chevrons on the sleeve of his tunic. Well done E.D.'

*Rev. J. M. Woodlock, S.J.*

SFX Liverpool Junior B 1922 Miss Carroll's class

*Junior B 1922 Miss Carroll's class*

## Trivia

If he had a fault it was an excessive concern for examination results. But he once said to our class 'you have nothing but your brains, and I am here to make sure you make the best use of them.'     1938

On negative side he had an excessive respect for us pupils. I think he thought we were better than we were. He readily talked about syllogisms to 4b and threw around phrases like "de facto", "post hoc ergo propter hoc", "ipsissima verba", "a priori", and "a posteriori" evidently assuming we would catch on straight away.     1936

*Two boys wearing College caps circa 1933*
*( boy on right is James Heery, later school captain 1935-36*

Once at prize-giving he announced some change or other for which there would have to be a prior trial. He smiled and said, 'Fiat experimentum in corpore vili'. Then he paused, remembering his audience, and said, 'Which roughly translated means "try it on the dog" '.     1935

I was with him in his room on one occasion. He was doing a Latin crossword. The stages were these:- trick Latin, find trick English, get back to trick Latin. He genuinely thought I might lend him a hand. I could not have been higher up the school than, maybe, 5a. He would not have been kidding me.     1936

He once told me he could do four things at the same time. He could, during a storm, read his office, count the lightning flashes, estimate the intervals and determine the rate of movement.     1937

The last time I visited him, he stopped at the foot of the stairs, hardly able to breathe, and said,'You will remember getting a stitch when running. That was because you had drawn in too much oxygen. I'm going to try that and breathe without moving until I feel dizzy. Then I should have enough oxygen to get me up in one go'. As far as I can remember it worked perfectly. 1946

In a religious doctrine lesson in 2B he told us that 'when we are told that Jesus met a certain man on the way down to Jericho, what was meant was an "uncertain" man.' 1933

After the War, that's to say in his old age and very frail, he was engaged in producing a decent English translation of the Aeneid. 1948

The College had been inspected by His Majesty's Inspectors in 1915, and it was inspected again in 1926 and 1937. The Inspectors had a number of criticisms: Fr. Woodlock's policy of appointing Old Boys to the staff - 10 of the laymen in 1937; the 'growing inadequacy of the building' for modern secondary school purposes; and the work of the scholastics - 'insufficiently equipped by training, experience and in some cases knowledge for the tasks given them.' (This contrasts with the Inspectors' comments about the Scholastics after an earlier inspection : ' ..struck by the devotion to their work both in playing with the boys in the field, but also in helping them in evening preparation and in the very careful correction of written work and the preparation of lessons'). A comment was also made about the governing body only meeting once a year. 'The Society is the real Governing Body. The other governors are men of straw - and not very good straw at that.'
Public Records Office, Kew  ED/109/3010 and Ed/109/3011

*Mr Checkland with Class 1935 (?)*

*Mr Jones with IVB 1937*

*Dr Grace with VI Form 1937(?)*

*Annual fixture against Everton 1920s*    *Dixie Dean*

LAST YEAR'S TEAMS.

# Football Match at Melwood, West Derby,

### THURSDAY, MARCH 25th, 1926,

Kick-off 3 p.m.

## St. Francis Xavier's College v Everton F.C.

. . . At the College at 5-30 p.m. . . .

### . . . MENU . . .

Sardines—Jacques Sharp.

Poulet des Joueurs d'Everton.

Jambon à la Banks.

Langue d' Alec. Troup.

Cuff's Bœuf Anglais.

Sawyer's Spring Salade.

Gelées à la Gibbons.

Compote de Fruits de Goodison.

Chedgzoy's Gateaux Melangés.

Delight de Turquish Raitt.

Dixie's Almonds and Dean's Raisins.

Bombe de Bob Irvine.

Les Boissons Mystérieuses de MacDonald.

Cigars.        Cigarettes.        Hardy Annuals.

## Interim

Fr. Brinkworth became Headmaster in 1937, but he only stayed for two years, after which he was transferred as Head to St. Ignatius' in London. He was very highly regarded and those who served under both him and Fr. Neylan have recorded that 'much bigger changes in the general life of the College occurred during Fr. Brinkworth's two-year stay than during the fourteen years under Fr. Neylan.'

# The Fr. Neylan Years : 1939 - 1953

'Fr. Neylan would acknowledge himself a "Laudator temporis acti." He would probably consider that no real contribution (save that of Revelation) had been made to the sum of human knowledge since the time of the Greeks: and that no discovery since that time (except perhaps tobacco) had increased human happiness. His standards were exacting, and any lesser achievement than an Open Major Scholarship might well be greeted as an almost total failure.' College Magazine 1953.

Fr Neylan was born in Clapham in 1895 and educated at Wimbledon College between 1904 and 1912, and then Oxford. He taught at Wimbledon and Stonyhurst before coming to SFX in 1939.

Formally, Fr. Neylan is associated with three developments in the life of the College in the 1940s. The Evacuation to North Wales in 1939, the purchase of the new site in Woolton, and the introduction of Greek to the curriculum. Informally, this period is remembered

REV. W. J. NEYLAN, S.J.
HEADMASTER 1939-1953

by many Old Xaverians for the severity and strictness of the discipline, in which the ferula figured too frequently for the likes of many. Some people - but not the writer - consider that this is a case of distance lending disenchantment. Fr. Brennan taught Latin under Fr. Neylan. A man in the best traditions of Fr. McHale, he managed to inject an atmosphere of fear and dread into his lessons that for some OXs is still only too vivid.

Fr. Neylan found the Evacuation or 'The Cambrian Captivity', as he liked to call it, very irksome. Parents soon made it plain that they too were not happy and wanted their sons to return home. Everyone was well pleased therefore, when after six months of life in rural Wales the pupils returned en masse - just in time to face the beginning of the worst bombing that Liverpool suffered.

The boys evacuated had been scattered around the district from Prestatyn to Rhyl to Dyserth and St Asaph. The brunt of the administration fell upon the able shoulders of Mr Bailey who was the billeting officer, together with Mr Birmingham and Mr Dunn, helped by Fr. McCann, Fr. Rogers, Fr. McPhillips and Fr. Woodlock. Fr. Neylan was content to leave the administrative and pastoral work to others, as he took up residence in Mia Hall, a large country house outside Rhyl. Here he taught his classics students - with their needs attended to by Elsie Crowney, the College cook, and by Miss Lewis, college secretary. There is no room to go into the details of this adventure. The reader is referred to The College Magazines of 1940 and 1941 for first hand accounts. It is a matter of regret that the many stories people have sent in about their experiences cannot be included here. The College re-opened fully for the summer term on April 11th 1940.

*Boys and Staff at Mia Hall, Dyserth, 1940*

The HMI Reports of 1926 and 1937 had made it plain that the building in Salisbury Street was inadequate for the needs of a modern secondary school. Fr. Woodlock had resisted any idea of a move and wished to extend around Salisbury Street and Haigh Street. (He said at one point that it was educative for outer-city middle-class boys to come into contact daily with the poverty of the inner city). But Fr. Brinkworth, who succeeded Fr. Woodlock in 1937, was persuaded of the need to re-locate and began to look for a suitable property. He tried to buy a six acre site in Wavertree, but that came to nothing. He was then replaced by Fr. Neylan in 1939.

Fr. Neylan set about looking for alternatives. Like Fr. Brinkworth, he considered and rejected sites in West Derby. The proximity of Melwood was an advantage, but no one wanted to enter into competition with St. Edward's, already well-established in the area. No record has been found to show which other districts of Liverpool Fr. Neylan visited, but attention soon focused on Woolton. There is an uncorroborated story that, as he tramped around Woolton investigating possibilities, Fr. Neylan was arrested at one point on suspicion of loitering in the area with intent. The solicitors acting on his behalf (in finding a property) advised him to put an advert in the Liverpool Echo. This was seen by the two ladies, Mrs Burman and Mrs Rubinstein, who owned the High Lee estate (previously owned by Sir Benjamin Johnson), and in the end a deal was done. But it was to be twenty years before the College was to transfer to Woolton.

Greek was re-introduced to the College by Fr. Neylan. It soon became successful and by the end of the 1940s it was more successful than any other subject in terms of university scholarships. This did not happen without criticism and resentment from other members of staff, since it was undoubtedly the case that Fr. Neylan brought irresistible pressure on the brightest pupils to take classics. This was a clear misuse of his position as Head. More than one father told Fr. Neylan that, if his son was to be compelled to take classics in the Sixth Form, he would move him to St. Edward's. Then, and only then, did Fr. Neylan back down. Be that as it may, of the College Oxbridge awards between 1942 and 1953 twelve were in classics, four in history, four in moderns, three in maths and two in science. It should be said that classics was strong in other schools at the time and remained so at SFX long after Fr. Neylan's time. Two SFX candidates who have had offers this year for Oxford for 2002 entry are studying classics.

In 1949 the College won all four of the Intercollegiate prizes. Senior and Junior in Latin and maths. This unique achievement was celebrated with a day's holiday and no doubt a great deal of deserved self-congratulation.

Two class photos from 1949 .

*Mr Britt-Compton with 3B*

*Mr Hornby with 4S*

153

In football, as has been already recorded, the 1940s were the most successful in the College's history, when we won the Senior Shield four times between 1941 and 1949.

*The Chicks 1946-47*

*First XI 1955-56*

*Colts XI 1950*

*First Eleven Cricket 1957*

*1947 Shield winners leaving the pitch at Goodison Park.*

*First XI 1952-53*

*College Lay Staff 1954 c.*

*Class photo 1950 c.*

*Class photo 1950 c.*

*Staff Dinner 1953.*

## Trivia

## Fr. Neylan

Reply from Fr. Neylan when asked for fire regulations :
  In the event of a fire make sure that those boys studying Greek get out of the building first.

Miss Lewis, get me Raspberry Hummock on the phone. ( i.e. Strawberry Hill, St. Mary's, Twickenham)

(On the phone) I am sorry, Reverend Mother, but this afternoon I have to watch a selection of my pupils propelling an air-filled leather sphere around an arena.

Whilst the boys were in Wales, Fr Neylan allowed the boys to smoke. The trouble was that he gave the impression to the younger boys that they had to smoke.

To a member of staff who had joined the NUT: You're a grammar school boy. If you have to join an organization, you should join the Association of Assistant Masters.

To his Sixth Form Class - on numerous occasions: What is the quickest way to disseminate information? Telegraph, telephone and tell a woman. (Fr. Neylan was a declared misogynist.)

To a sixth form pupil in class:  Are you contradicting me, X? No, Father , I am just offering an alternative explanation. Neylan goes berserk.

In three of the last four years of Fr. Neylan's spell he demoted three of his vice-captains. One for smoking in the Prefects' Room, one for cycling down Erskine Street without a cap, and one for expressing support for Attlee's social reforms. The last he also expelled for good measure.

Bert van de Put, (1915-1970) of Belgian descent, taught art at the College 1939-1952. For part of this time he lived in a small village near Mold in North Wales, Maeshafn, travelling in daily to Liverpool. In the thirties he did scene painting in London, and after leaving SFX he started to draw for Tiger Comics and continued doing the art work for Roy of the Rovers up to his death. He also drew the comic strip Brother Simon for Catholic Fireside, contributed to the Hotspur and the Victor, and did some of the art work for 'Wilson - the Wonder Athlete' and 'The Wolf of Kabul'.

*Fr. Neylan as seen by Mr van de Put, Head of Art*

**Putty Grace**

A loud bang heard from outside the classroom. ' Ah! our dear headmaster has done the decent thing at last.'

The bell for the end of lesson rings more urgently than usual. 'Ah! Miss Lewis is ringing for help'.

He always made a point of adding, if a king under discussion had no heirs, 'At least no legitimate heirs'. One day someone asked him who would get his money when he died. 'The Church', he said, 'I have no heirs'. Then from the back of the class, a pupil says quietly 'At least no legitimate heirs'. General laughter - including Putty.

Putty referred to the photo of Fr. Neylan in the Magazine which is reprinted at the beginning of this chapter. "A benign, charming and kindly headmaster, you would think. But I have seen Neylan as the Devil made him'.

He puts up a map of Northern France and ask us to find Brest. 'It's all right, boys, looking at Brest is not an occasion of sin'.

Putty's irreverence showed up with his play on catechism answers. Here the question about financially helping our priests was joined up with the one about worshipping statues. :
    Q.  Should we contribute to the support of our pastors?
    A.  We should not contribute to the support of our pastors, because they can neither see nor hear nor help us.

# The Fr. Warner Years : 1953 - 1961

*Fr. Warner (on left) and Fr. Taunton, the Rector, at High Lee*

The Warner Years were significant in a number of different ways. First and foremost, the move to Woolton ranks as a very great achievement, involving planning, financing, construction and moving. Bank managers, architects, builders and sundry suppliers - all succumbed to the Head's single-minded determination. A determination that was all the more remarkable in that for most of the time Fr. Warner was far from well. The College at Woolton is undoubtedly his 'monumentum aere perennius'.

The post-war 'fifties were hardly the best of times for major projects. Rationing had only just ended in 1954. Restrictions on building materials and planning developments were still very much in place. The country had four Prime Ministers in five years. Attlee, Churchill, Eden and McMillan. Progress of a sort was being made. Meter maids, yellow lines and motorways. In Fr. Warner's first year as Head, Hillary and Tensing had made it to the top of Everest, the Ashes were won, the Queen crowned and the first sub-four-minute mile had been run. The Mousetrap was going into its second year.

But perhaps even more important than the building programme were the policies Fr. Warner announced in his first two Proclamation addresses. He aimed 'to raise the standard of studies reached by the Upper School so as to meet the needs of boys who leave the College after taking GCE at Ordinary Level'. A re-direction of energies and resources - if that's what it was - away from the high-flyers and towards the 80% non-university pupils represented a seismic shift. The obsession with Oxbridge is a recurring theme in the College papers. In 1952 The Provincial at Proclamation declared that the success of a Jesuit College could be judged by the number of vocations to the priesthood *and* the number of Open Scholarships won.

The statement of Fr. Warner in 1954 stands out as the only policy statement in all the College records between the days of the Commercial School and the advent of comprehensive status that recognized in forthright terms the rights and interests of non-academic pupils and the duties of staff to attend to their needs. Acted on by the staff or not, and down to the credit of Fr. Warner or not, O Level passes improved by over 20% between 1953 and 1957.

A third major target for Fr. Warner was the 'careless and inchoate gabble, diffidently uttered that passed too often for speech'. Debating societies, drama groups, and elocution competitions were promoted during the fifties, as promised. The head also attacked 'the lack of taste, and even sense, in dress.' College blazers, maroon or navy blue were to be insisted on.

*Fr Warner and Fr. Taunton cutting the first sod at High Lee*

Sadly, Fr. Warner's Watch also saw the passing of the Old Guard - if a little perhaps-misplaced nostalgia may be permitted. Putty Grace, senior History master since 1923 retired in 1956 and died on February 11th 1957. 'Peg Leg' Frank Smyth also retired in 1956 after 32 years of service in the geography department. Willy Crook, with us since 1914, and Charlie Birmingham, here since 1922, both went in 1958. Natty Lucas took his leave in 1957. Fr. Tomlinson with many years service at SFX went to do the Provincial's bidding elsewhere in 1958, as did Fr. Brennan. The boys generally felt that departure of Fr. Brennan with his unfailing generosity in the matter of ordering "ferulas" would be something they would just have to cope with. Lofty Atherton sharpened his last College chisel in 1959. Les Bailey, steadfastly refusing to fade away, and George Ridge, a pupil in the 1930s, remained the only bridges between pre- and post-war. The well-deserved tributes to Miss Lewis and to Les Bailey can be found in the Magazines for both the years of their retirements and of their deaths.

## The Old Guard - 'Erant Gigantes in Diebus Illis'

1905 - 1941 Langford Mollard. Chemistry. 36 years
1914 - 1958 Willy Crook( a break in 1st World War). Maths. 40 or 44 years
1918 - 1959 Frank Checkland. 41 years
1919 - 1947 F.X. Bradshaw. Physics. 28 years
1922 - 1958 Charlie Birmingham. Chemistry. 36 years
1924 - 1956 Frank Smyth. Geography. 32 years
1924 - 1954 Dr. Frank 'Putty' Grace. Head of History. 30 years
1923 - 1949 Beaky Jones. Maths. 26 years
1926 - 1945 Harry Yare. French. 19 years

Other long-serving staff:

1927 - 1970  Miss Edna Lewis. School Secretary. 43 years
1928 - 1971  Les Bailey. Latin. 43 years
1929 - 1963  Evelyn Rice. College Cook. 34 years
1930 - 1963  Elsie Crowney. College Head Cook. 33 years
1949 - 1970  Fr. Adamson. English and RI. 21 years
1953 - 1973  Eddie Roberts. Geography and P.E. 20 years
1957 - 1979  Mr Lamb. Art. 22 years
1960 - 1995  Fred Devereux. History. 35 years
1967 - 1991  John Sherrard. Physics. 24 years
1966 -          J.P. O'Malley. Physics and still going strong
(With apologies to any missed who should be listed)

One of the strengths of the grammar schools has often been thought to lie in their out-of-hours clubs. Boys in the fifties at SFX had the option of chess, modelling (aeroplanes, boats and bridges), debating (unusually, a Fifth-form debating club as well as a Sixth Form), photography, and all the usual sporting activities of the day. A tennis club was formed in 1956. Football flourished but without a victory in either the Senior or the Junior Shield. Fr. Warner, George Ridge and Miss Lewis earned the undying gratitude of the Sixth Form for the organization of the Sixth Form Dances from 1955 onwards. There was a certain amount of reflected glory in the Oxford Blues awarded to Peter Sweeney and John Harding, and in the Blue at Cambridge for Mike Bushell. The Scratch Eights and Sixes were revived in 1956. That same year - 1956 - the College gave up the Saturday morning school and moved to a five day week.

Travel did not figure largely in the early fifties. London, Lourdes and camping trips to Prestatyn amounted to a fairly restricted programme. Dr. Grace and Fr. Gurrin are credited with organizing the College's first trip abroad in 1928 - to Belgium and the Rhine. It was decided to suspend visits to the Continent between 1939 and 1945. In the late 'fifties travel was in the air. Scotland, Paris, Germany, Belgium, London and Lourdes were on the itinerary. However the trip of the decade took place in 1956. Twelve boys cycled from Liverpool to Walsingham in Norfolk and back. The Magazine for that year has a heart-felt account by C. O'Neill (VI M).

Fr. Warner's direct influence on the College ended in 1961 with fears for his life. But in spite of severe illness, he lived on for another 20 years. His obituary was printed in the College Magazine for Autumn 1987.

## FATHER EDWARD JAMES WARNER, S.J.

Fr. Warner, who died in May, 1987, at the age of 84, holds a special place in the history of St. Francis Xavier's School, for it was during his tenure of the headmastership that the school was transferred to its present site at High Lee, Woolton, from Salisbury Street, Everton, where it had been located for over a century.

Edward James Warner was born in 1903 and was educated in London. After his conversion to Catholicism he joined the French province of the Society of Jesus in India. On his return to England in 1931 he went up to Oxford to read English Language and Literature and took a first-class honours degree in 1934. During the war he served as an army chaplain in Norway.

Fr. Warner came to SFX in 1950, and although his name will always be associated with the transfer of the school from Salisbury Street to Woolton, it should not be forgotten that his contribution to the school as a teacher of English would itself leave many in his debt. Fr. Warner was a thorough and painstaking scholar, who inspired in his pupils a knowledge and appreciation of English literature which remained with them for life as a legacy of their days at SFX. His methods were unashamedly didactic, for they had been formed in those happier days before 'creative' English had undermined literacy, and child-centred learning had made a virtue of ignorance.

Fr. Warner succeeded Fr. Neylan as Headmaster of SFX in 1953, and very soon his overwhelming concern was with the project of moving the school to the High Lee Estate at Woolton, which had been purchased in 1941. In 1957 the Building Fund was inaugurated and the architects were engaged to draw up plans for the new school. The plans were completed in 1959 and the first sod was cut on the 24th August. The foundation stone, which can be seen by the main entrance, was laid by Archbishop Heenan on 28th May, 1960. The staff and boys returned from holiday on 12th September to occupy the new buildings.

The burden of organising the transfer of the school to High Lee took a heavy toll of Fr. Warner's health. In February,

THE FIRST ELEVEN, 1960-61
*Back row (left to right)* : J. O'Leary, P. Williams, K. Darke, M. Pope, A. J. Gobbi, J. Duffy
*Front row (left to right)* : M. Redmond, B. Conwell, A. Dunn (*Captain*), P. Allison, J. Fay, J. Hagan

THE FIRST ELEVEN, 1961
*Back Row (left to right)* : D. Reynolds, P. Bailey, K. Darke, D. Kirwan, I. Samuel, G. Cullen (*Scorer*)
*Front Row (left to right)*: P. Halsall, A. Boyle, A. Dunn (*Captain*), M. Redmond, J. Harrison, C. Dunn

1961, he suffered a heart attack. Two further attacks followed, but after hospital treatment he returned to his tasks at the school. However, the burden proved too great, and at the end of the year he resigned for health reasons to be succeeded by Fr. A. D. Doyle. Fr. Warner's subsequent career was spent with distinction as Senior English Master at Beaumont College.

Those privileged to spend their days at school at High Lee will appreciate their debt to Fr. Warner if they reflect on how different those days would be if the school had not moved from the inner city to what is regarded by many as the best school-site in Liverpool. There can be no greater memorial to Fr. Warner's achievement. 'Si monumentum requiris circumspice.'

# The Fr. Doyle Years : 1962-1974

The decision by the Jesuits to withdraw from SFX in 1974 will stand out now for many people as the most momentous College event in this period. This is detailed at some length in Chapter 4 and there is nothing to add to that account. For much of the time the storm over this decision was brewing unseen and unheard. On the surface Fr. Doyle presided over a comparatively tranquil stage in the history of the College, whereas heads before and after him had had to cope with major changes and challenges in the full light of day. Clearly there was a need to bed down on the new site with some care, but consolidation and settling in perhaps took longer than they should, because of Fr. Doyle's style of management. As has been already mentioned, he was renowned both inside and outside the Order for an obsessive concern that every decision, no matter how small, should remain his and his alone. As a result, his years in office are not marked with what might be called a flurry of new initiatives. Retrenchment is a more apposite term - which for some became stagnation.

The concern for Oxbridge awards became once again the raison d'être for the College's existence, as it had been under Fr. Neylan. 'Academic standards' was the watchword and Open Scholarships the measure. Moral and social standards, too, were targeted. Behaviour, appearance and individual responsibility were all addressed and improved, which is much to Fr. Doyle's credit - along with the staff who loyally supported him. But as for the needs of all his pupils in the 1970s, for curriculum changes appropriate to the second half of the twentieth century, for fresh management and administrative structures, and for a receptivity to winds of social change - it is doubtful if Fr. Doyle had quite such a keen eye for any of these. Nonetheless two important curriculum developments deserve mention. The Sixth Form in 1963 was given a much wider choice with the introduction of 15 subject combinations: Moderns could now include Geography or Latin, Scientists Further Maths or Geography, and Classicists French, History or English. In addition, the appointment of a full-time music teacher (Mr J.N. Roberts) was a prelude to the subject being taught in every year. The absence from the curriculum of much in the way of creative subjects down through the years had left a gap in the education of more than one generation of pupils.

Proclamations saw a series of eminent bishops, judges, professors and doctors repeatedly call upon the pupils to work harder, stay at school longer, continue to practise their religion, and generally behave themselves. Politicians were not asked to speak as often as they used to, industrialists hardly at all, trade unionists never. In his Proclamation address the Head trod a path other Heads had trodden before him. He would urge the pupils of one class to pull their socks up, and congratulate the pupils of another class for having done so. Homework, hair and hard work are often referred to, and the co-operation of parents beseeched.

Dramatic performances were mounted regularly at first, but then gave way, as Roberts the Music, claimed to be the first full-time music teacher, built up a very respectable orchestra, starting in 1964. A new attitude was abroad. This was a real subject. HMS Pinafore, The Pirates of Penzance, The Mikado, and Trial by Jury were all great successes. The fledgling orchestra gradually spread its wings with regular performances at College functions - notably providing the entertainment on sports days. It is to the credit of the music department that a junior orchestra was trained as well.

TENNIS TEAM, 1969
*Standing left to right* : S. McDermott, P. Borland
*Sitting* : T. Starkey, M. Farrell (*Capt.*), A. Wilson, P. Bickerton

Skiing in Switzerland and climbing mountains in Scotland were the most popular amongst the school trips. In 1964 one group climbed sixteen mountains in one expedition, and another climbed the three highest peaks in the British Isles - Scafell, Snowdon and Ben Nevis - in twenty two hours. The less physical preferred Spain, Rome, Athens and Paris. Regular group visits were arranged to Lourdes, London, Stratford, Bonn and various parts of Ireland, with some intrepid individuals choosing to go solo to Poland, Canada and California. In 1969 Mr Whelehan and Fr. Laishley took a group on a classical odyssey

'CLASSICAL ODYSSEY'
*Left to right :* M. Walsh, Fr Laishley, M. Redmond, M. Spencer, D. McDonald, P. Jones, B. Temple, P. Brizell, P. Lewis, G. Lewis

which seems to have taken in every Roman site in Britain. (No doubt, Mr Whelehan and Fr. Laishley would have found it less stressful to have gone on the original trip with Odysseus.)

There were pluses and minuses in 1968. A new language laboratory was opened, but getting to it became a problem with the extended bus strike, which lasted from March to May. T. Ashplant received excellent notices for his performance in the school play as Sir Thomas More in A Man For All Seasons, as did a number of his fellow actors. The College came through a General Inspection in 1965 with credit.

1962 saw a revived chess club. In sport the major achievement went to the Juniors in 1972, who got to the final of the Junior Shield Competition and ended up sharing the award with St Kevin's. Swimming, badminton, basketball and athletics began to make stronger claims on pupils' time in Fr. Doyle's period of office.

## Obituary from College Magazine 1989

FR. ANTHONY DOYLE was the last Jesuit headmaster of St Francis Xavier's College. His departure in 1974 marked the end of an era in the school's history, which stretched back to 1842 when the school was opened by Fr. Francis Lythgoe SJ, its first headmaster, who had come to Liverpool from Stonyhurst College.

The news of Fr. Doyle's death at the Lourdes Hospital on Christmas Eve, 1988, was received with sadness by all who had known him during his years at SFX. It was fitting that many of his former colleagues were able to be present at the Requiem Mass for the repose of his soul, which was celebrated at the Church of the Sacred Heart, Blackpool, by Fr. Anthony Forrester, SJ, who had himself served for some years on the staff of SFX.

Anthony Dennis Doyle was born at Ilford in 1909. He was educated at Stonyhurst and entered the Society of Jesus in 1927. At Oxford he proved to be a fine classical scholar, and later he was to return to the university as Master of Campion Hall. In 1941 he was ordained, and subsequently became headmaster of St Michael's, the Jesuit College in Leeds. His first connection with SFX was made in 1948 when he took over for a term during the absence through illness of Fr. Neylan, the headmaster at the time. He returned in January, 1962, to succeed Fr. Warner, who had just completed the task of transferring the College from Salisbury Street to High Lee, Woolton.

Fr. Doyle's years as headmaster will be remembered by many as a period of consolidation, when the school established itself in its new surroundings after the upheaval of its move from the inner city, where it had flourished for over a century. If one were to offer a criticism it would be to suggest that the settling-in period was over-long. However, while it is true that no development, material or otherwise, took place under Fr. Doyle, it remains no less true that it was a time when the school's highest academic standards were vigorously maintained. Fr. Doyle was in the tradition of a type of headmaster which today has virtually become extinct. He discharged the duties of his office with an authoritarianism which left little room for consultation or delegation. To be called upon to assist in the simplest task of examination administration was deemed an honour and an intimation to the favoured member of staff that his career prospects were in the ascendant. It may be added that Fr. Doyle's defensive and protective attitude extended to the school's playing fields, much to the disappointment of the Old Xaverians. A story used to circulate that when Fr. Neylan was asked about the routine to be followed in the event of a fire, he replied that the important thing was to make sure that boys who did Greek got out of the building first. We can be confident that Fr. Doyle would have supported this order of precedence, for his enthusiasm for the Classics was boundless. The high point of his year was the news of the success of Classics candidates in the Oxford Entrance Examination, and during the years of his headmastership such successes were numbered in dozens. In later years, after 1974, Fr. Doyle was kept busy with parish work and teaching, including a period as headmaster in Blackpool. Failing health eventually forced him to retire, but he always found time to keep-up-to-date with the fortunes of SFX through the magazine, which he read from cover to cover.

## Trivia

In his youth he had a talent for cross-country and long -distance running.

Main contribution at St. Michael's Leeds was a very marked raising of standards and the instilling of real academic ambition into the boys .

Delegation seems to have been a concept outside his experience.

He was convinced that anyone who had read Greats could teach anything.

Famous for his notices that frequently began with 'No boy may....'

On moving to Liverpool in 1962 long hair was rooted out. Strict dress standards were insisted upon. The premises were preserved with great care - even kept under wraps. From Friday evening to Monday morning strict security was preserved

Re Vatican II : 'Lord, it could be the Reformation all over again."

# Brother Robert Power 1974 - 1979

As detailed earlier, Brother Robert Power succeeded Fr. Doyle in 1974, as the Brothers of Christian Instruction took over the running of the College. He served for five years, guiding the College through the difficult period which followed the departure of the Jesuits. The uncertainties of re-organization plans did nothing to make life easier, but during his time he maintained the highest standards in the spiritual, academic, sporting and social life of the College. The First Eleven won the Senior Shield twice - in 1975 and 1976. A Sixth Form Common Room was opened. Pupils started a College bookshop, which was immediately successful. Some unusual and more adventurous school trips were organized - including sailing a barge down the Grand Union Canal. What was needed at this stage was steadiness and order, and that Brother Power and the Governors provided.

# The Brother Francis Years : 1979 -

Brother Francis has served as Headmaster longer than any other Head or Prefect of Studies. Now in his twenty-third year, he has outlasted Fr. Woodlock by five years already. His term of office has been marked by considerable achievements for the College - in bold building programmes, in academic success, in state-of-the-art facilities and in Woolton's status and reputation.

It is thought inappropriate to analyse his contributions here in the same way as the other Heads have been looked at - for a number of reasons. In the first place, his work is not yet complete. Secondly, many of his important achievements have already been dealt with in detail in Chapter 4. Thirdly, it would be premature to start drawing conclusions on matters which could be

*Brother Francis O.B.E.*

said to be still in process, and, even if they are complete, whose details are not yet available for public scrutiny.

This section, therefore, will confine itself to descriptions of what has taken place at Woolton over the last quarter of a century, trying not to pass any judgements. The life of the College in the 'eighties will be dealt with separately from the 'nineties - and forgiveness is craved if the selection seems arbitrary and somewhat idiosyncratic.

## 1979 - 1989

The most momentous event of the Eighties affecting the College has to be the change of status from selective grammar to non-selective comprehensive. The birthrate had dropped dramatically. Families were deserting the inner city. As a result the Catholic Hierarchy in Liverpool had no option but to reduce 51 secondary schools to 15. SFX was one of the schools that survived.

At the re-named St. Francis Xavier's High School, pupil numbers doubled. Teaching staff increased from 40+ to 60+. New teaching skills and different teaching strategies had to be developed by the staff, many of whom were not used to teaching across an all-ability intake. Much to the credit of the staff and pupils the upheaval was not followed by any noticeable adverse effects on academic standards.

However, one regrettable result of the new dispensation was the loss of several loyal and long-standing servants either through transfer or retirement. The departure of James Whelehan and George Ridge - both with a 40+-year connection with the College - should not pass without notice and appreciation. George arrived as a pupil in September 1934 and retired in July 1983. His status as a Xaverian for nearly 50 years comes close to challenging the legendary Les Bailey who started as a boy in 1917 and retired in 1971.

As he coped with the strains of these adjustments, Brother Francis could have done without two sets of disruptions which marked the late 'eighties.

The teaching unions and the teachers' employers became involved in a prolonged battle nationally over pay and conditions of service. As a result some of our teachers were caught up in strikes and a 'work-to-rule' which on occasions seriously disrupted the ordinary life of the school. With good management and a fair amount of seat-of-the-pants driving - which some involved have described as aggressive confrontation - Brother Francis and the senior staff negotiated these difficulties without ever closing the College down, although some of the arrangements at times were very ad hoc indeed.

Although such industrial action caused something more than inconvenience at Woolton, it paled into insignificance beside the violent confrontations that attended the strikes of steel-workers, coal-miners, newspapermen and the demonstrations of the anti-poll tax rioters across the country.

The second disruption for the College was local and political. Education in Liverpool came in for a bumpy ride generally in the late 'eighties. Alongside much of the rest of local government in Liverpool, the school system suffered in the eighties as the Militant Tendency won control of the City Council. The Local Education Authority failed to provide the schools with the necessary resources. Teaching vacancies remained unfilled. Day-to-day maintenance was neglected. Minor works were constantly postponed. The College suffered in this along with other schools and the experience was a major factor in the 1998 decision to apply for grant-maintained status.

To turn to more internal and parochial matters. The Headmaster's comments at Proclamations are a clear indication that in many respects this decade was no different from any other. Satisfaction was expressed ' at progress in most aspect of College life'. There had been 'commendable and creditable success'. Over forty places had been secured at Oxbridge in the ten-year period under review; this included the ten places won in 1987 - a College record.

About forty Sixth Formers started on university degree courses each year. Eighty Fifth Formers - plus or minus - annually passed at least 3 GCSEs at C Level or above. But there were the usual warnings. 'Some results were disappointing'. 'Inadequate commitment to academic study'. 'Some areas of study need attention'. These contrast with the more forthright comments of Headmasters in the nineteenth century. '5A did little or no work during the year and their poor results are no more than they deserve.'

*Oxford awards 1987*

166

Activity at the College became that much more mobile with the gift of a minibus from the Parents' Association, and that much more technical with the College's first computer - a PET 32k - a TV and a video-recorder. The new fiction library was an immediate success and, for the record, the most borrowed book in its first year was The Rats by James Herbert. The last increase in accommodation had been the extension to the changing rooms in 1981 - the only addition since 1961. The opening of the new CDT and Art Block in 1989 was, therefore, something of a landmark.

Given what has been recorded in Chapter 2, it is a matter of some regret that dramatic activity hardly figures in the 1980s. Two pantomimes were performed  - *Snow  White* and  *Dirk Warrington* as well as a play by Dennis O'Gorman *The Way Out*. None of these was reviewed in the Magazine - still less reviewed in the tart and cutting style to which some of the 1930s and 1940s productions were subjected. At Christmas 1983 boys mainly from the Third Form under the direction of Ms. Wilkie with help from Brother Joseph put on *The Curse of the Mummy's Tomb*, which attracted attention.

Spectating rather than performing was more popular and it is recorded that the sixth form pupils of the 1980s saw half a dozen Shakespearean plays - *Julius Caesar, Macbeth, Hamlet*, and *The Merry Wives of Windsor* amongst them.

If dramatic activity and theatregoing were kept to a minimum, pupils' wanderlust was indulged to the full. From Israel to Hadrian's' Wall via Athens, Rome and Paris. Skiing in the French and Italian Alps. Hiking in The Lake District, the Peak District, the Yorkshire Dales, East Anglia and West Wales. Against all that it is nice to record a sense of balance was preserved with a trip to the Blackpool Illuminations, and some academic focus with several trips to the art galleries in London.

The College's sporting achievements were both general and particular. Past generations of SFX pupils had had a choice of soccer in winter and cricket in summer, with athletics waxing and waning, and a little desultory tennis on very badly maintained courts at Melwood. By the 1980s the choice was mouth-watering-basketball, badminton, soccer, cricket, five-a-side, swimming, cross-country running, golf and - with the opening of the Xaverian Club in 1987 - squash.

Pride of place in the particular achievements must go the Junior Team. They won the Junior Shield in 1982 ( v. Salesians 1 - 0), in 1984 ( v. St Margaret's 2 - 0). The First Eleven beat St Margaret's 3 -1 to win the Senior Shield in 1987, their first success since 1976.

In 1982 the Choral Society was re-formed and In 1985 the Ornithology Club was started. Brigadier Bill Bewley (OX 1956) came to speak at Proclamation magnificently attired in full-dress uniform complete with spurs. Other guest at Proclamation during this time were Dr John Watkinson, (OX 1948, industrialist) Bishop O'Connor, (OX 1945, Roman Catholic cleric), Lawrence O'Keeffe, (OX 1949, diplomat), Dr James Burns, (OX 1955, consultant pathologist and Presidentof the British Association in Forensic Medicine), Sir Peter Baxendell (OX 1943, industrialist), Sir Bernard Caulfield, (OX 1933, judge) and P.P. McCarthy (OX 1937 solicitor) - more cake-makers and fewer cake-eaters than heretofore.

Important though these landmarks were in their own way, none was more notable than the arrival at the College of our first female pupil. Elizabeth Emmott went on to underline her place in the College's history with an Oxford award to study Classics .

## Other Events at the College during the 1980s

| | |
|---|---|
| 1980 | The National Pastoral Congress |
| 1980 | Celebration of the Bi-Centenary of the birth of Jean- Marie Robert de la Mennais |
| 1982 | Careers Convention |
| 1989 | Merseyside Industrial Award. Four pupils won the prestigious Merseyside Industry and Commerce Award to Education with their development of a keyless car-locking system for Ford Motor Company. |

## Deaths

| | |
|---|---|
| 1979 | Fr. Tomlinson - identified for many pupils by his bicycle and his booming voice. |
| 1979 | Bert Kilburn - another legendary full-back for the Old Xavs who was a firm believer in the principle that, where a fullback was concerned, it was always better to give than receive. |
| 1981 | Evelyn Rice served in the College kitchen for forty years |
| 1982 | Brother Durkin, one of the first two Brothers to join the staff in 1964 |
| 1981 | James Baker - a Governor for 30 years |
| 1981 | Ossie Kelly - the prototype Old Xaverian full-back. |
| 1985 | Joe Alston, the Old Xavs' fixer par excellence. |

## Comings and goings

| | |
|---|---|
| 1981 | Brother Edmund arrived to teach Maths and Art |
| 1981 | Shirley Williams, Secretary from 1967 to 1981 and Miss Lewis' successor, left. |
| 1981 | Fr. O'Leary Chaplain since 1971 left. |
| 1983 | Mr Healy retired after 20 years on the staff. |
| 1983 | George Ridge retired. James Whelehan and Tony Lunt transferred to other schools. |
| 1987 | Hugh Donovan retired after 17 years in History Dept. |

After his first ten years as Headmaster Brother Francis could look back on some very difficult situations successfully negotiated. The decade closed with the Headmaster, Staff and Governors locked in a bitter struggle with both the Local Authority and the Catholic Hierarchy on the advisability of grant-maintained status.

An important aspect in the life of the College has been the encouragement Brother Francis has given to both the Parents' Association and to the Old Boys' Xaverian Association. This contrasts sharply with the attitude of some previous headmasters who at times seemed to regard these bodies as rivals rather than helpmates.

*Old Xaverian Cricketers 1950-1960*

*Basil d'Oliveira, Worcestershire and England cricketer, and Friends at the Centenary Dinner of the Old Xavs Cricket Club*

## 1990 - 2001

The College started the last ten years of the century dressed in the new clothes of a grant-maintained school. In 1996 this was embellished with title of City Technology College, which brought with it welcome developmental funds, and then in 2001 Foundation status. In the Spring of 2001 OFSTED Inspectors visited and on the whole the College came away with glowing testimonials. The College Choir deservedly won very high praise.

In reviewing the Magazines of the last twenty years, an impression is gained of a lively, varied and hardworking community, which could hardly do more for its pupils. One must be cautious. The writer only has the published appearances to go on - the record of the successes not the failures - presumably there were some. That more complete account will be written by someone else at some future date.

Those Old Xaverians, educated in Salisbury Street, will readily identify specific differences at Woolton for themselves, but there are some general features which sum up the state of affairs in 2002, as we prepare to celebrate a 160th anniversary.

'The finest school site on Merseyside' is a description that is often used of Woolton : the original buildings, the addition of the Warner Building and the De La Mennais Sixth-Form Centre, the smaller improvements and extensions - all go to make up a complex that is as expansive as the old site was restrictive. (It is perhaps worth recording here that the playing fields are still owned by and rented from the Jesuit Order; that land is not available for building.)

As for academic and classroom standards, people can read the OFSTED Reports and the Proclamation lists to judge for themselves the depth and breadth of the curriculum.

But in the end what tends to get lost in the tale of exam results is what is on offer to the pupils today outside the classroom. The number of sporting activities available has already been noted, although not the extra hours that staff in the P.E. Department are prepared to devote to keep such a programme up and running. Exactly the same must be said of the rest of the staff, who with equal devotion consistently provide a bewildering list of visits, activities and experiences. Touring the Kremlin, skiing in the Alps, singing at St. Peter's, canoeing down French rivers in the Ardeche, hardly a Roman villa left unvisited in England nor a mountain unclimbed, *Oliver* followed by *Mary Poppins*, and shenanigans at Alton Towers. None of this can come about without teachers giving up their spare time to plan, organize and chaperon. It is right that these notes should close by acknowledging their sacrifices.

*Some good friends and servants of the College*
*John McGlashan,    Bishop Vincent Malone.   Dr. James Burns,    Brother Francis,O.B.E.*
*(past Chair                                    (present Chair*
*of Governors)                                  of Governors)*

# The Epilogue

## Brain of Britain

### 14 A Grades for Broadgreen Boy

Jonathan Murphy got 13 A* grades & 1A in his GCSEs Summer 2001 and is now in the Sixth Form. It seemed appropriate to let him have the last word.

## IT'S SFX, BUT NOT AS WE KNOW IT
### OCTOBER 27th 2042
### by Jonathan Murphy

**The Future of Saint Francis Xavier's College**

Forget about teachers, ignore all lessons, burn all your school books! Get ready for rock concerts with an academic flavour, Michael Owen as headmaster, robot dinner-ladies (or robot dinner-men).

### St. Francis Xavier's College in 2042?

Liverpool Echo Headline July 2042:

**Sir Michael Owen**
Liverpool Footballer New Headmaster at SFX

What exactly will be going on at Woolton in 2042?

What do today's teachers and students think technology, society, education, religion, sport and music will look like, come our bi-centenary

It's SFX, but as you've never seen it before ........

The continuing IT revolution will ensure that education also continues to be re-vamped. The laptop and the electronic white board will take over from pen and paper. Senior staff believe that a good part of a teacher's work will be taken over by the internet. Teachers will not supply information, but they will be important in guiding, counselling, tutoring, directing and generally overseeing the work of students. The skills of the teacher in working one-to-one with his or her students or with very small groups will be the teaching skills most highly valued.

Technological development may also mean that it is truanting actually to go to school, as a high proportion of learning becomes home-based. By 2042 schools, colleges, universities, world-wide, will be open learning centres and libraries, visited electronically by the student working individually and under the tutorial direction of staff.

While some first year pupils wait for teleportation pads and holographic teachers, SFX sixth formers believe that standardised video conferencing will take their place with spells at the computer. Books in schools will be classified with the dodo - just a memory. Segregation of year groups into self-contained buildings are envisaged, but that flies in the face of what some see as a fluid and integrated system, responsive to the demands of individuals, not large groups. And co-education? It goes without saying.

But not everyone is convinced. Many teachers are more reluctant to over-state any educational revolution. After all, the SFX of 2002 is not too different from that of 1942. A nation-wide school timetable, a school-leaving age of eighteen, the elimination of the distinction between academic and vocational courses, students enrolled at different institutions for different units, education picked up at particular points in time for particular purposes, elements of work-experience judiciously integrated into the College course for everyone - these are all generally accepted as likely features at the College in mid-century.

Political change will affect the role of schools, as social and cultural shifts will be reflected in school life. The resurgence of local community is seen by some as a vital development, and the nature of schooling at SFX will be inseparably linked to Liverpool's social and Catholic community, as it always has been. "Education is simply the soul of society as it passes from one generation to another", said the writer and journalist, G. K. Chesterton. It is not unreasonable to predict that family life will revolve around schools, acting as community centres. With no age restrictions, enrichment courses will be attended by father and son alike.

As the school becomes the nucleus of society, cyber cafes may be sited here along with shopping malls and supermarkets. Social and emergency services, doctors' surgeries, public swimming pools and gymnasia seem destined to accompany polling stations as community links. The most convincing suggestion? All school dinners at the cyber cafe would be prepared by just two super robot dinner-ladies - or, of course, robot dinner-men.

Education has already shifted towards applied learning - with a view to employment. Doesn't it therefore make sense to have commercial business links with schools on site? BT information offices to aid computing, and Ford workshops for school engineering courses, an official training school for aspiring chefs. Academic excellence must still be the watch-word for these activities and others like them.

The College has a history of offering the maximum number of courses; separate sciences, Latin and Greek, IT and a GCSE and A Level in Physical Education have long been available. More and more varied offerings can be expected. (Popular options with students include DJ mixing, Hollywood directing and Calvin Klein modelling). Football coaching workshops and an A level course in football management are seen as natural consequences. Such sporting improvements are another aspect of strengthening business links. In recent years the English Premiership has been criticised for an abundance of foreigners. The solution is to develop British youth training schemes. With schools becoming a local amenity centre, SFX seems the ideal place for football giants - Liverpool and Everton F.C. - to locate a training academy.

Meanwhile, whispers still spread through the playground of stands and floodlights gracing the school fields. Pupils remain optimistic for a retired Michael Owen filling a PE vacancy - or even becoming head master. Alternatively, scientific developments suggest a solution. Many students have suggested that the computer-monitored thought patterns of Brother Francis might run the school from a bell jar. On the other hand, biotechnology could allow a suitable cloned individual to take over the reins. (Jennifer Lopez and Nicole Kidman were the most enthusiastic suggestions. Some Old Boys will be disturbed to learn that a sample of Fr. Neylan's DNA has been recovered from an old ferula. Will it be cloned in time for a Second Coming?)

However the role of the headmaster is a serious issue. The tradition of a religious priest or brother running the school remains a matter of growing local concern. Fewer vocations to the De la Mennais Order pose a threat. Circumstances may call for the College's first ever lay - and possibly female - principal . The decision over the next head would obviously affect the future of religion in the College. Pupils at rival secular schools, such as Bluecoat and Belvedere, predict current trends will continue and religion will decline in education.

Against this, one local parish priest has no doubts that there is still a deep spiritual understanding amongst the people. He looks to the past when faith-based schools fulfilled community needs. He believes that SFX's Christian education helps develop the original vision and understanding of faith in Christ. This will help pupils live out the faith, to find their place in society. It helps them to reach peace with themselves in life, and receive salvation with God in death. Brothers of the De La Mennais Order second this. They argue that religious instruction in the formative years helps provide a life-long moral awareness, part of which makes us whole as a person. With closer neighbourhood links, a community church and religious centre at Woolton seem a sensible project to work towards.

No one doubts that the choir under its music director will go on to achieve even greater honours. Well before 2042, the multi-million selling platinum album 'Heavenly Sequels 2' will have funded the school's music department, an SFX recording studio, and a home-grown group to eclipse The Beatles. Certainly such musical progression will attract media attention. 'Songs of Praise' will accompany the filming in the school of the new Channel 4 fly-on-the-wall television series, 'Big De La Mennais Brother.' Watching this, parents could see exactly what their children get up to at the College.

"O Romeo, Romeo! Wherefore art thou Romeo?" Perhaps all this media activity will re-start the College's theatrical department. The tradition of plays and pantos has halted recently, but the improved and professionally equipped school of 2042 could be producing shows for public performance on a regular basis. Referring back to Chapter 5, page 95, let us aim to present the play Constantine as a bi-centenary offering in 2042 - with all the splendour of Munich 1574.

Clearly then, with such revolutionary transformations, it will not merely be 'the same old SFX'. But the College will still be in a direct line from the SFX of times gone by. The individual spirit of Saint Francis Xavier's will endure. Despite the progression of technology, the rekindling of community and the uncertainty over the running of the College, the ethos of school life will prevail. The school's thrust for academic achievement will be sustained, the tradition of extra-curricular events put on for the community will be preserved. The Old Xaverian network will be extended. The College will still be SFX, just not as we know it.

"Boast not thyself of tomorrow, for thou knowest not what a day may bring forth." (Proverbs 27.1). The College will be in the safe hands of tomorrow's workers, inventors, teachers, politicians, headmasters, clergy, community members, parents and students. They will decide what surprises the future holds. The choice is theirs. But please, just trust me on those robot dinner-ladies (or robot-dinner men).

# **A**nnex 1 : Cardinal Acton and his Report to Propaganda

**C**rucial in this decision of Propaganda was the submission which the Sacred Congregation in 1841 had asked Monsignor Acton to prepare for it.

The Cardinal's Report to the Congregation put the Jesuits' case very eloquently and persuasively. Propaganda did not meet until February 1842 to consider his Report which proved wide-ranging in scope and visionary in content. Acton went beyond the level of argument, which had thus far obtained between Dr Brown and the Jesuits, and examined the full benefits which might be enjoyed by the Catholics of Liverpool if the Society of Jesus were given the opportunity of establishing itself firmly in the town. In an important section of his Report, entitled *Reasons for opening in Liverpool a church and house for the Jesuits,* he turned to the future possibility of developing secondary day-school education in Liverpool under the aegis of the Jesuits - a question which had not hitherto been raised.

The Congregation met and agreed that the Jesuits should be allowed to build a new church subject to rather stringent conditions. In the Decree no mention was made of the school, which Acton had included in his submission of his own accord. The claims Congregation were considering were solely to do with the plans for a new church in Salisbury Street.

The relevance of the arguments Acton deployed and the elegance of the language he couched them in make it worth reproducing extracts from his submission to Congregation. It is also pertinent in that this seems to be the very first mention of the possibility of a Jesuit secondary school in Liverpool.

The best account of the case put forward by Monsignor Acton is to be found in an article by Professor Maurice Whitehead (OX), Professor of Education at the University of Wales, Swansea, in the Proceedings of the North West Catholic History Society (Wigan 1990). With permission, the article is quoted below.

'Having first examined the contribution of the Jesuits, together with the Benedictines, as the sole missionaries in Liverpool in penal times, and the desirability of restoring the Jesuits to the position they had enjoyed in Lancashire prior to their suppression in 1773, Acton continued:

> .... we must also bear in mind the immense usefulness to the Catholics of Liverpool of the building of a new church together with a house in which new labourers can come together. This would be even more the case were it to incorporate a school for the education of the young. What is quite lacking in our large cities, starting with London itself, is a school for the social class which is not poor enough to attend charity schools but which is insufficiently affluent to go to the boarding schools which lie some miles outside the city.

> What is lacking is a school for the sons of people from this large social class, in which they can be instructed during the daytime, without leaving the parental home, in those subjects befitting their condition.

Acton went on to note that the ancient pre-Reformation schools in London were now in Protestant hands; and elsewhere in the capital a few small private schools run by Catholic lay people did exist but they could only cater for a small number of pupils. The situation in Liverpool was very different:

> .... I see no mention of these schools for the Liverpool area in the Catholic Almanac, where ... masters find it useful to list their schools so as to attract the attention of parents and increase the number of pupils. There are in Liverpool only three non-fee-paying schools for the poor - and Stonyhurst College, forty miles away, for those who can afford boarding fees.

From this I argue that the sons of shopkeepers and craftsmen and, on the whole, the sons of a large proportion of Catholic families are receiving such an education in the mixed schools run by Protestants.

In making suggestions for the beginning of Catholic secondary day-schools education, Acton was not pressurized by the interests of one party - least of all the Jesuits, who had never raised the question of opening a secondary school in Liverpool. Acton simply expressed his own opinion, based on his knowledge of Jesuit education in France and Italy:

It has often crossed my mind that it would be tremendously advantageous to open in London, Liverpool and in other large cities schools, at least for lower studies, like the Jesuit schools in the major Italian cities, where the youngsters spend a number of hours in the day. I am convinced that, if the Jesuits had schools of this type in Liverpool, the attendance would be most considerable. One would simply have to take the precaution of asking parents to pay a minimal monthly sum, as do the same Jesuits in Dublin, in order to forestall that aversion which many people feel in sending their sons to school without paying anything.

Acton's vision of a Jesuit college in Liverpool was of an educational institution having a moral and spiritual influence over its pupils long after their departure from the classroom:

Everyone then knows the spiritual advantage which can be gained from the existence of a Jesuit College in the town, not only for the young who attend it but also for those who have completed their period of studies, and who, with continuing affection for their former teachers, meet up with them again from time to time. Often amidst the temptations which beset the paths of young people, amidst the dissipation of the business world, it can be most beneficial to have access to the College which served as a bulwark to the innocence of tender youth, and to meet those same masters who instilled the sentiments of Christian piety, and who show themselves to be always ready to give fresh incentives in the ways of virtue.

Appending some statistics to his report, Acton showed the extent of non-Catholic educational activity in England in the early 1840s: the British and Foreign Schools Society,which existed to establish Non-conformists schools, and the Society for the Propagation of Christian Knowledge were making a significant contribution to education, while the National Society, which existed to establish Church of England schools, was educating over one million scholars in England and Wales. Such a situation demanded action from the Catholic authorities - and who better, he asked, could begin improving educational opportunities for the Catholic middle-class than the Society of Jesus.

# Annex 2 : Three Letters of Bishop Brown Conceding

The first is a letter from the Liverpool Archives, sent from Rome dated April 22 1842 to an unknown recipient in Liverpool. Only pages 1 and 2 survive. Page 3 and any subsequent pages are missing. The signature is therefore missing. It is almost certainly from Bishop Brown, who was in Rome at the time to negotiate this matter.

Dr Brown - or the recipient - has written at the top of the letter "The Pope's decision relative to the Jesuit's (sic) church. Confidential. To be kept till my death and then destroyed."

*My Dear Sir,*

*The affair is now decided. I believe I mentioned in a former letter to Dr Youens that we could not agree on the terms when I met the Cardinals in consultation in Easter Week and after two hours discussion Cardinal Mai proposed that this matter should be referred to the Pope. His Holiness gave his decision a few days ago and the terms are these.*

There follows a transcript of the Pope's decision, which lays down the terms mentioned earlier in this chapter.

*I send this to you for your information and that of Dr Youens, but I think it will be wise to refrain from communicating the precise terms of the decree to any one else, as yet at least. The delay of six years before the church is opened and the £10 per annum are additions made by His Holiness to the other terms which the General had offered me before, and which, I had said, were not quite sufficient security. I earnestly request that you and Dr Youens will use all your influence with the clergy in Liverpool to observe the strictest silence on the subject before all the laity without any exception and refrain from letting their looks even exhibit any signs of disappointment.*

*It is the Pope's decision and there are those who will be on the watch to see and report symptoms of dissatisfaction on the part of the Secular Clergy. I have been tried by a person who is intimate at Propaganda who was fishing to know my feelings - I quietly replied that I received the decision as being the will of God. I have since ascertained that these very words were reported to Propaganda the same day. I expected it would be the case and therefore was not surprised, and I mention this to you to show what caution is required at this time. Dr Baggs and another person who has been my confident in the whole affair say that the decision is more favourable than there was reason to expect and that Monsignor —(sic) has been foiled in his attempt to have things his own way.*

*Your letter arrived after the decision of the affair, but I showed it to Cardinal Acton on whom it has made an impression in favour of St Anthony's greater than anything I have hitherto said. I had repeated to him over and over again the same statements in every respect, but it seemed to me that he was hard of faith. Now that the die is cast I suppose his mind is more open to conviction. You mention 10,000 hearing mass every Sunday - of benediction and your choir that would be well thought of in.........*

This is the end of the second page. Further pages are missing. The handwriting has been compared inconclusively with a signed letter of Dr Brown.

It can be concluded that the recipient is not Dr. Lingard, one of the Bishop's regular correspondents, who would not be in Liverpool to act as Brown suggests. It is not to Dr. Youens, the Parish Priest at St Nicholas' and the obvious candidate as his closest supporter in Liverpool, since he is mentioned twice in the third person. The references to St Anthony's would indicate that Fr. Wilcock, Parish Priest of St Anthony's and a doughty protagonist in the dispute, is the most likely person to whom the letter is addressed.

Two more letters, written about the same time from Rome by Dr Brown to Fr. Lythgoe, are more measured.

*Dear Fr. Lythgoe,*

*His Holiness has been graciously pleased to arrange with his usual prudence the building of the church of St Francis Xavier in Salisbury Street in such a way as to afford, I hope, sufficient security for that of St Anthony's, and therefore I have now no hesitation in assuring you that I assent to it on the terms which have been agreed upon. I have no doubt but you will have been made acquainted with all the particulars of the arrangement or I would send you copy of the decision of His Holiness.*

*It seems unnecessary for me to add that it has always been my most ardent wish to see peace and harmony cultivated on all sides. I feel confident that the work, whenever it is commenced, will be prosecuted in an amicable manner in order to promote the honour and glory of God and peace and good will amongst men.*

*Yours etc George Brown*

Brown wrote again to Lythgoe in similar vein on 14 May 1842 from Rome.

*I cannot refrain from thanking you for the very kind and friendly manner in which you have expressed yourself towards me. ..........the members of the Society amongst whom I can number many personal friends and whose virtues have secured my sincere respect ...whose zealous and edifying attention to the sacred duties of the holy mission merits all praise....*

# Annex 3 : Catholic Liverpool 1800-1860

The founding of SFX College was intimately bound up with the difficult negotiations for the new church, for which the Jesuits had had to fight hard between 1840 and 1842. Much of the opposition - not all of it unjustifiable by any means - came from fellow-Catholics. But religious divisions and the conditions in Liverpool in the early nineteenth century are better understood if they are set in some sort of context.

The repressions of the Eighteenth Century would not have been entirely forgotten by Catholics alive in 1800. By an Act of Parliament of 1700 any Catholic running a school was liable to be imprisoned for life and in spite of the Roman Catholic Relief Act of 1791 and the Catholic Emancipation Act of 1829 antipathy towards Catholics was as strong as ever. From 1791 Catholics were allowed to open their own schools, but school-teachers had to register their names with the local Quarter Sessions. The Jesuits along with the other Orders were specifically excluded from the relaxations of the Emancipation Act. After the Reformation and the destruction of the monasteries and convents, the Jesuits had worked in secret throughout Lancashire for one hundred and fifty years, and the Catholics of Liverpool and the surrounding areas had good reason to be grateful to them.

## St Mary's Lumber Street - City's First Post-Reformation Catholic Church

Fr. Francis Mannock was the first Jesuit to take up permanent residence in Liverpool around 1700. He was succeeded in 1718 by Fr. John Tempest, also known as Hardesty, who is credited with the founding of St Mary's in Lumber Street off Old Hall Street - the first Catholic church in the city since the Reformation. It was probably no more than an upstairs room in a local Catholic house. The population of the city was about 7,000 at this time and there could have hardly have been 300 Catholics amongst them.

By 1740 St Mary's would seem to have been well-established and it was run by a Jesuit, Fr. Carpenter. But Catholics still lived on the edge, and on 30 April 1746 St Mary's was burnt down by a Protestant mob, enraged by The Young Pretender's march to Derby during the Scottish '45 Rebellion. The conduct of the priest in charge, who was caught in the church, was much admired and is mentioned in several contemporary records.

*'Before he quitted the church, Fr. Carpenter SJ opened his ritual and calmly read the preparation for death. Thinking his time had come, he put on his vestments, took out the Ciborium and made ready to present himself to the infuriated mob in Edmund (sic) Street. Two or three axes were applied to the door, and on its being demolished, the multitude stood aghast. A gangway was formed for the priest who passed into the house of a Presbyterian friend opposite who sheltered him from further insult.'*

There is a less lurid account in which the rioters treated the priests with respect and escorted them from the chapel with the Ciborium. Only then did they "tear up the benches and make a fire of everything combustible". This is probably more reliable since it is written by a Mr. Green whose mother was present.

For a while, Mass was celebrated in Dale Street at the house of Mr. Green, a celebrated Liverpool potter. St Mary's was rebuilt in Edmund Street, this time disguised as a warehouse. But a second Protestant mob burnt it down again in 1759.

The Jesuits built it a third time in Edmund Street. But, suppressed by Pope Clement XIV in 1773, they handed it over rather belatedly to the Benedictines in 1783. The Warehouse Chapel, as St Mary's was sometimes known, disappeared a third time, when a new St Mary's was opened on August 18 1844, designed by Augustus Pugin, the celebrated Catholic architect of the day and, with Charles Barry, responsible for the re-building of the Houses of Parliament in the 1850s. The Church finally fell victim to German bombs during the War.

Five years later the Benedictines opened a second church, St Peter's in Seel Street. In addition a Cornish Jesuit, Fr. John Price, had opened a chapel on the corner of Sir Thomas Street and Dale St. in 1780, working there on his own for over thirty years till his death in 1813. These three churches ministered to a Catholic population of about 5,000 until the expansion in the early 1800s.

*Fr Price's Chapel at the corner of Sir Thomas St. and Dale St., Liverpool.*

In 1825 The Mechanics Institute, which later became Liverpool Institute, rented the Chapel until its own premises were built in Mount St.

# New Catholic Churches 1800 - 1860

The massive Irish immigrations of the late eighteenth and early nineteenth centuries presented the few priests working in a hostile city with formidable challenges. Fourteen new churches were built between 1800 and 1861 in the struggle to provide for the spiritual needs of the steady stream of in-comers. St Francis Xavier's Church was to open in 1848, but only after the short but acrimonious quarrels amongst Catholics themselves described earlier.

### 1800 to 1830

Three churches were built in the first quarter of the century. A French priest, Fr. Jean Gerardot, a fugitive from the French Revolution, opened St. Anthony's in 1804 in Scotland Road. St Nicholas' Copperas Hill followed in 1807 under the secular clergy and St Patrick's in 1827. St Mary's and St Peter's made up the list.

### 1830 to 1860

As the population and the town boundaries grew, eleven more churches opened.

The Benedictines opened two - St Austin's, Grassendale in 1838 and St Anne's, Edge Hill in 1843. The secular clergy added St. Oswald's in 1842, St Joseph's in 1845, St Alban's in 1849, Holy Cross in 1850 and St Vincent de Paul's in 1852. St Francis Xavier's had opened in 1848. By 1861 Bishop Eton, Our Lady's Eldon St. and St Michael's had joined in serving the Catholic community.

In spite of the extreme poverty of the day these churches boasted some notable features. Augustus Welby Pugin was the architect for St Mary's and for the Gothic structure at St. Oswald's, whose spire and peal of bells prompted anti-Catholic elements to question whether they were within the law. His son, Edmund Welby Pugin was responsible for St Vincent's, Bishop Eton, and St. Mary's. In 1841 a fine stained glass window, also designed by Edmund, was unveiled at St. Nicholas'.

The altar at St Austin's had been imported from a Franciscan convent in Lisbon, while a large painting (1834) of the Crucifixion by the Dutch artist Nicaise de Keyser of Antwerp still hangs above the altar in St. Patrick's. The new St Mary's, in Edmund Street, built to Pugin's designs, was opened with great ceremony on 18 August 1844 and the celebrations continued for eight days. Bishop Goss commented later 'This is the church of my diocese'.

As for St. Francis Xavier's, the Jesuits had had to hoe a very hard row indeed. But finally the foundation stone was laid on 15 August 1842 and the completed church opened in 1848.

By this time the new school was beginning to grow, but the next fifteen years up to 1865 were not easy and there were alarms along the way. However, the College was open and eventually prospered.

# **A**nnex 4 : St Anthony's Letter - from the Parish Priest of St. Anthony's

Fr. Wilcock, Parish Priest of St. Anthony's, distributed this letter to his parishioners in February 1841.

# ST. ANTHONY'S, LIVERPOOL.

*We feel ourselves called upon respectfully to present to the Friends of the above Establishment, and to the Catholics of the Town, the following statement and observations on the part of St. Anthony's Society.*

## FOUNDATION OF ST. ANTHONY'S.

TO judge correctly of the condition of ST. ANTHONY'S, the particulars of that Establishment from its beginning should be known.

In or about the year 1805, the Rev. J. B. A. Gerardot, an exiled French Priest, partly by his own savings, but mainly by Public Subscriptions and Borrowed Money, erected a small Chapel dedicated to St. Anthony, with a convenient House for his own residence.

This was done under the express promise, that the Chapel should be made over to the Bishop ; but when the proper period arrived for fulfilling this engagement, the Rev. Gentleman insisted on conditions, which the Bishop could not grant, so that the promised transfer was never made.

In his last illness he bequeathed this property to the Society of Jesus, on condition they paid the mortgage thereon, should they accept it. Should they not accept it, he directed it to be sold, and the surplus of the proceeds over the mortgage to be given to the Dispensary, a public Institution for the sick.

Soon after his death, in 1825, by order of the Town Authorities, the Street in which his property stood was widened, and to make room for this alteration, a great part of the Chapel, and the whole of the Priest's residence, were taken down and removed. The remaining part of the Chapel was too small to be of any real service to the Liverpool Mission. The Bishop therefore declined making any effort to get it, and the Fathers of the Society declined accepting it as a legacy, under the above-named circumstances. It was therefore sold by the Executor to the Will, and the purchaser, who was a Catholic, allowed the Bishop the use of it as a Chapel, as long as he pleased to retain it.

The Catholic Population in that neighbourhood, principally by the continued influx of Catholics from Ireland, had become considerable, and the Bishop determined, in place of the remnant of the late Rev. J. Gerardot's Chapel, to erect a Church proportioned to the wants of a numerous and growing congregation. With this view he purchased a large and suitable plot of land, intending forthwith to commence the erection. But his good intentions were interrupted by legal proceedings concerning the land he had purchased. For years the law-suit continued, and for years the Bishop most anxiously awaited its termination to begin the building.

In the meantime the Catholic population in the neighbourhood kept rapidly increasing, till at length the want of a spacious Catholic Church became so manifestly urgent, that the Bishop resolved to delay no longer. He therefore consented to the purchase of another site of land ; and as land in that situation had greatly risen in value, the price was high. On this site, in the year 1833, the Church of St. Anthony's was erected. In its dimensions as it was designed for, so it was proportioned to a very extensive and populous district. The building, therefore, as well as the land, was highly expensive.

The requisite and costly appendages of a powerful Organ for the Church, and a residence for the Clergy sufficiently capacious to accommodate five or six clergymen, were also provided. Thus was formed the establishment of St. Anthony's, pronounced by many, who from all quarters, have seen it, to be hitherto the most extensive, and in many respects, the finest establishment for Catholic worship that has been raised in England since the pretended Reformation. The town applauded, and the Bishop sanctioned this proceeding with more than an implied promise of his special patronage and influence with the public, till the new establishment had received an opportunity of acquiring the means to liquidate, or, at least, greatly reduce, the heavy debts that had been unavoidably contracted.

There were two most urgent causes which compelled the conductors of this great work to take up these heavy burthens. In the first place, the only funds for the work were the voluntary donations of the wealthier class, and the weekly penny subscriptions gathered amongst the labouring Catholics of the town. Every possible exertion was made, and much in both these ways was collected during the progress of the building, but nothing like sufficient to bring the work to its completion.

In the second place, in consequence of the long delay which had occurred in commencing the building as above noticed, and the rapid increase of population in the district, the want of a Church in that situation had become so extreme, that the managers of the undertaking, prompted by the common feelings of charity, resolved to carry on the work, without any interruption, to its completion, by means of money borrowed upon interest, in the confident hope of being able to discharge, by donations and weekly collections, before any other large establishment was called for, the debts incurred for so urgent and charitable a purpose.

Had they acted otherwise, had they waited till a sufficient, or nearly a sufficient sum, to cover all expenses, was raised, St. Anthony's would not yet have been opened to the devotion of the public ; and the thousands upon thousands who now, for seven years, have enjoyed its advantages, must have remained up to the present period in spiritual destitution.

From this statement it will appear why St. Anthony's is so deeply in debt. For the Land and the Chapel there are still owing Twelve Thousand Two Hundred and Twenty-five Pounds, besides the debts contracted for the purchase of the Organ and the erection of a residence for the Clergy. These incumbrances would have been by this time much more materially diminished could the Bishop have afforded us that privileged protection, which he undoubtedly intended, and which he gave us every reason to expect.

But from the period our debts were contracted, up to the present moment, a regular continuance of various undertakings, similar to our own, have been allowed to share with us the resources of the town. To some of these the Bishops yielded through importunity or great necessity, and others were prosecuted in opposition to their wishes.

Much, however, has been done at St. Anthony's. During the erection of the Church, about Four Thousand Five Hundred Pounds were collected and paid. After the erection many bills were discharged. The original debt has been diminished Two Thousand Pounds; the annual interest, amounting to upwards of Five Hundred a year, has been paid. The sum of Five Hundred and Eighty-two Pounds has been expended in the purchase of land for an extensive School. That School is now nearly built at the cost of Two Thousand Three Hundred Pounds, of which a large portion has been collected; the rest we have ventured, for reasons hereafter mentioned, to add to our burthens, by taking it upon credit.

The present debt on St. Anthony's Chapel and Cemetery amounts, as stated in the last Report, to Twelve Thousand Two Hundred and Twenty-five Pounds, to which must be added the sum of Thirteen Hundred Pounds, taken up for the completion of the School.

Moreover, the Organ and residence of the Clergy are neither of them paid for. The interest on the debts for these, amounting to little less than a Hundred Pounds per annum, is affixed to the incomes appropriated to the Clergy, which are very moderate; but no complaint is made on this score.

For paying the annual interest on the debts of the Church and Burial-ground, amounting to Five Hundred Pounds per annum, we have no fund but the proceeds of the Cemetery itself.

It is given out, but not with truth, that the Cemetery produces Five Hundred Pounds yearly. The nett proceeds of the Cemetery, from its beginning to October last, (seven years), have not quite reached Three Hundred Pounds per annum; and of this, necessity has compelled us to apply a very considerable sum to meet Church expenses.

We cannot, therefore, maintain our ground without much aid from the voluntary benevolence of the people, supposing it were prudent to leave our debts standing as they are. But it would be most imprudent to do so; for should, by any occurrence, that benevolence fail, or be diminished, we must come to a dead stand. And, further—as long as the debts remain standing, our exertions are crippled, and we cannot maintain the number of Clergy that such an establishment as St. Anthony's requires, to effect the good that it is adapted to produce.

Under these circumstances we were desirous that the public should not be called on, at present, for means to erect a Church in Salisbury-street; because, without that additional call, we find ourselves nearly precluded from getting any assistance in our trying difficulties, by the great number of other calls already sanctioned.

The following Societies are all in active operation:—A Society at Seel-street Church, for the erection of a Church; a Convent and a Penitentiary at Edge-hill; another Society at St. Mary's, for the erection of a very extensive Church in place of their present Chapel; a third Society, under the direction of the Rev. John Maddocks, for the erection of a Church at the Old Swan; and the Rev. Gentlemen of Copperas-hill are soliciting help for the erection of a Convent in their district.

When all these Societies are actively engaged, under the influence of their respective Clergy, Friends, and Congregations, every one who knows Liverpool will be aware how much danger there is of a party spirit, and how little chance exists of obtaining much towards the liquidation of debts on establishments, which the public already possess.

We did, therefore, and we do, in our circumstances, deprecate the addition of another powerful call on the town, because we really did, and do think, that it will greatly add to the danger of our coming to a failure.

But from a garbled extract from one of our printed statements in February 1839, it is published, that we then acknowledged ourselves to be in so prosperous a condition as to recommend our Church to be left to its own resources, and that in future all donations and collections should be applied to the erection of the School.

We complain of this garbled extract, and beg here to insert our own statement:—

" DEEPLY does the Committee regret, that the want of means has hitherto compelled them to defer the second of " the two great and charitable purposes, for which the Society was established. Had an object of so much consequence to religion, " and to the interests of the Catholic community, as the intended School will be, when erected, been sooner attainable, by any exer- " tions in their power, it would not have been so long delayed; for, besides the strong desires they feel, on the general grounds of " charity, to provide a competent Free School, in a district crowded to excess with destitute Catholic children, there are many " other considerations that would have induced them, had there been a prospect of sooner succeeding, to commence, without " delay, so desirable an undertaking.

" The continued and insulting abuse heaped on Catholics, the often-answered, but for-ever-reiterated slanders and misrepre- " sentations, which are daily published to defame their religion, and the strenuous but ungenerous efforts of a powerful party to " keep down the Catholic, by withholding from him any share in the public resources of education, to which he, as well as others, " is made to contribute; are stimulations sufficient to goad the most apathetic to activity in their own defence.

" For is not the Catholic, under such circumstances, called upon, by every feeling of nature and religion, to attend to the " wants and safety of his little ones, to bring them often together; and as he values immortal life, to fortify them by timely, careful, " and constant instruction, against the snares of lying craft, and the misrepresentations of their enemies? and is he not also bound, " as he values their welfare in society, to spare himself no pains, in struggling to impart to them those temporal advantages of " education, of which a spirit of exclusion and mean injustice is striving to deprive them?

" If any thing be obligatory on man, these, in the case alluded to, are obligations; and obligations, the Committee beg to " observe, which, in the district of St. Anthony's, can never be discharged, till that district possess an extensive Free School.

    *    *    *    *    *    *    *    *    *

" In thus urging the immediate erection of the School, the Committee are not unmindful of the very heavy debt that still " encumbers the Chapel, and are glad of an opportunity of preventing any misconceptions, that might otherwise arise, on that " point, in the minds of the public, for the public may not be aware, that, perhaps, no institution has greater difficulties to contend " with than St. Anthony's.

" From the accompanying balance sheet of finances, it will be seen, that, notwithstanding great care, economy, and all the " exertions that have been made, the debt on the Chapel is still so great, that its annual interest amounts to a considerable rent charge " on the premises. Every year there are, also, a variety of incidental expenses, such as are noticed in the annexed accounts. Out " of their moderate incomes, the Clergy have to pay the interest of the money borrowed on mortgage, to erect their residence; and, " in addition, they have hitherto paid twenty-four pounds a-year for the interest of money taken up by them to build the organ.

" The Committee deeply deplore the necessity, but do not, and cannot, repent of having concurred to the acceptance of these " burthens. Without them, there could have been, for years to come, no competent Chapel for the district, and still less an adequate " mission to discharge its heavy and almost endless duties; and the spiritual destitution of the thousands, who now frequent, and " who, for the last five years, have been frequenting St. Anthony's, must have perpetuated its disastrous consequences.

" The good, therefore, that is, and has been done, amply compensates for the temporary inconveniences that have been, and " must, for some time longer, be endured.

"That their pressure will only continue for a time, the Committee feel confident.

" The natural resources of a large and increasing establishment, the liberality of charitable friends, occasional collections in " the Chapel, and the proceeds of the burial ground, will, they are convinced, not only defray what at present may be styled a rent " charge, but gradually reduce the incumbrance of debt, till it ceases to exist, and thus leave the Catholic public possessed of a " splendid and unshackled establishment, made over to them for ever by a deed of trust that is already executed and enrolled in " the High Court of Chancery.

" So convinced were the Committee of the correctness of this view of the Society's affairs and prospects, that they deemed it " incumbent on them, at the last general meeting, to recommend, and the Society have adopted the recommendation, that the Chapel " be left to its own resources, and that all future donations and collections be exclusively applied to the erection of the School."

We now reply to our objectiors.

The above is what you, by your mode of extracting from our Report, make us glory in, as unqualified prosperity.

Our statement is, and you saw it, that we were struggling with extraordinary difficulties: and still in our zeal we hoped, in the then state of the town, to keep ourselves up, and, by great exertions, to do a little more, and thus gradually work out our deliverance; and for the sake of obtaining a School, an object above measure wanted, we resolved to make the trial.

Could we have foreseen your proceedings, we should have then said, as we now say—if these things are allowed, instead of deliverance, St. Anthony's may look for dissolution.

We further believe, that the position of the intended Church in Salisbury-street would be seriously and permanently injurious to our establishment. Between our Church and the site on which that is to stand, a great part of the space is country, and for many years likely so to continue; and what there is of town consists of better streets than Catholics in general can afford to inhabit. There are only a few families—but those are nearly all the respectable families that belong to us, in that part of the town; and we do think it hard, that a Church should be so plaed as to take those from us, and leave us with almost nothing but the poor; whilst our chief and almost only revenue is the rent of pews, which even the labouring poor are in general unable to pay, and whilst one half of our Church is, by irrevocable contract, open to the poor gratis.

2ndly. On the other side of our district, a very large Church, in lieu of the present St. Mary's Chapel, is forthwith to be erected: this, again, will cause a material diminution of attendance at ours.

3rdly. Our Church, at present, is far from being filled, even on Sundays. At the two early Masses, seven and eight o'clock, hundreds more than ever attend could be accommodated: at the nine o'clock Mass, our gallery, in which there are sittings for four hundred persons, is nearly empty: and at the principal Mass, eleven o'clock, it is rarely more than half filled.

Whatever, therefore, may be alleged, on the strength of conjectural assumptions of population, experience testifies, that with us there is no want of church accommodation; and this case will be far stronger, very soon, when great St. Mary's is erected.

But it is alleged, that, in our first Report, we considered ourselves as justified in building at the distance of a mile from each of the next Chapels.

To this we reply, that the mile in that case consisted of continued streets, of which, many in each mile are densely inhabited by Catholics. No one surely will contend, that local circumstances, as well as distance, should not be considered in erecting Churches. In Dublin, there are large Churches well filled within a few hundred yards of each other. This would not be applicable to towns in England. Abstract distance, therefore, can form no criterion.

Again you say, you are, by actual measurement, a full mile from St. Anthony's, by the usual road on foot. We suppose, by these last words, you take into your measurement the foot-path across our church-yard. If so, it is clearly hard work to make out the mile.

But the great stress you lay on the word mile used in our first Report, is more than the word is entitled to; nor does it, in point of fact, make out, as you seek to do, a parallel case.

In using the word mile, precision or strict measurement were neither aimed at, or thought by us of great consequence. The distance and kind of streets between ours and the other Chapels were well known here. There could be no dispute but it was at least a mile, and well peopled with Catholics; and with noticing this, we were satisfied.

Now, in point of fact, a bare inspection of the map of Liverpool will show, that yours is by no means a parallel case with ours; for the distance from St. Anthony's to either Copperas-Hill or St Mary's, is far greater than the distance of Salisbury-street to St. Anthony's. Is it not also fair to observe, that St. Anthony's Church contains twice the extent of Copperas-Hill Chapel, and thrice that of St. Mary's, according to the dimensions stated in the Liverpool Directory? And is it incongruous, that, being so much more extensive, it should look for a more extensive district?

We have now given a plain and true statement of our case, accompanied with short replies to remarks that have been published to our disadvantage.

Our proceedings, have all along, been open, honourable, sanctioned by authority, and, if we know ourselves, undertaken solely for the advancement of Religion in the town. This object we have as much at heart as any others can have. It is in pursuit of this, our humble abilities have been exerted for years, with a diligence and perseverance equal to slavery; and we have taken up, in the cause, burthens, and entered into engagements which will render other years of exertion necessary.

These obligations we cannot cast off at pleasure. Our tent is pitched. We cannot pull it down, and carry it elsewhere, to make room for others.

If others come and strive to overpower us, either by a premature interference or encroachments, it then becomes our duty to refer the affair to the Bishop. This has been done, and both our late and present Bishop have pronounced their decisions in our favour.

ST. ANTHONY'S, FEB. 10TH, 1841.

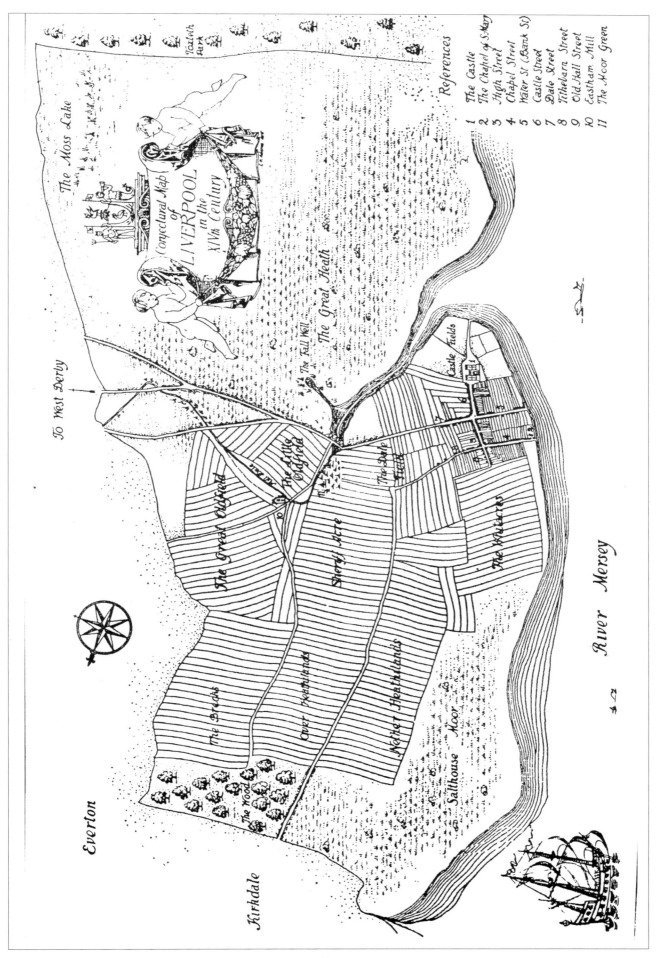

Conjectural Map of LIVERPOOL in the XIVth Century

References

1   The Castle
2   The Chapel of St Mary
3   High Street
4   Chapel Street
5   Water St (Bank St)
6   Castle Street
7   Dale Street
8   Tithebarn Street
9   Old Hall Street
10  Eastham Mill
11  The Moor Green

The Moss Lake

Toxteth Park

To West Derby

The Fall Well

The Great Heath

Castle Fields

The Great Oldfield

The Healthe Oldfield

The Dale Flatt

Shaws Acre

The Waterres

The Bricks

Over Heathlands

Nether Heathlands

Salthouse Moor

The Wood

Everton

Kirkdale

River Mersey

185

DRAWING (*from woodcut*) OF LIVERPOOL, MID-SEVENTEENTH CENTURY

St. Nicholas'                    Castle

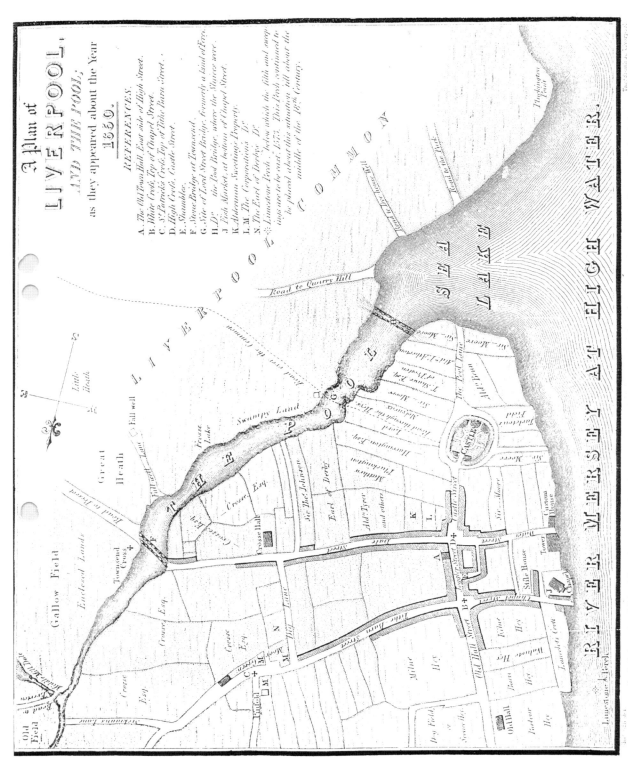

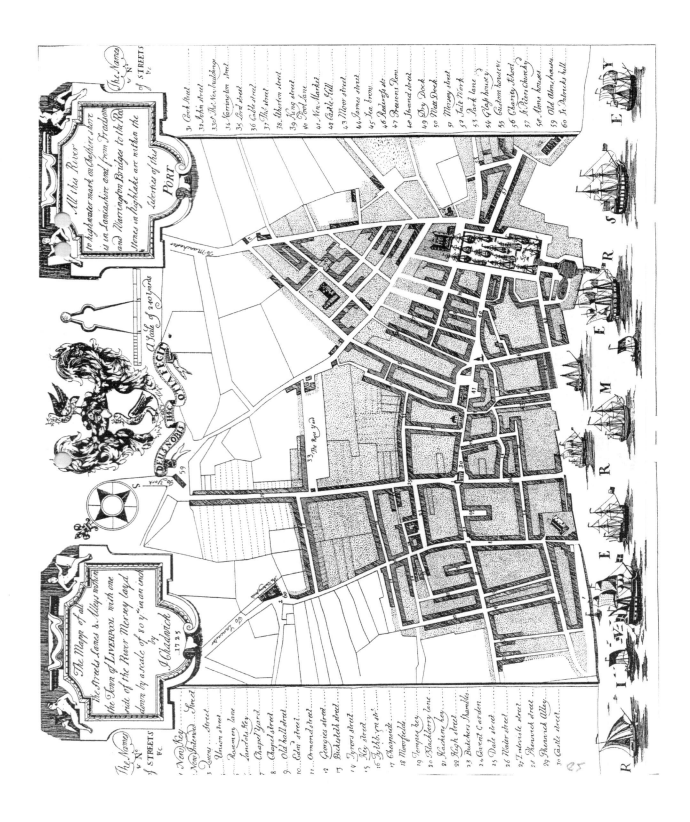

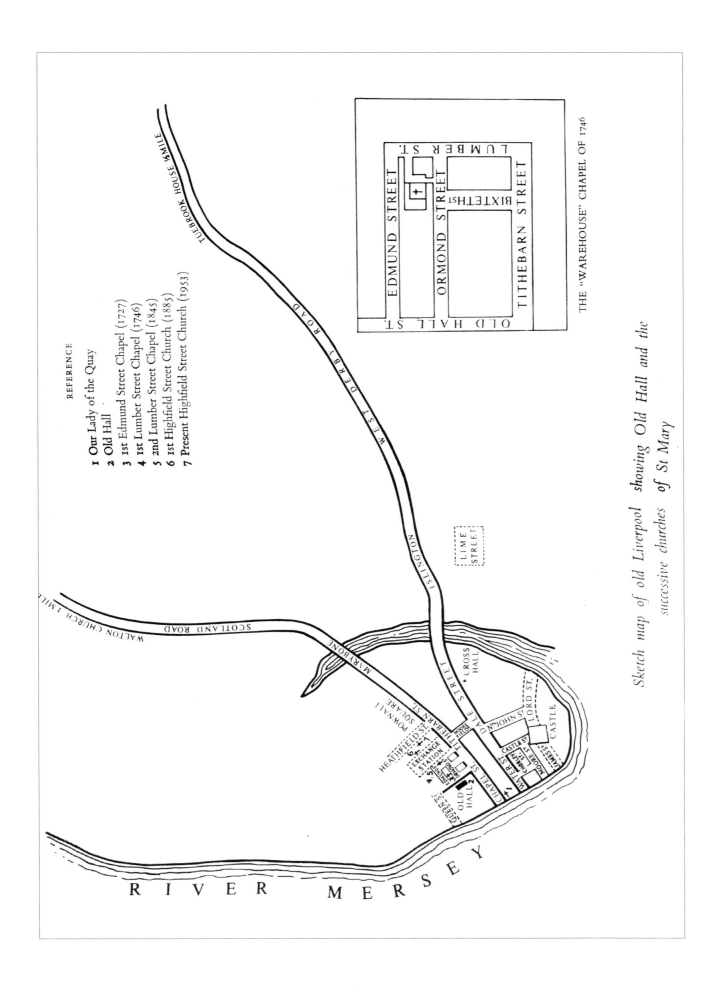

REFERENCE

1 **Our Lady of the Quay**
2 **Old Hall**
3 **1st Edmund Street Chapel** (1727)
4 **1st Lumber Street Chapel** (1746)
5 **2nd Lumber Street Chapel** (1845)
6 **1st Highfield Street Church** (1885)
7 **Present Highfield Street Church** (1953)

THE "WAREHOUSE" CHAPEL OF 1746

*Sketch map of old Liverpool showing Old Hall and the successive churches of St Mary*

# References

## Chapter 1

The Archive in Farm Street has been the main primary resource. Material catalogued under *Liverpool, St Francis Xavier's* has provided original letters and papers, which have both confirmed and enlarged on the details in Professor Whitehead's work. Files RW 1-7 are the main sources for letters referred to in Chapter 1. Files 2 and 7 are of particular interest.

RW/1 - The History of the College. Plan of SFX site Sept 1865 signed by Fr. Vaughan. Property owned by Jesuits in Shaw Street. References to Fr. Price's Chapel in Sir Thomas Street.

RW/2 - Salisbury Street Site Correspondence.

RW/6 - Opposition to New Church.

RW/7 - Letters re New Church 1840-51.

— 1st Annual Report of the Society of St. Francis Xavier January 24 1841.

Farm Street also has three sets of journals, each of which at times printed important articles on the early days of the College.

a. The copies of the parish magazine, *The Xaverian*, between 1884 -1919. Here are found the earliest contemporary references to the work of the College - particularly in the issue for April 1892, and in 1890s copies.

b. The copies of the *College Magazine*, which began publishing in 1920.

c. *Letters and Notices*, the Jesuits' own internal record of the affairs of the English Province, published quarterly since 1863.

In addition, the *Archdiocesan Archive of Liverpool : Parish Box Collections* have been used. This collection, *Box 49 : John Lingard (unsorted)* contains Bishop Brown's correspondence, amongst which is his final letter to Fr. Wilcock from Rome in 1842, after the Pope's decision was known. Reference has also been made to the Lancashire Archive in Preston.

There are two secondary sources for the College's early history in Chapter 1.

a. Fr. N. Ryan SJ (1948), *St Francis Xavier's Church : Centenary 1848-1948*.
In *Part 1 : I : The Prelude* Fr. Ryan deals with the part played by the Jesuits in Liverpool in the Eighteenth Century.
*Part 1 : II : The Interlude* deals with the struggles between the Jesuits and the Vicar-General.
*Part 1 : III : The Unfinished Symphony* deals with the building and the establishment of the Church and the College. Whilst this is an important reference, it gives no details of its sources.

b. Prof M. Whitehead,(1984), History of St. Francis Xavier's College 1842-1902.
PhD. thesis on the history of the College 1842-1902. As recorded in the Acknowledgements, this is a considerable volume of research. There are three copies readily available. One in the Jesuit Archive in Farm Street, one in the Liverpool Central Library in Liverpool, and one in the College Library in Woolton. The full text of Cardinal Acton's Report to Propaganda can be found in the Annex of Whitehead's thesis. The thesis was also used in the writing of most of the other chapters.

### Other references :

The most important of the books consulted for Chapter 1 is T. Burke, (1909), The Catholic History of Liverpool, London.

Archives of St Francis Xavier's Liverpool in the custody of Headmaster, SFX.
Archivum Provinciae Angliae Societatis Jesu, 114 Mount St. London.
Archivum Romanum Societatis - Jesu, Rome.


Beck, G.A., (ed), (1950), The English Catholics. Burns Oates, London.
(this includes the remarks ( p.72) of T.C. Anstey M.P., quoting Pope Gregory XVI).
Bossy, J., (1975), The English Catholic Community 1570-1850. Darton, Longman & Todd, London.
Muir, R., (1907), A History of Liverpool. Liverpool University Press, London.
Syers, R., (1830), The History of Everton. Robinson and Marples, Liverpool.
Waller, P.J., (1981), Democracy & Sectarianism. Liverpool University Press, L'pool.

**The Xaverian, Letters and Notices and the College Magazine have been referred to extensively in the remaining chapters.**

### Chapter 2
Building News and Engineering Journal, 19 May 1876.
Corran, H.S. (1984), Liverpool Collegiate School.
Huntingdon, P.S. (1979), Life and Work of Henry Clutton. London Univ. PhD. (unpubl.).
Tiffen, H.J.(1935), History of Liverpool Institute Schools 1825-1935. Tinling, Liverpool.
Whitehead, M. (1984), History of St. Francis Xavier's College 1842-1902


### Chapter 3
Farm St., AI/4 Prefect of Studies Conference 1888-1923, pp. 12-15. SFX April 14-15th.
Devereux, F., (1992), St Francis Xavier's 1842 - 1992. SFX's Sesquicentennial.
Sadler, M.E., (1904), Secondary Education in Liverpool. Eyre & Spottiswoode, London.
The Xaverian, 1896 - for numbers on roll.
Tiffen, H.J.(1935), History of Liverpool Institute Schools 1825-1935. Tinling Liverpool.


### Chapter 4
Dent. J., (1968), The Education Act 1944. ULP, London.
Liverpool - St Francis Xavier's File. Voluntary Aided Application. 5.2.56. File 55-57.
Liverpool - St Francis Xavier's File. Withdrawal of the Jesuits: Farm St. (closed).
Partington, J.A., (1967), The History of the System of Direct Grants to Secondary Schools.
Durham University, Unpublished Thesis.


### Chapter 5
Fulop-Miller, R., (1930), The Power and Secret of the Jesuits. Putnam, London.
McCabe, W.H. SJ, (1983), An Introduction to Jesuit Theater. IHS, St Louis.
Motter, T.H.V., (1929), The School Drama in England. Kennikat, Washington.
Schwickerath, R. (1904), Jesuit Education: History & Principles. St Louis MO, Herder.


### Chapter 6
Farm St., AI/4 3/7/88, Letter of Fr. Tarleton to Provincial re science curriculum
Whitehead, M., (1986), *The Jesuit Contribution to Science and Technical Education in Late-Nineteenth-Century Liverpool.* Annals of Science, 43(1986), pp 353-368.


### Chapter 7
Public Records Office, Kew. HMI Inspections.
{ED/109/3010 (1926) and Ed/109/3011(1937)}

## Bibliography

Alexander, W.P. and Barraclough, F., (1953), County and Voluntary Schools. Councils and Education Press, London.
Andrews, L., (1976), The Education Act, 1918. Routledge, London.
Barnard, H.C., (1947), A History of English Education from 1760. ULP, London.
Beck, G.A., (ed.), (1950), The English Catholics 1850-1950. Burns Oates, London.
Binney, M., (1984), Our Vanishing Heritage. Arlington, London.
Bossy, J., (1975), The English Catholic Community 1570-1850. Darton, Longman & Todd, London.
Burke, T., (1909), The Catholic History of Liverpool. London.
Corran, H.S., (1984), Liverpool Collegiate School. Liverpool.
Central Office of Information, (1994), Education Reforms in Schools. HMSO.
Curtis, M., (1963), Church and State in English Education. McMillan, London.
Curtis, S.J., (1948), History of Education in Great Britain. University Tutorial Press, London .
Dent, H.C., (1968), The Education Act, 1944. University of London, London.
Docking, J. (ed.), (2000), New Labour's Policies for Schools. Fulton, London.
Evans, K., (1975), The Development and Structure of the English Educational System. ULP, London.
Fulop-Miller, R., (1930), The Power and Secret of the Jesuits. Putnam, London.
Garrold, R.P., (1909), Boys of St Batt's. McDonald and Evans, London.
Garstein, O., (1992), The Counter-Reformation in Scandinavia. Chap. 2 in Oberman, H.A.,
Of Christian Thought. Brill, London.
History of Education Society, (1970), Studies in the Government and Control of Education since 1860. Methuen, London.
Hughes, J., (1927), Concise History of Catholic Liverpool.
Hunting, P.S., (1979), The Life and Work of Henry Clutton. London Univ. PhD. (unpubl.)
Little, B., (1966), Catholic Churches since 1623. Hale, London.
McCabe, W.H., (1983), An Introduction to the Jesuit Theater. Institute of Jesuit Sources, St Louis.
McCullough, G., (1994), Educational Reconstruction. Woburn Press, Ilford.
Martin, C., (1979), A Short History of English Schools. Wayland, Hove.
Meredith, P., (1992), Government, Schools and the Law. Routledge, London.
Murphy, J., (1971), Church, State and Schools in Britain, 1800 - 1970. Routledge, London.
Motter, T.H.V., (1929), The School Drama in England. Kennikat, Washington.
Muir, R., (1907), A History of Liverpool. Liverpool University Press, London.
Neal, F., The Liverpool Experience.
Partington, J.A., (1967), The History of the System of Direct Grants to Secondary Schools. Durham University MA Thesis (unpublished).
Pevsner, N., (1969), Buildings of England : Lancashire. Penguin, London.
Public Schools Commission, (1970), The Report on Independent Day Schools and Direct Grant Grammar Schools, Vol. 1. (The Donnison Report). HMSO, London.
Sadler, M.E., (1904), Report on Secondary Education in Liverpool. Eyre & Spottiswoode, London.
Schwickerath, R., (1904), Jesuit Education: History & Principles. Herder, St Louis MO.
Stonor, R.J., (1957), Liverpool's Hidden Story. Birchley Hall Press, Wigan.
Sutherland, G., (1973), Policy-Making in Elementary Education 1870-1895. OUP, London.
Syers, R., (1830), The History of Everton. Robinson, Liverpool.
Tiffen, H.J., (1935), History of Liverpool Institute Schools 1825 -1935. Tinling, Liverpool.
Trautmann, K., (1890), Ober-Ammergau und sein Passions-spiel.
Wainwright, D., (1960), Liverpool Gentlemen. Faber, London.
Waller, P.J., (1981), Democracy and Sectarianism. Liverpool UP, Liverpool.
Ward. B., (1915), Sequel to Catholic Emancipation. Longman, London.

# INDEX

Acts : Forster Education Act 1870, 58, 63
Sandon Act 1876, 58
Technical Instructions Act 1889, 58, 63
Local Taxation (Customs and Excise ) 1890, 59
Elementary Act 1891, 58
Voluntary Schools Act 1897, 58
Education Act 1902, 60 - 2, 65
Education Act 1918 (Fisher), 67
Education Act 1936, 67
Senior Public Elementary Schools ( Liverpool ) Act 1939, 67
Education Act 1944, 67 - 68
Education Reform Bill 1988, 76
School Standards and Framework Act 1998, 81
Acton , Cardinal, xiii, 27, 54, 175 - 177
Adamson, Fr. SJ, 43, 160
Anstey, T.C., xii
Arrupe, Fr. SJ, 74, 118
Ashplant, T., 163
Assembly Hall, 37
Atherton, 'Lofty', 159
Athletics, College and Intercollegiate, 123-125

Bailey, L., 44, 65, 120, 126, 151, 159, 160, 166
Baxendell, P., 167
Beardwood, P., 103
Beck, Archbishop, 72
Bellerive School, 68, 69
Belvedere School, 68, 69
Bewley, Bill, 135, 167
Birmingham, C., 65, 113, 159
Balfour, 60
Bird, R. SJ, 19, 21, 24, 26
Bradshaw, F.X. 65, 113, 159
Brennan, Fr., SJ, 137, 151, 159
Briggs, Bishop, 19, 21, 22
Brinkworth, Fr. SJ, 67,  151, 152
Brothers of Christian Instruction, 53, 72 - 74, 82 - 84
Brothers on Staff  1960s - Durkin, Melody, Mahon, Power, 84
Brothers on Staff  1970s - Brothers Augustine (Chem.), Bradley (Head of Middle Sch.), Malcolm (RE), Cullen, Slattery,  Thomas), 84
Brothers on Staff  1990s - Brothers Edmund (Maths,) and James (Music), 84
Brown, Bishop, 19, 24, 26, 27, 54, 55, 175 - 178
Broughton Hall School, 68
Bryce Commission, 54
Board of Education Circular 1381 (1926), 68
Building Development Society, 44
Burke, D., 108
Burns, J., 167
Burton, F., SJ, 117
Bushell, M., 131
Butler, R.A.B., 67

Caesar's Friend, criticism, 86 - 88
Cast of Caesar's Friend, 86
Cast of Henry IV Part I, 103
Cardinal Allen/Heenan, school, 75
Cardinal Newman Building, 49, 75, 78
Cardinal Newman School, 49, 75
canonical distance, xiv, 25
Case of Derek Hatton's Sandwiches, 76
Catholic churches, L'pool, 1800-1860, history  of, 179 - 181

Catholic Institute, 28, 55, 63, 98
Caulfield, B., 167
Characteristics of Jesuit Education, 74, 118
Checkland, F., 65, 120, 131, 159
Classical School, 28, 54, 55, 85
clubs and trips, 159, 160, 163, 165, 167, 169
Clutton, H., 34 - 37, 47
College Choir, 105 - 106, 167, 169, 173
College Prospectus, 57
Collyns, Fr., 32, 38
Commercial School, 28, 54, 55, 85, 112
Community House, 48
Compositions, 114
comprehensive schools, 53, 74 - 76
Computing and Information Technology Department, 85
Concertatio, 114
Conference of Catholic Bishops, 81
Crook, W., 65, 159
Crowney, E., 151, 160

de la Mennais Sixth Form Centre, 29, 50, 51, 78, 169
Department of Education and Science, 68 - 69, 74, 76
Devereux, F., 43, 51, 74, 77, 81, 160
direct grant school, 53, 65, 59, 68 - 71, 74
Domestic Science College, 64
Donnelly, Fr. SJ, 111 - 113, 138 - 139
Doyle, A.D. SJ, 72 - 73, 118, 161 - 165
drama, Jesuit School Plays, an article, 94 - 97
drama, College Dramatics - a Retrospect, an article, 100 - 102
drama, Jesuit conditions for acceptable, 93 - 94
drama and the teaching of morals, 93
drama, the rapid development of, in Jesuit colleges, 94
drama at SFX in the Nineteenth Century, 97 - 98
drama, decline and revival, 1860-1880, 99
drama at the College in the Twentieth Century, 103 - 105

electoral Reform Society, 77, 79
elitism, 115,118, 120, 133
elocution, 103
Emmott, E., 166, 167
Emmott, M., 113
evacuation, 53, 151 - 152
events listed, 1980s, 168
Evening Continuation Schools, 64

Feeder Parishes:
(Christ the King, St Paschal Baylon, St Mary's (Woolton), St Clare's, St Gregory's, Our Lady of Good Help, Our Lady of the Annunciation (Bishop Eton), Our Lady of the Assumption, Holy Family, St Andrew's, and St Mark's.), 75
Feeley, Terry, 108
ferula, 135 - 138
First Eleven, football, 125 - 128, 150, 154, 161
footballers, representative honours, 131
Foundation School, 53, 81 - 83, 169
Fransoni, Cardinal, 26
Francis, Brother, O.B.E. Headmaster, 53, 75 - 84, 85, 110, 113, 119, 165 - 169
French domestic architecture, 35 - 37
Fr. Parry Shield, 123 - 124
Fulop-Miller, 93
Funding Agency for Schools, 77, 81

The Gables, 46, 84
Gallwey, Fr. SJ, 34
Garrold, R.P. SJ, ( Boys of St. Batt's & A Fourth Form Boy),
    107, 110
Gerard, Fr. SJ, 59, 111 - 112, 139
Gerardot, J., Fr., 181
Gilbert and Sullivan operettas, 104
Gillick, J. SJ, 119 - 120
Golden Jubilee, 58
Gregson, J., 108
Grace, F.W.W., vii, 47, 65, 107, 120, 131, 137, 158, 159, 160
grant-maintained status, 76-81

Harding, J., 131
Harris, R. SJ, 34, 37, 33, 39, 56, 99, 135, 136, 138 - 139, 141
Harris Memorial Organ, 39
Heenan, Archbishop, 44, 161
Her/His Majesty's Inspectors / OFSTED, 55, 61, 62, 141,
    142, 148, 152, 169
The Hidden Gem, 57 , 99
High Lee, 43 - 51 (passim),  75, 76, 78, 151, 152, 158, 160,
    161, 163
HMS Conway Training Ship, 141
Hodge, W.,( downs and variava ), 42
Holder Bursaries, 56
Hope University, 42
Hopkins, G. Manley, Fr. SJ, ( Felix  Randal), 108 - 109
Hunting, P.S., 37

Ignatian education, 116-129
Inter-Collegiate Examinations, 114, 153
Irish Christian Brothers, 55, 137

Jesuit Colleges other than SFX, 60, 61
Jesuit drama and its influence on French and Spanish
    theatre, 97
Jesuit drama and its international ramifications, 96 - 97
Johnson, Fr. SJ, 31, 32
Jones, ' Beaky', 137, 159
Junior Shield, 53, 125, 128, 160, 167

Kensington Science and Art Department, 58, 112

Laishley, Fr. SJ, 163
Lamb, Mr., 160
La Sagesse School, 68
Learning Resources Centre, 48
Lewis, E., 70, 151, 157, 158, 160
Liberal Education Bills of 1906 and 1908, 62
Library, 44
Liverpool City Council/ Education Committee, 62, 63, 65,
    67, 69, 71, 74, 75, 76, 77 - 81
Liverpool Collegiate, 27, 54, 63, 64, 74, 112
Liverpool Daily Post, 69
Liverpool Echo, 55
Liverpool Institute for Boys, 54, 63, 64, 74, 112
Liverpool Institute for Girls, 54, 74
Liverpool Mercury, 17
Liverpool Museum, 64
Liverpool Public Library, 64
Liverpool School Board, 63
Liverpool School of Tropical Medicine, 64
Liverpool University, 64
London Oratory, 77
Lucas, N., 65, 115
Lythgoe, R. SJ, 17, 19, 21, 23, 25, 26, 27, 54, 178
Lythgoe, F. SJ, 30, 31, 163

Macbeth, 90
Maths Dept, - Salisbury St.- Mr Dunn, Mr Crook, Mr Jones, 113
        Woolton - Mr. Healy, Brother Edmund,
        Mr. Benton, Mr. Bright 113
McCabe, W.H., 91, 93, 94
McCann, Fr. SJ, 120, 143, 151
McCarthy, P. 167
McDowd, 90
McGovern, J., 108
McHale, Fr. SJ, 53, 61, 113, 136, 138, 141
McMorrow, Fr. SJ, 137, 138
Melling, Fr. SJ, 122
Melwood, 46, 53, 121, 122, 123, 150, 167
Militant Tendency, 75, 166
Ministry of Education, 68, 69, 74
Mollard, 113
Morant, R., 60
Motter, T.V. H., 93, 97
Murphy, J., 171
music, 162

Nautical College, 64
Neylan, W. SJ, 43, 46, 51, 53, 68, 70, 107, 118, 135, 137,
        151 - 158
Northern England Educational Conference, 90
Notre Dame Everton Valley, 68, 69
Notre Dame Mount Pleasant, 68
Note Dame/ St. Julie's, 75
Nugent, Monsignor, 55

O'Connor, Bishop SJ, 49, 167
OFSTED Report, 115
O'Keeffe, L., 108, 167
O'Malley, J.P., 113,160
Old Xaverians, Association , Sports and Social Club, 49, 51,
        99, 164, 168
O'Leary, Fr., Chaplain, 84
Oswald, Brother, de la Salle School, 71
Our Lady of Assumption School, 49, 75
Our Lady of Compassion, Formby, 36
Oxford Local Examinations, 56, 57, 114
Oxford University, 77, 159. 162, 163, 164, 166, 167

Parents' Association, 72, 167, 168
Passion Play of Oberammergau, 94
Patrick, Brother Superior, 71, 72
Petillon, J., Superior General, 50
Plays - *The Safety Match, The Admirable Crichton,*
        *The Baby Elephant, The Ten Minute Alibi, and*
        *cast of Ten Minute Alibi, 89,*
        *The Naughty Nephews, the Prince and the Page, 99,*
        *The Cornish Buccaneer, Aladdin, Barcelona, 100,*
        *The Walrus, and The  Carpenter, The Burglar Alarm,*
        *The Tide of Life, The Bear, The Laburnum Grove.*
        *The Old Bull, Jack and The Beanstalk, Ali Baba,*
        *Cinderella, Robin Hood, Sherlock Holmes, Dracula,*
        *Star Trek, A Man for All Seasons, Wanted Mr. Stuart,*
        *The Billion Dollar Saint, Trial by Jury, Pinafore,*
        *Mikado, 99,*
        *Thwarting of Baron Bolligrew, Snow White, Dirk*
        *Warrington, The Way Out, The Curse of the*
        *Mummy's Tomb, Joseph, Oliver, Mary Poppins,*
        *The Last  Night of the Proms,104 - 105, 162, 167*
Pope Clement XIV, 179
Pope Gregory XVI, xiii, 24, 27, 177, 178
Porter, T. SJ, 32, 34, 37, 138

Power, Brother, Headmaster, 69, 72, 73, 84, 165
Prefects of Studies, 1842-1919, 138
Prefect of Studies Conference 1909, 62 - 62
Price,J., SJ & Sir Thomas St, Chapel, 180
Proclamation Speakers, 167
Provincial, 19, 21, 24, 26, 27, 34, 71, 72,  99, 111, 113
pupil roll, 66, 142

Ratcliffe, R. SJ, 99
Ratio Studiorum, xv, 91 - 93, 114
Raymond, P. (G. Quinn), 108
Reade, Kevin, 90, 103
Regulations of Secondary Schools 1907, 64
religious education, 115 - 121
Reynolds, Fr. SJ, 107
Robinson, Andrew, 106
Rice, E., 160
Ridge, G., 133, 160, 166, 168
Roberts, E., 160
Royal Institution, 63
Ryan, N. SJ, 32

Sacred Congregation de Propaganda Fide, xiii, xiv, 17, 22,
          26, 27, 126, 175, 177
Sadler, M., 60, 63, 64
Saint Anne's, 22
Saint Anthony's, 19, 21, 24, 26, 27, 174, 178, 181, 182 - 184
Saint Austin's, 22, 181
Saint Domingo House, 27, 54, 55
Saint Edmund's School, 68, 69
Saint Edward's College, 28, 55, 68, 69, 74, 152
Saint Elizabeth's, 69
Saint Francis Xavier's Bilateral (Campion School), 42
Saint Francis Xavier's High School, 53, 75, 165
Saint Ignatius, 74, 91, 118, 119
Saint Mary's, L'pool, 22, 179
Saint Mary's, Southampton, 73, 84
Saint Mary's, Twickenham, 84
Saint Peter's, Seel Street, 22, 63, 180, 181
School of Art, 64
School for the Blind, 64
School of Commerce, 53
School for the Deaf and Dumb, 64
School of Hygiene, 64
Science Dept. -  Woolton - Messrs. Sherrard, O'Malley,
                Prescott, Blackhurst, Matthews,
                Brother Augustine, Dr. Emmott, 113
science teaching, 55, 57, 58, 59, 111 - 113
Schwickerath, R., 93,
Scott, Councillor, 78 - 80
'Scouse', 133 - 134
Scratch Eights, 130
sectarianism, 67, 69
Senior Shield, 53, 125 - 127, 160, 165,
Sergeant, Fr. SJ, 111, 113
Sermin, Fr. SJ, 48
Shaw, Brother SJ., 120
singing gallery, 38
Smyth, F., (Peg-Leg), 159
Society of St. Francis Xavier, 20, 21, 22, 24, 26, 27
Sodality Chapel, 39
Somerville, Fr., SJ, 117, 119
Sports other than football and athletics, 131, 168
Stonyhurst College, 17, 20, 24,  99, 111, 114, 122
Sumner, R., SJ, 97, 98
swimming pool, 48, 131
Sweeney, P., 131

Tarbuck, J, 109
Tarleton, Fr. SJ, 111
Taunton, Fr. SJ, 112, 158, 159
Technical Instruction Committee, 63
Tomlinson, Fr. SJ, 159
Traynor, Monsignor, 68, 69

under-achievers, 159

van de Put, 88, 157
Vaughan, R. SJ, 34, 37, 38,  59, 111, 112, 113
Vaughan, Cardinal, 58
Vicar Apostolic, xii, 19, 21, 24
voluntary aided, 53, 67, 68, 69, 71, 74, 81, 82, 83

Walker Art Gallery, 64
Walton, J, 39
War Decorations ( First  World War ), 66
War Memorial, 65, 145 - 146
Warner, Fr. SJ, 44, 50, 53, 71, 137, 118, 138, 158 - 161
Warner Building, 29, 50, 78, 169
Watkinson, J., 167
Whelehan, J., 163, 166
whisky money, 59
Whitehead, E. ,107, 108
Whitehead, M., 27, 111, 113, 175
withdrawal of the Jesuits, 71 -74
Wilcock, M. Fr., 19, 24, 178, 182
Woodlock, J. SJ, 53, 65, 67, 122, 131, 135, 136, 143 - 148, 152

Yare, H., 159